Windows® Phone 7 for iPhone® Developers

Kevin Hoffman

⋏Addison-Wesley

800 East 96th Street, Indianapolis, Indiana 46240 USA

Windows® Phone 7 for iPhone® Developers

ISBN-13: 978-0-672-33434-4
ISBN-10: 0-672-33434-8

Library of Congress cataloging-in-publication data is on file.

Printed in the United States of America

First Printing: August 2011

Trademarks

All terms mentioned in this book that are known to be trademarks or service marks have been appropriately capitalized. Pearson Education, Inc. cannot attest to the accuracy of this information. Use of a term in this book should not be regarded as affecting the validity of any trademark or service mark.

Warning and Disclaimer

Every effort has been made to make this book as complete and as accurate as possible, but no warranty or fitness is implied. The information provided is on an "as is" basis. The author and the publisher shall have neither liability nor responsibility to any person or entity with respect to any loss or damages arising from the information contained in this book.

Bulk Sales

Pearson offers excellent discounts on this book when ordered in quantity for bulk purchases or special sales. For more information, please contact:

U.S. Corporate and Government Sales
1-800-382-3419
corpsales@pearsontechgroup.com

For sales outside of the U.S., please contact:

International Sales
+1-317-581-3793
international@pearsontechgroup.com

Editor-in-Chief
Greg Wiegand

Executive Editor
Neil Rowe

Development Editor
Mark Renfrow

Managing Editor
Kristy Hart

Project Editors
Jovana San Nicolas-Shirley and Elaine Wiley

Copy Editor
Barbara Hacha

Indexer
Lisa Stumpf

Proofreader
Seth Kerney

Technical Editors
Bruce Johnson
Nate Dudek

Publishing Coordinator
Cindy Teeters

Cover Designer
Gary Adair

Senior Compositor
Gloria Schurick

I want to dedicate this book to the women in my life:

Angelica, Isabella, and Jerrah.

Behind every good man is an even better woman, and behind every good author is a woman with the patience of a saint and a perpetually running coffeemaker.

Table of Contents

About the Author

Kevin Hoffman (Windsor, CT) is an enterprise programmer who has extensive experience with both Windows Phone 7/Windows Mobile and Apple's iPhone platforms. Currently chief systems architect for Oakleaf Waste Management, he specializes in mobile and cloud development. He writes *The .NET Addict's Blog*, served as editor-in-chief of *iPhone Developer's Journal*, presented twice at Apple's World Wide Developer's Conference, and has authored and co-authored several books, including *WPF Control Development Unleashed: Building Advanced User Experiences* and *ASP.NET 4 Unleashed*.

Acknowledgments

Thanks also go to the staff at Pearson, in particular to Neil Rowe, who has impeccable taste in beer and has somehow managed to put up with me for years.

We Want to Hear from You!

As the reader of this book, *you* are our most important critic and commentator. We value your opinion and want to know what we're doing right, what we could do better, what areas you'd like to see us publish in, and any other words of wisdom you're willing to pass our way.

You can email or write me directly to let me know what you did or didn't like about this book—as well as what we can do to make our books stronger.

Please note that I cannot help you with technical problems related to the topic of this book, and that due to the high volume of mail I receive, I might not be able to reply to every message.

When you write, please be sure to include this book's title and author as well as your name and phone or email address. I will carefully review your comments and share them with the author and editors who worked on the book.

Email: feedback@samspublishing.com

Mail: Neil Rowe
Executive Editor
Sams Publishing
800 East 96th Street
Indianapolis, IN 46240 USA

Reader Services

Visit our website and register this book at informit.com/register for convenient access to any updates, downloads, or errata that might be available for this book.

Introduction

Twenty years from now you will be more disappointed by the things you didn't do than by the ones you did do. So throw off the bowlines. Sail away from the safe harbor. Catch the trade winds in your sails. Explore. Dream. Discover.

Mark Twain

This chapter provides you with a brief introduction to the material that will be presented in this book, as well as some insight into the writing style, how best to read this book, and more. Hopefully, after reading this introduction, you will know whether you want to continue reading this book or skip it and go find the latest book in the *Twilight* series in another section of the bookstore.

I know that it's hard for a book about mobile device programming to compete with angst-ridden vampires in love, but there is a tremendous amount of extremely good information in this book. This isn't just another reference guide. In addition to all the code samples, comparisons between iOS and WP7, and tutorials, I also try to provide as much insight as possible based on my experience building applications for both platforms. If you squint hard enough and cross your eyes while reading, you might learn a few useful patterns, tips, or tricks. If you manage to read all the way to the end, you might even learn how to survive the zombie apocalypse, or at least learn how to write some software that will help you and your Windows Phone survive it.

Who Are You and Why Should I Care?

I've been writing mobile applications for a long time. One of the first truly mobile applications I wrote was an app that ran on a PalmOS Symbol Barcode reader that could be used by people in warehouses to scan products on shelves. Once plugged back into a workstation (if you're wondering if I really am old enough to pre-date Wi-Fi, you are correct, and no, I do not have an 8-track player in my car), the app would then check an inventory system that maintained level information of hazardous materials.

After my tour of duty with PalmOS, I spent some time in the PocketPC/Windows CE realm writing applications for form factors of all shapes and sizes, even tablet PCs before they became hip and trendy. More recently I wrote code for Windows Mobile using the .NET Compact Framework. Eventually the iPhone came out and I started writing code for the iPhone and, obviously, I have since become hopelessly addicted to building applications for Windows Phone 7.

In addition to writing code for mobile platforms, I've been writing and co-writing books on virtually all aspects of the .NET Framework for the past 10 years, since before .NET 1.0 was released to the general public. I spoke at Apple's Worldwide Developer Conference (WWDC) two years in a row. The first time I compared the developer experience of building apps with Windows Presentation Foundation (WPF) with desktop application development using Cocoa for the Mac. The next year, I compared the .NET Compact Framework to the first release of the iPhone SDK.

I am a language nut, whether that language involves telling a computer what to do or conversing with a human. Over the years I've dabbled in Spanish, Hindi, Japanese, and explored programming languages such as Ruby, Python, Pascal, Delphi, VB, VB .NET, C, C++, Objective-C, C#, Java, Haskel, Scheme, and a whole bunch more that I'm probably forgetting.

Helping developers compare and contrast similar platforms and learn awesome new technology is in my blood; it's what I do for a living, it's what I do for fun when I get home from work, and now it's what I'm doing with this book. Asking me to slow down and do less of what I love would be like asking me to only eat half of a peanut butter cup, which is obviously a completely ridiculous request.

Why Should I Read This Book?

Hopefully by now you've figured out that this book provides an introduction to development with Windows Phone 7 (WP7). What sets this book apart from some of the other introductory books about WP7 is that it takes a more holistic approach and includes information and comparisons about how "the other guys" do it—in this case, "the other guys" are iPhone developers.

If you've written an iPhone or iPad application, thought about writing an iPhone application, have touched an iPhone, or have simply seen an iPhone commercial, you are part of the target audience for this book. In fact, even if you don't know what an iPhone is (what rock have you been hiding under?), you will still be able to use this book to learn what you need to build WP7 applications.

If you're more interested in building applications that do something useful than you are about learning 500 different ways to print "hello world," this book is for you. If you want useful advice and a gradual progression through the entire WP7 SDK and how it relates to the iOS SDK, this book is for you.

If you want to build mobile applications and your ultimate goal is to get those applications into the Windows Phone application Marketplace, this book is for you. Finally, if you are a human being currently capable of both reading and breathing, this book is for you.

You don't need any prior knowledge of any specific programming language or platform to use this book. You'll be gradually introduced to the C# programming language, the Silverlight framework, and Extensible Application Markup Language (XAML) for building user interfaces; wherever applicable, you'll see comparisons with how these new concepts relate to iOS programming. As new concepts are introduced, you'll be given the tools and background information you need to incorporate those into functioning applications.

What's in This Book?

As you have probably guessed by now, the first thing you will encounter in this book is an introduction. Then the book takes you on a tour of the Windows Phone 7 programming environment, all the while providing comparisons with the iOS programming environment. Even if you aren't an iPhone programmer, these comparisons provide useful information and insight about mobile device programming in general. The following is a breakdown of the chapters you'll find in this book.

Early in the book I will do a lot of comparison between the iOS environment (especially regarding the Objective-C programming language) and the Windows Phone 7 environment. This is to help ease the transition for iPhone developers into the world of WP7 programming. As the book progresses and the platforms diverge and take their own unique paths, I will do less detailed comparisons and bring up iOS concepts only when necessary or when it gives me an excuse to tell a really good story.

Chapter 2: C# and Objective-C, Second Cousins Twice Removed

This chapter provides you with an introduction to the C# programming language and the basics of the .NET Framework that support this language. I also compare some of the basic tenets of Objective-C programming with C# programming, including how these languages are similar, how they differ, and where they came from.

Chapter 3: Object-Oriented Programming

Now that we've got a basic linguistic foundation for writing code in C#, I take you on a tour of some of the basics of object-oriented programming with C#. This chapter discusses concepts such as encapsulation, members, inheritance, contracts, and interfaces, and illustrates how these concepts are implemented in both Objective-C and C#.

Chapter 4: Event-Driven Programming

This chapter covers an incredibly important concept in object-oriented programming and one that is even more important in Silverlight-based user interfaces: events. In this chapter I cover the means by which code gets notified that something important took place, and I compare and contrast that with the "delegate pattern" that is so popular in iOS. This is where the real nuts and bolts of how to build applications starts.

Chapter 5: Rendering and View System Basics

As much as some of us programmers would like to be able to do everything without a single piece of user interface, we need to acknowledge that there is a user interacting with our application and users need to see the app. This chapter describes how Silverlight goes from the XAML markup and code we write to a fully rendered, interactive user interface. The knowledge you get from this chapter will help you as you progress throughout this book to create rich, compelling user interfaces.

Chapter 6: From Xcode to Visual Studio

This chapter is all about the Integrated Development Environments (IDE). Xcode is a powerful tool that has been around on the Mac since long before the first iPhone application was built, and Visual Studio has been around for much longer than Windows Phone or its predecessor, Windows Mobile. A developer's familiarity and level of comfort with an IDE is directly related to how productive the developer is in building applications for that platform. This chapter provides you with the information you'll need to be productive in Visual Studio 2010 and points out some key differences and similarities between Visual Studio and Xcode.

Chapter 7: Introducing Expression Blend

Taking the tools discussion out of the realm of pure code and into the realm of the designer, this chapter talks about Microsoft's Expression Blend tool. Until Microsoft released Blend, it was probably one of the last companies I would've accused of having a good design tool. However, Expression Blend is an absolutely incredible tool and, in the hands of a capable designer or even a half-talented developer, can create absolutely amazing user interfaces. In addition to coverage of Blend, this chapter also provides some comparison points with Apple's design tool, Interface Builder.

Chapter 8: Using Basic UI Elements

This chapter gives you a preliminary walkthrough of the tools in your toolbox that will allow you to build basic user interfaces. Here you'll learn tips and techniques for using XAML (the declarative UI markup language used by Silverlight and Windows Phone 7) and code. You'll build a few basic UIs and see demonstrations of all the basic controls that ship with the WP7 SDK.

Chapter 9: Using Advanced UI Elements

This chapter builds on what you learned in the previous chapter and introduces new controls and new techniques for working with controls, including animation, perspective transformation, navigation, and much more.

Chapter 10: Using Hardware and Device Services

A smartphone wouldn't really be a smartphone without a bunch of hardware and system services that make it "smart." This chapter shows you how to use all the "smart" features of your phone, including the accelerometer, GPS location, interacting with photos, contacts, email, SMS, and much more—even how to control the built-in FM radio that is present on all Windows Phone 7 devices.

Chapter 11: Introduction to Application Tiles

Application tiles are the large icons that show up on the start screen of your phone after you have slid the background image up and away. This chapter teaches you everything you need to know about creating the images for these tiles, including building schedules to change the tile images, changing the tile count, and more.

Chapter 12: Using Push Notifications

Push notifications provide developers with incredible amounts of power and flexibility, both for iOS and Windows Phone 7 applications. They allow you to send raw data notifications to running instances of your applications as well as send "toast" notifications, and even dynamically change the image and count of your application's tile. This chapter shows you everything you need to know about building push notification applications, including walking you through a demonstration app that shows you how to build an application tile that updates with the current status of the zombie apocalypse (I wasn't kidding when I said you'd learn how to use WP7 to survive the zombie scourge).

Chapter 13: The Phone Execution Model

Now that you know a little about building user interfaces, using push notifications, and working with application tiles as well as system-level features and smartphone hardware, this chapter gives you an overview of the phone execution model. In this chapter you learn about what happens when a user presses the Back button to leave your application versus. pressing the Home button, techniques for holding onto information between invocations of your application, and what a "tombstone" is and how it is used.

Chapter 14: Local Storage on the Phone

The iPhone, iPod Touch, and iPad all have access to Core Data, a relational database object-relational mapping API for iOS. Windows Phone 7 has no such ORM tool, but there are tons of options for storing and retrieving data on the phone that are in many cases so easy that developers won't even miss not having access to an ORM such as Core Data.

Chapter 15: Building Smart Clients

Now that you know how to store and retrieve data locally on a WP7 device, this chapter discusses the finer points of building "smart clients." Smart clients are applications that typically store local data but augment that by synchronizing data with web services. This chapter shows you everything you need to know about accessing web services, making web requests, and even parsing common web service data formats such as Google Data (YouTube feeds), RSS, Twitter, and more. In this chapter you'll build an application that displays the most recent YouTube videos uploaded by a user, follows a user's Twitter feeds, downloads blog post data from an RSS feed, and displays the blog post text in an embedded browser control.

Chapter 16: Separating Your Concerns

By the time you reach this point in the book, you should have a significant amount of syntax and basic knowledge under your belt. You know your way around Visual Studio and Windows Phone 7 and you're starting to get the hang of things, but you're also noticing that as the sample code gets more complex, it's starting to get hard to read and you figure it would be hard to maintain in a production environment. This chapter introduces you to the concept of Model-View-ViewModel (MVVM) and how separation of concerns and good programming practices can help save your application from being strangled by its own complexity.

Chapter 17: Unit Testing and TDD

If you took the lessons from the separation-of-concerns (MVVM) chapter to heart, you're on the right track toward building testable applications. This chapter shows you how to create automated unit tests, how to run those tests, and introduces you to the concepts behind test-driven development (TDD) and how that can all be implemented to help your development life cycle for your WP7 applications.

Chapter 18: Building Connected Social Games

Some of the most popular types of applications downloaded from the Apple App Store are casual gaming experiences or social applications with some element of fun. In other words, not hard-core 3D high-budget gaming experiences, but fun applications designed specifically for the "quick in and out" mobile form factor. This chapter is full of game theory, design considerations, advice, and patterns that you should take into account if you plan to build social connected applications or games for WP7. Also included in this chapter is an overview and comparison between Xbox Live for WP7 and GameCenter and GameKit for iOS.

Chapter 19: Securing WP7 Applications

Security is an important part of virtually every application and isn't just limited to simple username and password login functionality. This chapter is full of information about the various ways in which you can secure your application and the trade-offs you must pay for those types of security. There is thorough coverage of data encryption and the best (and worst) ways to implement this type of security.

Chapter 20: Debugging and Troubleshooting

Surely you have *never* written an application that has had bugs, performed poorly, or operated in unpredictable ways. However, as I'm sure you know someone *else* who has had these problems, this chapter can help your "friend" debug and troubleshoot his application. This chapter contains tutorials on using the debugger, working with breakpoints, and even an overview of static analysis and code metrics.

Chapter 21: Deploying Applications to the Marketplace

Congratulations, you've made it through the entire book and haven't given up and gone back to the *Twilight* section of the bookstore to read about vampires in love. Instead, you've stuck with it, and you've learned a wealth of information about building Windows Phone 7 applications. Now you've gone off on your own and built your own application and you're ready to submit it to the Marketplace to make your millions and become famous. This chapter contains everything you need to know to test your application on a device, get registered as a developer, and submit your application to the Marketplace.

Summary

So you're standing in the book store (or sitting at home in your favorite chair) and you've read through what you can expect to see in this book. As you read through this book, I highly recommend that you do so with a copy of Visual Studio nearby so that at any moment you can put the book down, type in a code sample, and start messing around with the code to see what happens. No matter how expertly I have managed to write any of the chapters, they are no substitute for good old-fashioned tinkering. So read on, tinker as much as possible, and enjoy the book!

C# and Objective-C: Second Cousins Twice Removed

I always call my cousin because we're so close.
We're almost like sisters, and we're also close because our moms are sisters.

Britney Spears

This chapter provides you with a comparison of the two programming languages involved in iPhone and Windows Phone 7 Development: Objective-C and C#. You see where these languages are similar, where they differ, and how they support the complex application development frameworks for their respective platforms.

The first section of this chapter deals with the origins of each language. The chapter then continues with coverage of some of the most basic concepts of C# and how those apply to iPhone developers.

The Origin of Objective-C

Objective-C's lineage starts further back than that of its younger counterpart, C#. In the 1980s, Brad Cox and Tom Love ran a company called Stepstone. While at this company, Brad Cox attempted to fuse what he saw as the best qualities of the Smalltalk programming language with the utility and power of C. He did this by modifying a standard C compiler to add some of the features of the Smalltalk language.

His first working prototype was called OOPC, which stood for Object-Oriented Programming in C. Love and Cox formed a new company, Productivity Products International, and in 1986 Cox published the first definitive description of the Objective-C programming language.

In 1988, NeXT (the company Steve Jobs started when he left Apple) licensed the use of Objective-C from Stepstone and made its own Objective-C compiler. Eventually, NeXT stopped trying to make hardware and focused on its custom software development environment, which included NeXTStep and the open standard on which it was based, OpenStep.

After Apple acquired NeXT in 1996, it used OpenStep in its new operating system, Mac OS X. This acquisition gave Apple the Objective-C development tool Project Builder, and the UI design tool Interface Builder.

Eventually Xcode replaced Project Builder, and Xcode and Interface Builder have undergone radical growth throughout their histories. Today, Xcode and Interface Builder (which is now an integrated part of Xcode as of version 4) can be used to build Mac applications as well as iPhone, iPod Touch, and iPad applications using the Objective-C programming language.

> ### Note
> Xcode can be used to build applications with other languages as well. For example, you can use Xcode to build Cocoa applications for the Mac using the Ruby programming language. For the rest of this book, however, we will focus only on the capabilities and features of Xcode as they pertain to iOS development with Objective-C.

The Origin of C#

Back in 2000 and 2001, Microsoft was hard at work trying to build a new runtime as a successor to its component services runtime, COM+. While building this new runtime, Microsoft discovered that the runtime it was building solved more problems than just what it was trying to fix with COM+, and it was eventually repurposed and re-dubbed the Common Language Runtime (CLR). While searching for an end to a problem called "DLL Hell" that had plagued COM (Component Object Model, a binary-based, tightly-coupled application composition model), Microsoft had constructed something with far broader scope.

This runtime is a managed environment that serves as a host for managed code, written in any of the languages that were built for the CLR. These languages include Visual Basic .NET, IronPython, IronRuby, and of course, C#.

In 2001, I was writing C# code using the command-line compiler (a beta at the time) and had started work on my first .NET technical publication. I was so convinced that C#, and .NET in general, was going to change the way developers wrote software that I dove headfirst into learning this powerful new framework.

The chief architect behind the design of the C# programming language is Anders Hejlsberg, who was also heavily involved in the design of other popular programming languages, including Turbo Pascal and Delphi.

The first version of C# was released in January 2002, and the most recent version of the language, version 4.0, was released in April 2010 alongside the 2010 release of Visual Studio.

Silverlight, one of the frameworks that enables application development on Windows Phone 7, was originally released in 2007 after a brief run being referred to as "WPF/E," or "WPF Everywhere." Silverlight, which is the framework used for application development throughout this book, is a cross-platform subset of the .NET Framework and the UI functionality that originally came with WPF (Windows Presentation Foundation).

Silverlight and XNA are two different application development frameworks available to Windows Phone 7 developers, both of which sit atop the .NET Framework and the CLR, allowing developers to write code for either environment in C#. Silverlight is a framework that uses the familiar control hierarchy concept for building applications, whereas XNA is used for games and is an engine wrapped around the "game loop" concept.

Language Basics

This next section takes you through some of the basics of the two languages, such as differences in core syntax as well as a discussion of method calls versus message passing. Chapter 3, "Object-Oriented Programming," builds on the rest of this chapter and provides a comparison of object-oriented programming techniques with both languages.

Core Syntax

First, let's take a look at some basic Objective-C that you might find in a typical iPhone application. Listing 2.1 shows some sample Objective-C code that should look familiar to an iOS developer.

Listing 2.1   **Sample Objective-C Code to Fetch an Image from a URL**

```
NSString* urlString = @"http://www.site.com/images/pic.png";

NSData* imageData = [[NSData alloc] initWithContentsOfURL:
                    [NSURL URLWithString:urlString]];

UIImage* image = [[UIImage alloc] initWithData:imageData];
[imageView setImage:image];
[imageData release];
[image release];
```

Listing 2.2 shows some basic C# that you might find in a Windows Phone 7 application. Despite there being quite a few differences in how the languages work and their syntax, both are still fairly easy to read for programmers with at least a basic understanding of C-derived languages.

Listing 2.2   **Sample C# Code to Fetch an Image from a URL**

```
WebClient wc = new WebClient();
wc.OpenReadCompleted +=
    new OpenReadCompletedEventHandler(wc_OpenReadCompleted);

wc.OpenReadAsync(new Uri("http://www.site.com/images/pic.png ",
                 UriKind.Absolute));
...

void wc_OpenReadCompleted(object sender, OpenReadCompletedEventArgs e)
{
    StreamResourceInfo sri =
      new StreamResourceInfo(e.Result as Stream, null);
    BitmapImage imgsrc = new BitmapImage();
    imgsrc.SetSource(sri.Stream);
    MyImageControl.Source = imgsrc;
}
```

Don't worry if either of these code samples seems confusing at the moment; by the time you get to the end of this book, all of the preceding will seem like second nature to you.

From the previous two code listings, you should be able to fairly quickly see a couple of things about how C# and Objective-C are similar and where they differ. One of the most important differences to keep in mind is that although Objective-C is a superset of C and can compile any ANSI C code, C# is a managed language that is only C-like and is inspired by C++ (despite rumors you might have heard indicating that C# was inspired by Java). This means that functions as they exist in C aren't possible in C#. Any executable code in C# must occur inside a class (we'll talk about OOP in the next chapter).

Another key difference in core syntax is that in Objective-C, as in C and C++, there are header (.h) files and code implementation (in C these are .c files; in Objective-C, these are .m files). C# does not separate code between header and implementation, and all code resides within C# (.cs) files.

At their core, they both share the following core syntactical similarities:

- Type declaration of members follows the same C-style syntax (for example, `int x; double y;`).

- Both use semicolons as executable statement delimiters.

- Both use curly braces (`{` and `}`) to mark the beginning and end of code blocks.

- Both are easily integrated to third-party projects.

- Both share many looping keywords and syntax, such as for, while, and so on.

As we progress throughout the book, you will see more and more ways in which C# and Objective-C differ and how the UI Frameworks (Silverlight and Cocoa Touch/UIKit, respectively) are vastly different.

One other syntactical difference to keep in mind that will often irritate many unprepared Objective-C developers is Boolean statement evaluation. In C (and thus, Objective-C), any expression that evaluates to nonzero, including negative numbers, is considered true. This is not the case in C#, and you will see that idiomatic C# rarely, if ever, has an if statement that occurs without a logic operator specifically to avoid this type of confusion.

For example, the following snippet of Objective-C is quite common because of its C roots:

```
if (memberVariable)
{
    // do something, knowing that memberVariable is not null/non-zero
}
```

Whereas the same evaluation would rarely appear in idiomatic C# and is usually written like this:

```
if (memberVariable == null)
{
    // do something, knowing that memberVariable is null
}
```

Or, to test for null (or empty) strings, you often see code that looks like this:

```
if ((memberVariable == null) || (memberVariable == string.Empty))
{
    // do something, knowing that memberVariable is null or empty
}
```

In this code block, C# takes advantage of logic short-circuiting so that the second condition will not evaluate if the first condition can be used to make the whole statement true. In other words, if the memberVariable is null, it will never attempt to compare it with string.Empty.

C# also has the concept of nullable primitives. In short, you can have a nullable integer or a nullable decimal. It might seem odd to Objective-C programmers, but such constructs can come in handy from time to time, especially when communicating with databases or converting data from disparate sources.

The following few lines of code illustrate how to declare nullable primitive types and how to test to see whether those types have values assigned to them:

```
int? nullableInt;
Nullable<decimal> nullableDecimal;

// do something to the variables
if (nullableInt.HasValue)
{
```

```
    // do something, knowing that the value isn't null
}
```

In C#, testing for whether a value is null is often a bit trickier than the equivalent in Objective-C, so C# programmers out of habit generally make very explicit logic statements.

Method Calls and Message Passing

When we start talking about message passing in Objective-C and method calling in C#, this is where we really start seeing some fundamental differences in the languages.

In Objective-C, to get an object to do some work for you, you have to send it a message. This concept of message passing can be traced directly to Objective-C's Smalltalk heritage.

In conceptual form, message passing is a much less tightly coupled way of getting objects to do work than invoking methods. When you invoke methods in C#, you are executing a specific piece of code at that specific time, by invoking whatever method matches the signature that you're calling.

To indicate that you're sending a message in Objective-C, you enclose the target of the message and all of the parameters to that message in square brackets ([and]), as the following code snippet shows:

```
[car accelerateTo:65 inUnits:MPH withLightsOn:NO];
```

In this example, the car object is said to receive the `accelerateTo:inUnits:withLightsOn` message. What's interesting here is that the Objective-C runtime does not need to know at compile time whether this object will respond to this message. Sure, a warning will appear in Xcode if it doesn't appear as though the object will respond, but that will not prevent the code from compiling. In fact, in Objective-C, you can add messages to which an object will respond at runtime. In this sense, Objective-C is more dynamic than C#.

The same action, when done as a C# method call, would look something like this:

```
car.Accelerate(65, SpeedUnits.MPH, false);
```

Unlike Objective-C, this method call is statically checked at compile time. If a method matching this signature does not exist at compile time, the build will fail. There are dynamic extensions to C# that can make this distinction a little fuzzy, but they are beyond the scope of this book.

Both of these are fairly easy to read, although I would definitely make the case that the Objective-C message passing syntax, in the hands of a good developer, can make for more easily read, self-documenting code.

Before you get discouraged and start thinking that maybe C# isn't up to the task of building your application, C# 4.0 (both in and out of the WP7 SDK) introduced a new but infrequently used feature: named parameters. This allows developers to invoke methods C#-style, but to still label the parameters in a way that feels comfortable to them as Objective-C developers. You can rewrite the previous method call like this:

```
car.Accelerate(mph:65, units:SpeedUnits.MPH, lightsOn:false);
```

In this version of the method call, it is much easier to tell exactly what is being passed to the method and what the method expects. Just by using named parameters, your code becomes a lot easier to read, and code that's easier to read is easier to maintain.

A Note on Conventions and Named Parameters

I highly recommend that developers who are planning to write code for both environments get into the habit of using named parameters when writing their WP7 code. It will make the context switching between iOS and WP7 development far less jarring and will actually promote a good practice of making your code as self-documenting as possible. In short, skip named parameters only for the simplest, most obvious of methods. Trust me, when you put down your WP7 project for four weeks to work on your iOS project and then come back to a WP7 project without a single named parameter, you will want to stab yourself with a rusty, blunt object. So, save yourself the trip to the ER and embrace named parameters.

Memory Management

Whenever iOS and .NET developers get into the same room, things typically remain civil and often lighthearted for a long time. Then someone mentions that the iPhone doesn't have garbage collection. This is when the steak knives, slings, and USB rocket launchers come out and a war begins. Memory management on mobile devices is an enormously important topic—and one that is equally important to developers of iOS or WP7 applications, regardless of whether the runtime has a garbage collector.

This section provides a discussion of reference counting—the memory management system on iOS devices—and garbage collection, the memory management system on WP7 devices. Even if you are a seasoned .NET developer, I highly recommend that you read through this section because, as you will see, it is possible to cause memory-related application crashes even in a garbage-collected environment.

Reference Counting and Object Ownership

Reference counting is the means by which allocated objects in memory in Objective-C are deallocated. One of the core skills of any iOS developer is the ability to get a firm grasp of retain/release counts.

For those of you reading this who don't know what retain and release mean, they are messages that are sent to objects to increase or decrement the reference count. When an object wants to take ownership (indicate to the system that it doesn't want said object freed from memory until it specifically says it's done with it) of another object, it sends it the retain message. When it is done with the other object, it sends it the release message and, in good practice, the variable is set to nil (called nil in Objective-C, null in C#).

When your code sends an object the release method and, as a result, the object's reference count reaches zero, the object is free for deallocation. It will be removed from memory when its reference count reaches zero.

This particular type of memory management is a solution to the classic problem where two objects are working with the same data in memory and one object finishes and disposes of that memory before the other one finishes. With reference counting, both objects can safely work with the data, and neither will dispose of the allocated memory until the shared object's reference count reaches zero.

One big problem with reference counting in iOS is that it can quickly become difficult to keep track of which code has been retaining your objects and which code is releasing. Something that happens all too often is a memory leak: Objects are allocated and retained and never released, either holding into the same memory for the lifetime of the application, or worse—continually consuming more and more memory until the application crashes. If you have a memory leak in a loop, chances are, the application will at some point crash.

Thankfully, tools that come with the iOS development SDK include tools for tracking down memory leaks and out-of-control allocation, and with practice, iOS developers can get pretty adept at hunting down and eliminating memory leaks.

That iOS developers often spend a tremendous amount of time hunting down and eliminating problems that stem from retain/release cycles is what causes the knife-wielding bar brawl mentioned earlier. iOS developers often think C# developers are lazy or write inefficient code because their code is garbage-collected. C# developers often think iOS developers are doing everything the "hard way" because they're manually managing reference counts.

Garbage Collection

C# removes the burden of manually maintaining reference counts from the developer. When you write code in C# that instantiates classes (you will learn more about working with C# classes in the next chapter), you use the new keyword. When your code is done with an object, many times you can allow the variable pointing at that object to go out of scope, and the garbage collector will eventually take care of that object. Take note of that word, *eventually*, because it will be important in the next section on finalization.

C# uses a managed heap. This is unlike the way heap memory is managed in Objective-C. Allocation cost on a management heap is significantly faster than that of a typical C runtime heap. The trade-off occurs with the act of garbage collection. Before we can understand what happens during garbage collection, we need to understand how the runtime knows the difference between good memory and garbage memory.

With Objective-C, the programmer tells the runtime what is garbage by manually decrementing an object's retain count to zero, which will free the object from memory automatically.

The CLR (and through that, C#) does something called *root counting*. Whenever you create an object on the managed heap with a strong reference (a variable in scope contains a pointer to that new object), the runtime keeps track of that instantiation. In memory, it maintains a graph of object roots. So, you could have a Car object that has a member variable pointing to a Wheel object, which in turn has a member variable pointing to a Brakepad object, and so on. The CLR knows that there is a root path from the Car object to the Brakepad object.

If, while the application is running, the variable `myBrakePad` (which was holding the reference to the instance of the `BrakePad` class) is set to null, the object to which the `myBrakePad` variable used to point becomes orphaned. In other words, there is no longer a root path from any "live" object to that newly orphaned object. This means that the object will be garbage collected, *but not necessarily right away*.

At a time of its choosing (an algorithm too complex and out of scope for this chapter), the CLR's garbage collector will make a pass through the managed heap. In doing so, it will find the instance of the `BrakePad` class sitting there without any roots (no "live" object has a direct or indirect reference to that object). This is when the garbage collector will decide to finally dispose of the memory associated with that object.

Garbage Collection in Depth

If you really want to know the ins and outs of how the garbage collector works in the CLR for Silverlight or the desktop and server runtimes, you should check out the following book: *Essential .NET, Volume I - The Common Language Runtime*, by Don Box and Chris Sells. It's an older book, but the coverage it provides on how the garbage collector works is unparalleled.

This is where I think it's appropriate to pause and try to let some of this sink in; C and C++ programmers can often get very confused at this stage because this is not how they are used to disposing of memory. It also provides a good lead-in to the next section on finalization.

Garbage collection in the CLR is an asynchronous process that is done completely out of band with whatever the application happens to be doing. All effort is made to delay a garbage collection event until an appropriate, and hopefully idle, moment. However, if the heap is full, the CLR will do a garbage collection (GC) pass. GC passes are extremely taxing on the application itself, and performance can be degraded considerably during a GC pass.

The reason I mention this, and stress it so much here, is that when building desktop applications with .NET, or even Silverlight applications (which still run on a desktop processor with desktop RAM), developers often forget that the garbage collector is even there. Things just work, and they often work fairly well, so few people stop to think about optimizing their memory usage. This becomes a far more important matter for mobile developers, where a particularly long and taxing GC pass can cause your app to seize up and stop responding for a second or two.

The following list contains a few things you should keep in the back of your mind as you build your WP7 applications to make them as GC-friendly as possible:

- A simple rule of mobile applications: Don't hold memory you don't need. Don't create instances of anything unless you need them. This can be a particularly hard habit to break if you're coming from a desktop development world where "objects are cheap."

- Big data is easy to allocate, slow to garbage collect. Always make sure you aren't keeping references around to something your app doesn't need at the moment. By big I don't just mean size in bytes, I mean graph complexity. If you have an object that points to another that points to another and so on, that increases the number of roots that need to be tracked, and when this object is collected, increases the number of root paths that need to be traversed during a collection pass.

- Try to keep churn to a minimum: Don't instantiate a bunch of things in a loop, then set their references to null, and then instantiate a bunch more things. By "churn," I mean the production of a large number of orphaned objects within a short period of time. A GC pass with a few thousand small objects can be just as taxing as a GC pass over a large object graph.

- Analyze your app. There are a number of tools available within Visual Studio (also out of scope of this book, but references and books on the subject abound) that allow you to profile your application as well as your application's heap performance. You can even watch when collection passes occur. Don't skip this step. You can delay it while you're in initial development and prototyping, but don't push an app to the marketplace unless you know your app is playing nice with the heap.

Cleaning Up After Yourself—Object Finalization

Finalization is related directly to the act of garbage collection. In languages such as C++, objects are disposed of using what is called *deterministic finalization*. All that really means is that when you "free" or "dealloc" an object, it's gone. It disappears at that exact moment in time, and a clean-up method called a *finalizer* is also invoked just before that memory is reclaimed. This is *not* how the CLR and C# work.

When an object goes out of scope, or when the variable pointing to that object is set to null, the object will *eventually* be garbage collected. You absolutely cannot guarantee when an object is going to be disposed, nor can you guarantee the order in which it is disposed.

C# developers often take advantage of an interface known as `IDisposable` (more on interfaces and classes will be discussed in the next chapter). When an object implements this interface, it means that its `Dispose()` method will be invoked by the runtime just before the garbage collector reclaims the memory for that object. This gives your object a chance to clean up whatever mess it made before daddy finds it on the floor with the Legos scattered everywhere.

I won't cover too much in this book about building disposable objects, except where appropriate in the course of illustrating other examples. If you're curious about how that all works as well as other detailed mechanics of the C# language itself, you might want to pick up a copy of *C# 4.0 Unleashed,* by Bart De Smet.

Finalization Order

The runtime doesn't guarantee the order in which finalization occurs through objects that are marked as disposable. Going back to the car object with a pointer to a wheel object with a pointer to a brakepad object, you cannot guarantee that the brakepad object will be disposed before the wheel object. You cannot even guarantee that the car object will be disposed last.

If you write code that executes when an object is disposed (remember, at some arbitrary time after being marked for collection), that code must never access member variables that are also going to be disposed, because doing so might "reawaken" the member variable, short-circuit the collection process, and prevent the object from being collected, creating a memory leak that only an iPhone developer could truly appreciate. See, having a managed heap doesn't mean you can't crash your app with memory problems.

Summary

In this chapter, you got a look at what the core syntax of C# looks like, as well as some good background on where Objective-C and C# came from. This chapter discussed some of the ways in which these languages are similar and how they differ at the lowest levels.

In the next chapter, we'll continue the language comparison discussion with a look at how both languages deal with various object-oriented programming concepts and talk about terminology that might seem confusing at first.

Object-Oriented Programming

Certainly not every good program is object-oriented, and not every object-oriented program is good.

Bjarne Stroustrup

This chapter will cover some of the core concepts of object-oriented programming (OOP) and how they apply to both iPhone and Windows Phone 7 programming. Regardless of the type of application you plan to write, or the platform on which you plan to write it, you will need to utilize and understand some basic object-oriented principles and concepts.

Most developers are already familiar with concepts such as inheritance, contract-based (interface) programming, members, methods, encapsulation, and more. However, those concepts each have different implementations and even different terminology on different platforms. This chapter will help clear things up and show you how the core tenets of OOP are implemented in iOS and WP7.

Why OOP?

If you're reading this book, you probably do not need to be convinced that object-oriented programming is a good thing. However, as the chapter quote from Bjarne Stroustrup so eloquently puts it—not all OOP is a good thing. Like any tool, if used inappropriately, it can make a royal mess of any well-intentioned project.

We create classes as a way to group logically related data and behavior that's all geared toward performing a certain task. When these classes are written properly, they exemplify the benefits of OOP: increased reuse and the creation of testable, reliable, predictable applications that are easy to build, easy to maintain, and easy to change.

On mobile devices, we have classes that encapsulate information and behaviors for all kinds of things from reading GPS coordinates, to displaying text, to accepting input. Without a carefully architected suite of classes that abstract all the capabilities of a device, we would never be able to rapidly and reliably produce software for that device.

The same is true for the applications we build and the code we write. Without our own ability to create reusable classes, even the relatively small amount of code we write for mobile applications would be impossible to maintain and deliver applications on time and on budget.

Building a Class

Throughout the rest of this chapter we're going to be building a class that has progressively more functionality. The goal is to walk you through the process of designing and building a full-featured class for both the iPhone and Windows Phone 7 so that you can compare and contrast and map your existing iPhone skills (if any) to how classes are created in C#.

To demonstrate class creation, we need some behavior and data that we want to model. Throughout the rest of the chapter we'll be working on a class that might show up in a game. Because we are good little programmers that have been following the advice of those who know better, this class will model just behavior, logic, and data encapsulation and will not have anything to do with UI. In short, this class is a pure model and not a view.

The class we're going to build as a starting point is a class that models the logic, data encapsulation, and behavior of an object that can participate in combat in a hypothetical mobile game. We'll call this class a *Combatant*.

To start with, we'll create an empty class. In Listings 3.1 and 3.2, respectively, you can see the code for the Objective-C header (.h) and implementation (.m) files. Listing 3.3 shows this same (utterly empty, and completely useless up to this point) class in C#.

Listing 3.1   **Combatant.h**

```
@interface Combatant : NSObject {

}

@end
```

In the preceding code, you can see the stock contents of an Objective-C header file as they would look immediately after creating an empty class using an Xcode template. There really isn't much to see here. The important thing to keep in mind when learning C# is that C# classes do not separate the code into header and implementation files.

Listing 3.2   **Combatant.m**

```
#import "Combatant.h"

@implementation Combatant

@end
```

The preceding code is the implementation file for an Objective-C class. This is where all the actual implementation code goes, whereas the header file is used to allow other code that references this class to know how the class behaves and what data it exposes.

Listing 3.3   **Combatant.cs**

```csharp
using System;

namespace Chapter3
{
    public class Combatant
    {
    }
}
```

Finally, Listing 3.3 shows the same empty class implemented in C#. If you created your own empty class by adding one to a WP7 project, you probably noticed a whole bunch of extra using statements. For clarity, I removed those from Listing 3.3. There's not much to see here, and we haven't gotten to any of the fun stuff. The purpose of this section was to help you get your head around the difference between how classes are stored on disk in iOS and C#, and we will progressively go through more OOP comparisons throughout this chapter.

Encapsulating Data

One of the most important things that any class can do is to encapsulate data. This is one of the main reasons for the original use of object-oriented programming.

Data encapsulation involves a few key concepts that each programming language implements differently:

- Store member variables
- Provide wrappers around accessing those variables
- Add scope and security (for example, read-only) to member variables

Objective-C in its earlier days had somewhat limited support for what most modern programming languages call properties, but now has full and robust capabilities for data encapsulation that rival those of C#.

The best way to see data encapsulation in action is to look at some code with member variables in it. In these next few code listings, we're going to add member variables to the Combatant class that will model some of the properties of a combatant that we know the game engine might need, such as hit points, armor class, damage class, and a few other details.

Listing 3.4 shows how we might declare properties in the header file of an iOS application.

Listing 3.4   **Combatant.h with Member Variables**

```
@interface Combatant : NSObject {
}


@property(nonatomic, assign) int maxHitPoints;
@property(nonatomic, assign) int currentHitPoints;
@property(nonatomic, assign) int armorClass;
@property(nonatomic, assign) int damageClass;
@property(nonatomic, retain) NSString *combatantName;
```

This should be fairly familiar to most iOS developers. We have a couple of int-based properties to store values such as hit points and armor class, and there is a string property for storing the combatant name. Using the @property syntax, we can specify that the autogenerated accessor for the combatantName property will automatically retain the string. In C#, we don't need to worry about retaining strings as a precaution against unintended disposal like we do in Objective-C. Listing 3.5 shows the implementation that automatically synthesizes the getter and setter accessors for the properties declared in Listing 3.4.

Listing 3.5   **Combatant.m with Member Variables**

```
#import "Combatant.h"


@implementation Combatant
    @synthesize maxHitPoints, currentHitPoints, armorClass, damageClass,
combatantName;
@end
```

In the implementation (.m) file, I'm using the @synthesize keyword to instruct Xcode that it should autogenerate accessors for those properties. How Xcode does so is governed by the information in the header file in the @property declaration. If I wanted to, I could manually override this autogeneration process and supply my own accessor for specific properties, or even replace a get or a set accessor.

Listing 3.6 shows the C# version of the Combatant class, including the automatic implementation of the property get and set accessors.

Listing 3.6   **Combatant.cs with Member Variables**

```
using System;
using System.Net;
using System.Windows;


namespace Chapter3
{
    public class Combatant
    {
```

```
    public int MaxHitpoints { get; set; }
    public int CurrentHitPoints { get; set; }
    public int ArmorClass { get; set; }
    public int DamageClass { get; set; }
    public string Name { get; set; }|
    public Point Location { get; set; }

    public int HitPointPercent
    {
        get
        {
            double pct =
             (double)CurrentHitPoints / (double)MaxHitpoints;
            return (int)Math.Floor(pct * 100);
        }
    }
  }
}
```

Listing 3.6 shows the basic `Combatant` class with several public properties that use a shortcut syntax available in C#. This shortcut syntax allows the developer to leave the get and set implementations blank. When these accessors are left blank, the compiler will automatically generate a private member variable to back the public property and do all the required plumbing on behalf of the developer. This type of "automatic property" is also available in iOS.

The `public` keyword in front of each of the property names indicates that the property is visible and accessible from any class in any assembly. If the keyword were changed to `internal`, the properties would be available only to other classes within that assembly. Finally, the `private` keyword indicates that only that class has access to those members. You will learn about the `protected` keyword later in the chapter when we get into inheritance and object hierarchies.

The last property, `HitPointPercent`, shows an example of how you can create a read-only property that computes its value dynamically based on other properties. This shows another example of data encapsulation in that it allows the developer to hide the complexity of a calculation behind a simple property. In this example it's a simple percentage calculation, but you can imagine how this kind of technique can come in handy when modeling complex business objects with very detailed rules and logic. Also note that we have to typecast each of the integer values in the division calculation to a floating point value; otherwise, the / operator would assume integer division and return 0 instead of a fractional value.

Adding Behavior

Now that you've got a class that encapsulates data, you want to add behavior to it. Behavior in classes is added in the form of methods, which are functions that execute within the scope of an instance of a class.

Methods in Objective-C typically have their signature defined in the header (.h) file and the implementation defined in the implementation (.m) file. In C#, the method is defined directly on the class and there is no header used for exposing the method signature.

Some of the behavior that we want to add to our Combatant class might include attacking another combatant and moving. Listings 3.7 through 3.9 illustrate how we go about adding methods to the class to give our class some behavior. A good general rule is to think of members (or properties) as nouns on a model, whereas behaviors (or methods) should be considered verbs on a model.

Listing 3.7   **Combatant.h with Behavior**

```
@interface Combatant : NSObject {
}

- (void)attack:(Combatant *)target;

@property(nonatomic, assign) int maxHitPoints;
@property(nonatomic, assign) int currentHitPoints;
@property(nonatomic, assign) int armorClass;
@property(nonatomic, assign) int damageClass;
@property(nonatomic, retain) NSString *combatantName;
```

Listing 3.7 shows the header for the Combatant class, including the property declarations as well as a method signature for the Attack method.

Listing 3.8   **Combatant.m with Behavior**

```
#import "Combatant.h"

@implementation Combatant
    @synthesize maxHitPoints, currentHitPoints, armorClass, damageClass,
combatantName;

- (void)attack:(Combatant *)target
{
    // obviously this should be more complicated...
    target.currentHitPoints -= rand() % 20;
}
@end
```

Listing 3.8 shows the Objective-C implementation of the `Attack` method. This method operates on a supplied instance of another combatant to allow it to do damage to the other target. It's important to keep in mind here that in Listing 3.8's Objective-C code and in Listing 3.9's C# code, both classes are using encapsulated accessors to manipulate the other objects; they are not modifying internal variables directly.

Listing 3.9   **Combatant.cs with Behavior**

```csharp
using System;
using System.Net;
using System.Windows;
using System.Diagnostics;

namespace Chapter3
{
    public class Combatant
    {
        public int MaxHitpoints { get; set; }
        public int CurrentHitPoints { get; internal set; }
        public int ArmorClass { get; set; }
        public int DamageClass { get; set; }
        public string Name { get; set; }
        public Point Location { get; private set; }

        public int HitPointPercent
        {
            get
            {
                double pct =
                 (double)CurrentHitPoints / (double)MaxHitpoints;
                return (int)Math.Floor(pct * 100);
            }
        }

        public void MoveTo(Point newLocation)
        {
            this.Location = newLocation;
            Debug.WriteLine("Combatant {0} just moved to ({1},{2})",
                this.Name,
                this.Location.X,
                this.Location.Y);
        }

        public void Attack(Combatant target)
        {
            Random r = new Random();
            // obviously oversimplified algorithm...
```

```
            int damage =
            (this.DamageClass - target.ArmorClass) * r.Next(20);
            target.CurrentHitPoints -= damage;
        }
    }
}
```

In Listing 3.9 there are a couple of minor changes to the access modifiers for some of the class members, and we have the implementation of the `Attack` and `MoveTo` methods. What you might notice is that the `CurrentHitPoints` property now has an access modifier of `internal` for the set accessor. This means that only classes within the same Assembly as `Combatant` are able to modify that property. This allows your "game engine" to freely tweak combatant health but does not allow code outside the core engine to modify that data directly. This forces all changes to hit points to go through only authorized routes.

Additionally, the `Location` property now has a private access modifier. This means that only the `Combatant` class itself can modify its own location. This forces changes to the `Combatant`'s location to go through the `MoveTo` method, which is the only acceptable means for moving a `Combatant`.

The reason I mention these here is because C# has much finer-grained control over access modifiers for methods and members than Objective-C, allowing you to place much more firm control over which code can and cannot affect certain pieces of data. Although this might seem like an unimportant detail, it becomes incredibly important when you are writing code that other developers will consume. An entire type of "accidental side effect" bugs can be eliminated by preventing unwanted changes to your member variables and properties.

Inheritance

In this section of the chapter we're going to take a look at how we can use inheritance to create specialized derivatives of the original `Combatant` class. For example, we might want to create a particular type of combatant that cannot move, such as an automated turret or a stationary cannon. Another kind we might want to create might be combatants that get an extra attack because they are so quick. Finally, we might want to create something completely unusual, such as a drunken attacker who never hits for more than one point of damage at a time.

Figure 3.1 shows the class hierarchy diagram that we want to create from the existing `Combatant` class. As you can see, we want to create three new classes:

- `ReallyDangerousCombatant`
- `StationaryCombatant`
- `DrunkenCombatant`

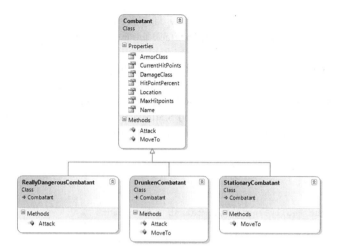

Figure 3.1   Class inheritance hierarchy diagram.

Building these classes in either C# or Objective-C is pretty straightforward. C# gives us a bit more fine-grained control over what the inheriting types can do and see, so we'll make more use of the access modifiers than we do in Objective-C.

In Listings 3.10 and 3.11, I show a sample derivative class called `ReallyDangerousCombatant`, written in Objective-C, that does double damage. This is inheritance in its most basic form—creating a child class that provides behavior that supersedes that of the parent.

Listing 3.10   **ReallyDangerousCombatant.h**

```
#import "Combatant.h"

@interface ReallyDangerousCombatant : Combatant {
}
@end
```

And the implementation of the "really dangerous" combatant class:

Listing 3.11   **ReallyDangerousCombatant.m**

```
#import "ReallyDangerousCombatant.h"

@implementation ReallyDangerousCombatant

- (void)attack:(Combatant *)target
{
    [super attack:target];
    target.currentHitPoints -= 12;
}
```

In Listing 3.11, you can see that the really dangerous combatant first asks its parent class (indicated by the super keyword) to attack the target. Then it does its own damage to the target. This really dangerous implementation will always do 12 more damage than a regular combatant would do because of the inheritance hierarchy.

In the interest of saving space and spending more time focusing on the C# implementations of these classes, I won't include the listings for DrunkenCombatant.h, Drunken-Combatant.m, StationaryCombatant.h, and StationaryCombatant.m. The following three listings show the C# implementations for the new derived classes.

Listing 3.12   **ReallyDangerousCombatant.cs**

```
namespace Chapter3
{
    public class ReallyDangerousCombatant : Combatant
    {
        public override void Attack(Combatant target)
        {
            base.Attack(target);

            // attack again for good measure!
            base.Attack(target);
        }
    }
}
```

Listing 3.13 shows how we can use inheritance and child classes to make a combatant that is so drunk it can't possibly win a fight and has an incredibly hard time moving where the game tells it to move:

Listing 3.13   **DrunkenCombatant.cs**

```
using System;
using System.Windows;

namespace Chapter3
{
    public class DrunkenCombatant : Combatant
    {
        public override void Attack(Combatant target)
        {
            target.CurrentHitPoints -= 1; // never do any real damage
        }

        public override void MoveTo(Point newLocation)
        {
            Random r = new Random();
```

```
        Point realLocation =
          new Point(r.NextDouble() * 30, r.NextDouble() * 30);

        this.Location = realLocation;
      }
    }
}
```

And now let's take a look at using inheritance to create a combatant that refuses to move at all (such as a stationary turret gun):

Listing 3.14   **StationaryCombatant.cs**

```
using System.Windows;

namespace Chapter3
{
    public class StationaryCombatant : Combatant
    {
        public override void MoveTo(Point newLocation)
        {
            // do nothing
        }

    }
}
```

No matter how many times the game engine might ask this combatant to move, it will do nothing in response.

Inheritance Versus Switching on Data

This is an argument that continues today, no matter your choice of platform or language, so long as it supports OOP. Take the example of a `StationaryCombatant`. What we've done is build a child class such that any time it is asked to move, it simply refuses. Another alternative to this might be to create a Boolean property called `IsStationary`. Then the base class can check the status of the `IsStationary` property in its `Move` method. This prevents the need for creating an entire subclass for the purpose of stationary objects.

This might seem like a simpler solution at first. But this is the top of a slippery slope. Fairly quickly, your simple base class becomes little more than a garbage truck filled with properties and data—a massive storage bin that holds information that might be used only by 1% of all instances of that object. This is just the beginning of the troubles.

Now your simple `Move` method has become convoluted and filled with enormous if statements. In many cases, the logic can become nested and nearly impossible to read. When someone goes to make a change to your `Move` method, it can potentially break functionality for specialized instances of your class (such as for `Combatants` where `IsStationary` is true). Several design patterns are violated by these giant if statements, but in the interest of keeping things simple in this chapter, I won't go into their names or definitions here.

To sum up: If you can solve your specialization issues with inheritance and interfaces (discussed in the next section), that is often a much cleaner, more maintainable and reliable solution than filling a single "bloat master" class with inordinate amounts of properties and logic.

Programming with Contracts

Contracts are different from class implementations. A contract merely defines the requirements of a particular class; it does not actually control the class implementation. To continue the combatant analogy: A `Combatant` base class defines behavior that all child classes can inherit. A `Combatant` contract defines the behavior and data that must be implemented by any class wanting to call itself a combatant.

Let's walk through an example while assuming we're still building a game engine. If we go with a straight inheritance hierarchy, we might be limiting the types of interactions we can model. Assuming single inheritance (which is the case for both Objective-C and C#), anything that can do damage to a player (via the `Attack` method) must inherit from `Combatant`. This presents us with a problem: What about complex inanimate objects with a unique inheritance hierarchy but that cannot inherit from `Combatant`?

Let's say the player is walking through an alley and is struck by a car. Vehicles in this game might require their own inheritance hierarchy, probably starting with a base class such as `Vehicle` or `MovingObject`. Given that we don't have the capability to do multiple inheritance, how do we allow noncombatant objects to do damage to players without messing up the `Combatant` object hierarchy? The answer is contracts.

Contracts are called *protocols* in Objective-C and *interfaces* in C#, but they serve identical purposes. Contracts define a minimum set of required properties or methods that must be implemented by a particular class. They do not enforce any restrictions on inheritance hierarchies. It is critically important here to remember that two classes, each with entirely different inheritance hierarchies, can implement the same interface.

So let's take a look at the `Combatant` class. The `Attack` method does two things (which might give us a clue that we can start refactoring there): It figures out how much damage to do to an opponent, and then it asks the other combatant to take that damage. If we take out the function of taking the actual damage and make that a requirement on an interface called `ITakesDamage`, we start getting some real flexibility in our game engine. This interface has a requirement that anything implementing that interface must implement a method called `TakeDamage`.

Listing 3.15 shows the `ITakesDamage` interface in C#, and Listing 3.16 shows the new `Combatant` class, refactored to separate out the concern of doing damage to be something that satisfies the interface requirement.

Listing 3.15   **ITakesDamage.cs**

```
namespace Chapter3
{
    public interface ITakesDamage
    {
        void TakeDamage(int hitPoints);
    }
}
```

Listing 3.16 shows the refactored Combatant class to implement the interface.

Listing 3.16   **Combatant.cs (Refactored to Implement IDoesDamage)**

```
using System;
using System.Net;
using System.Windows;
using System.Diagnostics;

namespace Chapter3
{
    public class Combatant : ITakesDamage
    {
        public int MaxHitpoints { get; set; }
        public int CurrentHitPoints { get; private set; }
        public int ArmorClass { get; set; }
        public int DamageClass { get; set; }
        public string Name { get; set; }
        public Point Location { get; protected set; }

        public Combatant()
        {
            this.CurrentHitPoints = this.MaxHitpoints;
        }

        public int HitPointPercent
        {
            get
            {
                double pct =
                  (double)CurrentHitPoints / (double)MaxHitpoints;
                return (int)Math.Floor(pct * 100);
            }
        }

        public virtual void MoveTo(Point newLocation)
        {
```

```
        this.Location = newLocation;
        Debug.WriteLine("Combatant {0} just moved to ({1},{2})",
            this.Name,
            this.Location.X,
            this.Location.Y);
    }

    public virtual void Attack(Combatant target)
    {
        Random r = new Random();
        int damage =
            (this.DamageClass - target.ArmorClass) * r.Next(20);
        target.TakeDamage(damage);
    }


    public void TakeDamage(int hitPoints)
    {
        this.CurrentHitPoints -= hitPoints;
    }
  }
}
```

The new Attack method on the Combatant class now determines the amount of damage to be done and then calls the TakeDamage method to affect the target. Now that the Combatant class isn't the only thing in the game engine that can be damaged (anything that implements ITakesDamage can now be harmed), we can create classes like the PincushionTarget (shown in Listing 3.17), which can be harmed by players but is not a combatant.

Listing 3.17   **PincushionTarget.cs**

```
public class PincushionTarget : ITakesDamage
{
    void TakeDamage(int hitPoints)
    {
      // take points out of pincushion target
    }
}
```

For reference, Listing 3.18 shows what the protocol definition might look like in Objective-C. Objective-C does not use the uppercase "I" prefix naming convention but rather uses the word "Protocol" as a postfix. To achieve a similar goal in Objective-C, we would create a protocol called TakesDamageProtocol like the one shown in Listing 3.19. I show you this because protocols are used extensively throughout iOS and in UIKit, so recognizing how those patterns translate into C# patterns can be very useful.

Listing 3.18   **TakesDamageProtocol.h**

```
@protocol TakesDamageProtocol
- (void)takeDamage:(int)hitPoints;
@end
```

Namespaces Versus Naming Conventions

As you have been going through the samples in this chapter, you might have noticed that the C# classes always exist within a namespace. Namespaces in C# are designed specifically to avoid naming collisions as well as to aid in organizing hierarchies of logically connected classes, enums, and structs.

In Objective-C and throughout all of Apple's libraries, either for the iPhone or for traditional Mac development, you will see that there are no namespaces. The decision was made for Objective-C to not support the concept of namespaces (which are available in many OOP languages, including C# and C++). Instead, Apple has opted for a standard by which classes belonging to a particular family, purpose, product, or company all begin with a common two-letter prefix in all capital letters.

For example, a combatant class written by someone named Kevin Hoffman might actually be called `KHCombatant` rather than simply `Combatant`. Further, that same class written by a company called Exclaim Computing might be written as `ECCombatant` or `XCCombatant`.

Naming collisions within iOS applications are rare because you will encounter these collisions only if your application is making use of a library, framework, or class that contains classes named identically to yours. The rare chances of naming collisions in this situation are usually eliminated with the use of the two-letter prefix naming convention.

Extending Other People's Classes

The last topic I want to cover in this chapter is the capability to extend classes written by other developers or companies without actually having the source code to those classes. Keep in mind that in both iOS and C#, extensions to third-party classes can access only class members and methods to which your code would normally have access. In other words, you cannot use class extensions to circumvent encapsulation methods surrounding private or protected members.

C# gives us a facility called *static extensions*, which is roughly analogous to the concept of categories in the Objective-C world. When a static extension to a specific class is in scope of the current code block, that code block can invoke methods on the extension class as if those methods actually belonged to the original class.

Let's assume that we didn't write the `Combatant` class and that it's sealed and we cannot inherit from it. We want to be able to add a method to the `Combatant` class that makes the object move in a square, as if it was square dancing. Perhaps this effect is a custom spell that can be cast on our combatants that gives them an irresistible urge to get their hoedown on.

We can accomplish this custom extension to the `Combatant` class using the code in Listing 3.19.

Listing 3.19   **CombatantSquareDancingExtension.cs**

```
using System;
using System.Net;
using System.Windows;
using System.Windows.Controls;
using System.Windows.Documents;
using System.Windows.Ink;
using System.Windows.Input;
using System.Windows.Media;
using System.Windows.Media.Animation;
using System.Windows.Shapes;

namespace Chapter3
{
    public static class CombatantSquareDancingExtension
    {
        public static void SquareDance(this Combatant dancer)
        {
            Point origin = dancer.Location;
            Point step1 =
              new Point(origin.X, origin.Y - 1); // move forward
            Point step2 =
              new Point(step1.X - 1, step1.Y); // move left
            Point step3 =
              new Point(step2.X, step2.Y + 1); // move back
            Point step4 =
              new Point(step3.X + 1, step3.Y); // move right
        }
    }
}
```

Although there are no hard and fast rules about naming conventions used for building extension classes, I like to follow a simple naming scheme: *[OriginalClass][ExtensionDescription]Extension.* The presence of the suffix Extension immediately tells me and any other developer looking at this class that it is not a complete class on its own; rather, it provides additional functionality to some other class. The class being extended is the first section of the name of the extension class. So in our example, a class that extends the `Combatant` class by providing square dancing capabilities would be called `CombatantSquareDancingExtension`.

If the code in Listing 3.19 is in scope, it should be perfectly legal (and possibly amusing) to invoke the `SquareDance` method of any object that is (directly or through inheritance) of type `Combatant`.

Summary

In this chapter, you were given a brief overview of some of the core concepts of object-oriented programming (OOP) and how they apply to the tasks of building iOS and Windows Phone 7 applications using Objective-C and C#, respectively.

Those of you who have been programming for a long time might have found some of these concepts remedial, but the key here was to introduce you to the syntax required for day-to-day programming in an object-oriented programming language such as C#. As you progress through the rest of the book, we will be using things like encapsulation, inheritance, properties, methods, interfaces, and extensions extensively, and if you don't have a firm grasp on those concepts now, the rest of the book will be very difficult to read.

If you have read through this chapter and feel as though you now have a decent understanding of how to write OOP code in C#, you are well prepared to dive deeper into the world of building Windows Phone 7 applications and continue with the rest of the book.

Event-Driven Programming

Transmitted at the speed of light, all events on this planet are simultaneous. In the electric environment of information all events are simultaneous, there is no time or space separating events.

Marshall McLuhan

This chapter provides an overview of an often underrated aspect of modern programming frameworks: events. In many cases when comparing Objective-C to C#, there are subtle linguistic differences while the core concepts remain the same.

This chapter gives you an overview of what true event-driven programming is, how such programming is accomplished in Objective-C, and finally, how this same type of programming can be accomplished in C# within the context of a Windows Phone 7 application.

What Is Event-Driven Programming?

The subject of event-driven programming is an area in which Objective-C and C# differ greatly and at a core, fundamental level. An event isn't just a single thing. When an event of some importance occurs, you have three pieces of information that are typically required to take appropriate action in response to that event:

- The object sending the event—This object knows someone is interested in the event that has occurred and is responsible for dispatching that event to all subscribers.

- The event itself—The sender needs to tell the receivers exactly what happened and provide sufficient context.

- The event subscriber or receiver—As far as C# is concerned, if a tree falls in the woods and there are no event subscribers to be told about it, nothing happened. When an event occurs, those objects interested in that event are told and are given the previous two pieces of information: the event sender and the context information about the event itself.

As you read through this chapter, you will see how Objective-C's "delegate pattern" is used and how that relates to the publish-and-subscribe event-driven model espoused by the .NET Framework.

Another common misconception among both newbies and veterans in the C# world is that events are applicable only to the user interface. For example, most programmers can tell you that events are generated when you tap a button with your finger or when you submit text to an input control. However, far too many programmers don't know that events can be both useful and powerful when used throughout all levels of your application, not just the UI. You will see extremely powerful examples of how essential event-driven programming is for WP7 when we get to a discussion on asynchronous programming and communication with external services.

Using the Delegate Pattern in Objective-C

Objective-C doesn't use events the same way that C# does, and this is often a source of confusion when programmers are trying to relate their skills from iPhone development to the .NET Framework or WP7 development.

In iOS (and virtually all other Mac-based development using Objective-C) something called the *delegate pattern* is utilized almost exclusively for event-driven programming. This pattern works as follows:

If a class needs to inform another class about something, or obtain information from another class, a reference to that object is stored as a delegate. This delegate isn't like a C# delegate (which is roughly analogous to a C function pointer). Instead, this delegate is more like the dictionary definition of the word: the class is delegating functionality to another class.

For example, one of the most common control types in iOS programming is the UITableView. This control displays data arranged in vertical rows. The individual cells in these rows can be highly customized, but no matter how customized the control might be, it still performs certain core functionality the same way.

Rather than having some other class push data into the table view, the table view asks for data. This allows the table view to maintain its own optimization so that it asks only for the data it knows is going to be rendered on the screen (or will be rendered very soon). In addition to delegating the data source to another class, the UITableView also delegates the methods that respond to user events to another class, such as when a row is selected, when the view state changes into edit mode, and so on. There are even methods delegated to other classes for telling the table view how many groups there are, the style that should be used for the groupings, and for providing a custom cell to the view for each row being rendered.

For those familiar with .NET programming, this pattern might seem entirely backward. .NET programmers, especially those used to Windows Forms or ASP.NET programming, are used to gathering the data themselves and then stuffing the data into a control through some kind of data-binding mechanism. The concept of the controller being a passive participant that is invoked only when the UI control needs it often seems very strange indeed.

However strange it might seem to C# developers, this pattern is incredibly powerful and works amazingly well for iOS. Each type of delegate is required to expose a certain set of methods (some of which are optional, a very important point) so that the class utilizing the delegate can be assured that all delegated functionality is provided.

The agreement between a delegate and the class doing the delegation is very often defined explicitly in the form of a protocol. For example, the UITableViewController class is a handy controller that comes pre-equipped to conform to the two different protocols required by the UITableView control: UITableViewDelegate (the protocol that deals with handling events that occur within the control) and UITableViewDataSource (the protocol that defines how a delegate must provide rows, cells, groups, and other data for the table view).

Table 4.1 shows just a few of the methods that are part of the two delegate protocols that define the communication between the UITableView control and your application. As you will see later in this chapter, this pattern is very different from the way Silverlight controls communicate with your application in Windows Phone 7 applications.

Table 4.1   Some Delegate Methods for iOS Table View Controllers

Protocol	Method	Description
UITableViewDelegate	`tableView:willSelectRowAtIndexPath:`	Used to perform actions before selecting a row
UITableViewDelegate	`tableView:didSelectRowAtIndexPath:`	Invoked after a row has been selected by the user
UITableViewDataSource	`tableView:cellForRowAtIndexPath:`	Returns a configured cell to be rendered by the table view in the appropriate place
UITableViewDataSource	`numberOfSectionsInTableView:`	Returns the number of section groups in the view
UITableViewDataSource	`tableView:numberOfRowsInSection:`	Returns the number of rows in a given section

The important thing to remember here when looking at the delegate pattern is that it often appears backward or passive when compared to traditional C# data-binding patterns. This is true, but the delegate pattern accomplishes far more than just data binding—it bundles together logically associated operations, defines them with a protocol, and then allows any control to be supplied with data or other parameters by any class.

When used properly, the delegate pattern can contribute to highly cohesive applications with very well-defined boundaries and loose coupling between the UI, the models, and the controllers. Developers familiar with Mac and iOS programming will know how deeply ingrained the concept of Model-View-Controller is within the entire framework.

As you will see in the next section, C# events operate in a different fashion entirely because they solve a different set of problems.

Using Events in C#

Whereas a delegate is a class that conforms to a specific protocol and is agreeing to perform a certain set of logically related behaviors for another class, an event is a single occurrence of some fine-grained activity worth mentioning. To further differentiate the delegate pattern from C# events, an iOS will have only one delegate at a time (although they can be switched dynamically at runtime) whereas an event can have multiple subscribers at once and can notify them all simultaneously of the same event.

In idiomatic C#, you will rarely see people make use of the delegate pattern (although it is entirely possible and often quite elegant when paired with interfaces). Instead, events are exposed on an object as endpoints to which consumers can subscribe.

To continue our example from the previous chapter with Combatants, let's expose a few events on the Combatant to make the game engine more flexible and reactive. A few of the events we might want to expose are the following:

- When a Combatant is hit
- When a Combatant hits another enemy
- When a Combatant dies

The game engine can subscribe to these events to perform specific actions when these events occur. For example, when a Combatant dies, the game engine can broadcast a message to all connected players indicating that some combatant has died as well as who did the killing. If you've ever played a multiplayer combat game, this particular pattern should seem familiar; most of us have seen scrolling messages on the bottom of our screens indicating that a buddy just stepped on a landmine or took a sniper bullet in the face.

Listing 4.1 shows a new Combatant class (simplified to only contain things pertinent to demonstrating events and C# delegates). It exposes the three events previously discussed and contains wrapper methods for invoking these events. You will see this pattern very often in C# code because every event notification needs to be guarded by a check to see whether there are any subscribers. This type of plumbing work is handled for you automatically when you subscribe to Silverlight's UI events.

Listing 4.1   **Combatant.cs (Showing Events)**

```csharp
using System;
using System.Net;
using System.Windows;
using System.Windows.Controls;
using System.Windows.Documents;
using System.Windows.Ink;
using System.Windows.Input;
using System.Windows.Media;
using System.Windows.Media.Animation;
using System.Windows.Shapes;

namespace WindowsPhoneApplication1
{
    public delegate void DidGetKilledDelegate(
      Combatant killer, Combatant target);

    public delegate void DidHitTargetDelegate(
      Combatant attacker, Combatant target, int hitPoints);

    public class Combatant
    {
        public event DidGetKilledDelegate OnGotKilled;
        public event DidHitTargetDelegate OnHitCombatant;
        public event DidHitTargetDelegate OnHitByCombatant;

        public int HitPoints { get; set; }
        public string Name { get; set; }

        public void Attack(Combatant target)
        {
            // obviously this would be algorithm-based in a real game
            bool didHit = true;
            int hitPoints = 42;


            if (didHit)
            {
                NotifyHitCombatant(target, hitPoints);
            }
        }

        public void TakeDamage(Combatant attacker, int hitPoints)
        {
            this.HitPoints -= hitPoints;
            NotifyHitByCombatant(attacker, hitPoints);
            if (this.HitPoints <= 0)
```

```
            {
                NotifyGotKilled(attacker);
            }
        }

        private void NotifyHitByCombatant(Combatant attacker, int hitPoints)
        {
            if (OnHitByCombatant != null)
            {
                OnHitByCombatant(attacker, this, hitPoints);
            }
        }

        private void NotifyGotKilled(Combatant attacker)
        {
            if (OnGotKilled != null)
            {
                OnGotKilled(attacker, this);
            }
        }

        private void NotifyHitCombatant(Combatant target, int hitPoints)
        {
            if (OnHitCombatant != null)
            {
                OnHitCombatant(this, target, hitPoints);
            }
        }
    }
}
```

The code in Listing 4.1 shows a couple of interesting things. The first reinforces what I mentioned earlier about how events are signals to broadcast a notification about a single important occurrence to multiple subscribers. This differs greatly from the delegate pattern.

Next, you might have noticed that C# has a keyword called `delegate`. This is not the same kind of delegate you might be familiar with in Objective-C. This delegate is roughly analogous to a function pointer in C. The `delegate` keyword in Listing 4.1 assigns a method signature to a named type. For example, the method signature

```
void (Combatant killer, Combatant target)
```

is assigned to a named type (which is a descendant of type `delegate`) called `DidGetKilledDelegate`. Putting the postfix `Delegate` on the end of the type name is a naming convention that I prefer, and I think it helps keep the code as self-documenting as possible.

So, now that you have code that publishes events (Listing 4.1), let's take a look at some code that consumes events. In this case we'll write a barely functional stub of a game engine. It acts as a factory to create instances of Combatants and, once instantiated, subscribes to all their events. Listing 4.2 shows the implementation of this game engine class and the implementations of the methods that are called in response to the various combatant events.

Listing 4.2   **GameEngine.cs**

```
using System;
using System.Net;
using System.Windows;
using System.Windows.Controls;
using System.Windows.Documents;
using System.Windows.Ink;
using System.Windows.Input;
using System.Windows.Media;
using System.Windows.Media.Animation;
using System.Windows.Shapes;
using System.Diagnostics;

namespace WindowsPhoneApplication1
{
    public static class GameEngine
    {
        public static Combatant CreateCombatant()
        {
            Combatant c = new Combatant();
            c.OnGotKilled += new DidGetKilledDelegate(c_OnGotKilled);
            c.OnHitByCombatant +=
              new DidHitTargetDelgate(c_OnHitByCombatant);
            c.OnHitCombatant +=
              new DidHitTargetDelegate(c_OnHitCombatant);

            return c;
        }

        static void c_OnHitCombatant(
          Combatant attacker, Combatant target, int hitPoints)
        {
            BroadCast(attacker.Name + " hit " +
              target.Name + " for " + hitPoints.ToString() +
              " hitpoints.");
        }

        static void c_OnHitByCombatant(
          Combatant attacker, Combatant target, int hitPoints)
```

```
    {
        BroadCast(target.Name + " was hit for " +
          hitPoints.ToString() + " by " + attacker.Name);
    }

    static void c_OnGotKilled(Combatant killer, Combatant target)
    {
        BroadCast(killer.Name + " killed " + target.Name +
          "! OH NOEZ!!1ONE");
    }

    static void BroadCast(string msg)
    {
        // ordinarily there would be network code here
        // to broadcast to the entire game
        Debug.WriteLine("[Game]: " + msg);
    }
    }
}
```

Listing 4.2 shows how a C# class might subscribe to events published by another class. Note that the += operator, normally used for adding to an existing number or in-place string concatenation, is also used to add an instance of a subscriber delegate to the event's subscriber list. Likewise, you can use the -= operator to remove that instance of a delegate from the event's subscriber list. One thing you cannot do, however, is remove a subscriber that you didn't add. In other words, two different pieces of code written by two different developers, even though subscribing to the same event, cannot modify each other's event subscriptions.

Global Events and NSNotifications

So far we've seen how to handle events in a typical publish-subscribe pattern. However, if you look closely at the code in Listing 4.2, you'll notice that the events to which the code is subscribing are exposed by objects that have local scope. In other words, we can only subscribe to (and receive events from) those objects that our code can "see." It is not immediately obvious how we might broadcast events throughout our entire application to which any object may subscribe, regardless of scope or object lifetime.

iOS has a very robust solution to this problem. The NSNotificationCenter class is a static (global scope) class that exposes a singleton property called defaultCenter. This property serves as a hub for a robust publish-and-subscribe mechanism. Any object may post notifications through the global notification center and any object may listen for notifications published by the notification center. Notifications can have unique (string) identifiers so that objects can subscribe to only certain types of notifications.

This notification center functionality works with two simple operations: adding an observer (subscribe) and posting a notification (publish).

Several very important (and often low-level) events are publicized through the notification center. For example, when the iPhone is rotated, the default notification center for the currently running application publishes a notification. Your app can either listen to that notification directly (not recommended), or the UIKit Framework will listen to it for you and provide a higher-level abstraction around the concept of rotating the UI to deal with orientation changes.

If you want to code something like this in C#, it is pretty simple to do. In addition, some helper toolkits and frameworks (such as some MVVM implementations that we'll talk about later in the book) already include facilities for publishing and subscribing to global notifications.

The super-quick and easy way to accomplish global notifications in your C# application is to use static classes that expose static events. To this end, we'll add a few static events to the GameEngine object that indicate when a game has started, when it has been paused, and when it finishes. Any object, regardless of lifetime or scope, can subscribe to these events and execute code in response to them. This revised GameEngine object is shown in Listing 4.3.

Listing 4.3   **GameEngine.cs (with Static Events)**

```
using System;
using System.Net;
using System.Windows;
using System.Windows.Controls;
using System.Windows.Documents;
using System.Windows.Ink;
using System.Windows.Input;
using System.Windows.Media;
using System.Windows.Media.Animation;
using System.Windows.Shapes;
using System.Diagnostics;

namespace WindowsPhoneApplication1
{
    public delegate void OnGameStartedDelegate(DateTime startTime);
    public delegate void OnGamePausedDelegate();
    public delegate void OnGameFinishedDelegate();

    public static class GameEngine
    {
        public static void Start()
        {
            if (OnGameStarted != null)
                OnGameStarted(DateTime.Now);
        }
```

```
public static void Stop()
{
    if (OnGameFinished != null)
        OnGameFinished();
}

public static void Pause()
{
    if (OnGamePaused != null)
        OnGamePaused();
}

public static void Resume()
{
    if (OnGameResumed != null)
        OnGameResumed(DateTime.Now);
}

public static Combatant CreateCombatant()
{
    Combatant c = new Combatant();
    c.OnGotKilled += new DidGetKilledDelegate(c_OnGotKilled);
    c.OnHitByCombatant +=
      new DidHitTargetDelgate(c_OnHitByCombatant);
    c.OnHitCombatant +=
      new DidHitTargetDelegate(c_OnHitCombatant);

    return c;
}

static void c_OnHitCombatant(
  Combatant attacker, Combatant target, int hitPoints)
{

    BroadCast(attacker.Name + " hit " + target.Name +
      " for " + hitPoints.ToString() + " hitpoints.");
}

static void c_OnHitByCombatant(Combatant attacker,
 Combatant target, int hitPoints)
{
    BroadCast(target.Name + " was hit for " +
      hitPoints.ToString() + " by " + attacker.Name);
}

static void c_OnGotKilled(Combatant killer, Combatant target)
{
```

```
            BroadCast(killer.Name + " killed " + target.Name +
                "! OH NOEZ!!1ONE");
        }

        static void BroadCast(string msg)
        {
            // ordinarily there would be network code here
            // to broadcast to the entire game

            Debug.WriteLine("[Game]: " + msg);
        }

        public static event OnGameStartedDelegate OnGameStarted;
        public static event OnGameFinishedDelegate OnGameFinished;
        public static event OnGamePausedDelegate OnGamePaused;
        public static event Action<DateTime> OnGameResumed;
    }
}
```

At this point, the code in Listing 4.3 should look pretty straightforward. There are new methods on the game engine that will trigger various events such as Start, Stop, Pause, and Resume. At the end of the listing you can see where I've declared the four new events.

If you have been looking closely, you'll notice something a little different about the way I've declared the OnGameResumed event. I didn't use a strongly typed delegate that was declared at the top of the namespace like I did in previous listings. Instead I made use of a few shorthand features in C# like Generics and the generic type called Action<T>.

Generics allow classes to be associated with a particular type by the code creating the instance, rather than by the class itself. For example, rather than creating a list of objects that can be any type by using an instance of the List class, I can create a list of combatants by creating an instance of List<Combatant>. Generics allow me to supply one or more type parameters to a class when instantiating it. If you want to know more about Generics and other low-level details of the C# language itself, you might want to pick up a copy of *C# 4.0 Unleashed,* by Bart De Smet.

The second change to the last event declaration is the use of Action<DateTime>. The Action<T> class is a generic class that provides a kind of shorthand for delegates that have a void return type. As you can see, writing Action<DateTime> once before the event declaration is much easier to read than creating a custom delegate type and then using that to declare the event. Anytime you see Action<T> you can translate that in your mind to "a void-returning delegate that takes a parameter of type T." There are also variants of Action that take multiple parameters to accommodate more parameters in the event handler.

Beware of Static Classes and Properties

Although I showed you that using static classes and event properties is one way of providing for a global event notification system in your application, you must take this advice with a grain of salt.

C# applications are garbage-collected. This means that a process runs in the background and cleans up your messes as you make them, freeing the memory allocated to objects that are orphaned or no longer in scope. Static classes and the properties they expose never leave scope. This means they are never orphaned and the memory allocated to them will never be reclaimed.

In short, if you can avoid the use of static classes and properties for anything (events or otherwise), do so. Before you create a bunch of static events on a class for global notifications, make sure that the effort is necessary. If you can deal with locally scoped event handling, do that instead; your memory footprint will be smaller, and garbage collection cycles will be quicker.

Summary

In this chapter, you were given a brief overview of event-driven programming from both an iOS and a Windows Phone 7 perspective.

In iOS (as well as Cocoa on the Mac) development, the delegate pattern is used extensively to allow objects to communicate with each other using known and agreed-upon contracts called protocols. The delegate pattern is used for everything from invoking methods in response to user events to supplying data to controls of different types, and it can be used by developers when building their own custom frameworks. The delegate pattern is typified by a passive feel where, rather than pushing data and functionality at controls, the controls passively request data and functionality on an as-needed basis. Even if you never use this pattern in your WP7 development, you should know and respect this pattern because it enables so many of the development features that make iPhone programming so compelling and powerful.

This chapter then moved from discussing the delegate pattern to discussing how events are handled in C#. You saw how to expose event properties, how to publish events, and how to subscribe to those events. Finally you saw how to utilize static classes and event properties to expose global events.

With the knowledge of OOP you gained in the previous chapter combined with the event-based programming knowledge in this chapter, you should be reaching a point where you are getting ready to start writing your first WP7 application.

5

Rendering and
View System Basics

Painting is poetry that is seen rather than felt, and poetry is painting that is felt rather than seen.

Leonardo DaVinci

This chapter provides an overview of how the underlying control rendering systems work on both the iOS and Windows Phone 7 platforms. This chapter is not about the controls themselves (there will be plenty of chapters on that later in the book). Rather, this chapter provides a review of the UIKit view system, including a brief discussion of coordinate systems, points versus pixels, and more.

This chapter next introduces you to Silverlight from a low-level perspective. Here you will see how Silverlight composes declarative UI elements and then renders them onto the screen and allows users to interact with those controls.

Having this kind of low-level knowledge of the plumbing of the view rendering systems might not seem all that useful now, but after you start rolling up your sleeves and writing some very serious WP7 applications and controls, you will be thankful that you have a basic understanding of what is going on under the hood and how that relates to the workings of a typical iOS application.

Review of the UIKit View System

If you have done any iPhone programming, you know that everything visible to the user is dealt with in layers. Think of it like a deck of cards. At the very bottom of the deck is the table. This is a UIWindow. Although you can technically have more than one UIWindow, only one window is displayed to a user at any given time.

The window, despite being an object, does not have any visual aspects. Unlike a typical desktop window, there is no close box, no minimize button, no context menu, nor even a title bar.

Every visual control in iOS inherits directly or indirectly from UIView, even the UIWindow. Think of the views as cards. Each one of these cards is placed on the table (inside a UIWindow's list of child views). New cards placed on the table can be placed in any orientation at any location. This means that new cards can cover up old cards or can exist without occluding any other view (card) beneath them.

Now that you're thinking about a table with a pile of cards scattered on it, imagine looking through a cardboard tube down at a small section of that table. That cardboard tube is the rendering area for the iPhone, iPod Touch, or iPad's screen. Any card that you can see while looking through that narrow tube is rendered, and anything else outside the tube is not displayed to the user, nor can any touches or other user-generated events affect those cards.

In short, everything you see and interact with in iOS is the direct result of a tree of nested views. Every UIView has a list of child views that are rendered on top of that view. Remember that view composition on iOS is done from the *bottom up*. To put that another way, child views occlude or cover over their parents. You can use all sorts of tricks with transparency and varying levels of opacity to create incredibly cool effects and user interfaces that rely on nothing more than clever view composition. In fact, clever view composition, good static images, and alpha blending are often used to create compelling and fast user interfaces without very much overhead.

Displaying Graphics and Rendering in iOS

One of the most important things to remember about displaying and positioning graphics, controls, images, or anything else on iOS are coordinate systems and view transformations.

The coordinate system starts with the origin at the top-left of the view. This is always the origin of the actual view (although the view may be transformed to appear to have a different origin when the device is rotated). The X coordinates continue upward from 0 heading to the right, whereas the Y coordinates increase growing downward from the origin. Unlike a center-origin system, views that are positioned entirely in negative coordinates are not visible.

When views are rendered in iOS, the `drawRect:` method is used to perform any custom drawing that the developer wants done within that view. Then each of the current view's subviews is told to draw itself. This process is done recursively until every view in the view hierarchy has been given a chance to render itself, *from the bottom up*.

Finally, it is important to remember that in iOS, any time you refer to a coordinate or a size, you are referring to it in terms of *points* rather than *pixels*. This distinction provides a scalable layer of abstraction between the physical pixel coordinates of the device and the developer. The iPad, iPod touch, and the iPhone 4.0's "retina display" all have different screen resolutions and pixel densities.

The iOS rendering engine (often referred to as Quartz) utilizes scalable vector graphics. By having developers express locations and sizes in terms of points rather than pixels, their applications can work in environments with varying pixel densities and still have the UI maintain the same relative appearance. Obviously, developers can choose to create different UIs for different devices (for example, using the larger resolution but lower pixel density of the iPad versus smaller resolution and higher pixel density of the iPhone 4), but having the unifying concept of a device-independent *point* rather than tying developers to pixels is freeing.

Finally, the last important point to mention about layout and rendering in iOS is that whether you use Interface Builder or Objective-C, the end result is that views are controlled programmatically. A view defined in Interface Builder is just executing code on your behalf, whereas a custom view you've written is controlled entirely by your own Objective-C code. As you will see in the following discussion of Silverlight, Silverlight places more emphasis on a declarative, markup-style way of defining user interface elements.

Introduction to XAML and Silverlight

As you already know if you're an iOS developer, UIKit is the collection of controls and APIs used for producing the user interface for iPhone and iPad applications. The Windows Phone 7 counterpart is Silverlight, a collection of controls and APIs used for building user interfaces on Windows Phone 7 (and also on the web with the larger and more powerful Silverlight 4).

One thing that iOS and other developers often find difficult to adjust to is XAML. Extensible Application Markup Language (XAML) is an XML dialect that Silverlight uses for declarative user interface construction. If you've ever done any development for Android or Flex, you might already be familiar with the concept of using declarative XML for user interfaces.

XML is handy for a couple of reasons. The first is that it is easy for software to read and write, which makes XAML "designer-friendly." The second reason is that XML is human-(well, those humans who belong to the subspecies *homo developus*) friendly as well. This means that developers can choose to type in the XML for their UI by hand, with the aid of a design tool, or use a combination of both.

Using XML to build UI isn't really a new concept. What is unique to XAML is that XAML isn't just a proprietary dialect that can be used to produce UI elements like the XIB file format for iOS or the view XML used by Android.

XAML is actually a generic, all-purpose *instantiation language*. This means that instead of requiring a design tool or some kind of parser to have detailed knowledge of the underlying UI framework (like Interface Builder's XIB files), XAML has no such tight coupling. XAML can be used to instantiate any .NET object types and is even used for non-UI purposes, such as the Windows Workflow Foundation (WF) in enterprise application development.

As you will see throughout this book, just about every piece of user interface (and even some things that are not visible) can be represented as XAML. As you see the code samples in this book, keep in mind that the XAML you're looking at is really nothing more than a declarative, designer-friendly view of a set of object instantiation and configuration statements.

Take a look at the following bit of XAML. It creates an instance of an object of type `Customer` and then sets several properties, including properties which are themselves instances of other objects like `Address`.

```
<cust:Customer
    FirstName="John"
    LastName="Doe"
    PhoneNumber="888-555-1212">
    <cust:Customer.Address>
        <cust:Address
            Line1="12 Somewhere St"
            Line2=""
            City="Somewhere"
            State="CA"
            Zip="90210"/>
    </cust:Customer.Address>
</cust:Customer>
```

In the preceding XAML, we're using an XML namespace prefix. In XAML, we can associate an XML namespace prefix with a .NET namespace. In the preceding sample, we might have associated the `cust` XML namespace prefix with the `MySamples.Customer` namespace using the following XAML:

```
xmlns:cust="clr-namespace:MySamples.Customer"
```

Keeping in mind that XAML has no tight coupling to any UI system and is just a generic way of instantiating via XML, we can assume that the preceding XAML is functionally equivalent to the following C# block:

```
Customer c = new Customer()
{
    FirstName = "John",
    LastName = "Doe",
    PhoneNumber = "888-555-1212",
    Address = new Address()
    {
        Line1="12 Somwhere St",
        Line2="",
        City="Somewhere",
        State="CA",
        Zip="90210"
    }
};
```

When learning Windows Phone 7 or Silverlight programming for the first time, a lot of developers have trouble adjusting to the XAML syntax. If you keep in mind as you learn that XAML is just an XML substitute for C# instantiation, the learning curve might be a little less steep.

In this next section, you'll learn how Silverlight takes the objects you instantiate with XAML (or with C# behind the scenes) and creates the rich, touch-responsive UI that makes Windows Phone 7 such a great platform.

Introduction to Silverlight Layout and Rendering

The goal of any UI subsystem is to get things displayed on the screen as quickly as possible and respond to user events related to things on the screen just as quickly. Silverlight for Windows Phone 7 is no different. It is designed to render as quickly and efficiently as possible while still allowing for rapid response to user-generated events such as touches, swipes, and double-taps.

Often when developers talk about rendering systems, they tend to lump together the concepts of the layout engine and the rendering engine. In Silverlight, layout and rendering are two different activities and we really should avoid grouping them together into a single "do everything" engine.

Whereas everything in an iOS UI can have its roots traced to a `UIView` of some kind, all the visual components of a Silverlight user interface derive from the `UIElement` class. This base class forms the top of the class hierarchy for just about everything a user will see in a Windows Phone 7 application. It is at the `UIElement` level that objects have the beginnings of animation properties, the capability to detect user interaction with the element, and the capability to be measured and arranged.

The Two-Pass Mantra: Measure and Arrange

Understanding the two-pass method for laying out Silverlight controls is crucial to your ability to effectively build any UI more complex than a simple "Hello World" application.

The following sentence is probably the single most important rule to remember when trying to figure out how your UI is going to render: *Silverlight renders from innermost element out, bottom-most element up; measure first then arrange.*

Every UI element in a tree is measured in the order I mentioned (innermost element out, bottom-most element up). These elements are asked for their desired size by having their `Measure` method invoked. When this method is invoked, the UI element should then update its `DesiredSize` property.

The call to `Measure` is done by the parent, which passes in the available space for the child. This entire process is done recursively. When the measure process has completed, each UI element in the tree has been given a chance to size itself according to the size of the parent container in which it resides. The entire tree has now been measured.

After the entire tree below a given container has been measured, the UI elements are then positioned and rendered on the screen. The important thing to remember here is that the end result of the measure-arrange process is different depending on the type of layout container performing the process.

For example, the elements contained within a `Grid` control are laid out according to the row-and-column layout defined by column and row definitions and the assignment of UI elements to specific rows and columns. Elements contained within a `StackPanel` are laid out sequentially, either horizontally or vertically. A single element (which can itself be a layout panel) contained within a `Border` simply appears surrounded by a border. Regardless of the layout mechanism used by the parent panel, the measure-arrange process is still invoked in the same fashion.

To recap, the Measure pass is where the desired size of each element is determined, and the Arrange pass is where each child element's size and position are finalized.

Take a look at the following XAML (don't worry if it doesn't make much sense to you yet; it will as you progress throughout the book). Pay close attention to the order in which the child elements appear and how each element is nested within a parent panel. Figure 5.1 shows how these elements are measured and then arranged to produce a rich display.

```
<Grid x:Name="ContentPanel" Grid.Row="1" Margin="12,0,12,0">
<Border BorderBrush="AliceBlue" BorderThickness="2">
    <StackPanel>
        <TextBlock Text="Hello"/>
        <TextBlock Text="World"/>
        <StackPanel Orientation="Horizontal">
            <TextBlock Foreground="Yellow" Text="Hello "/>
            <TextBlock Foreground="Yellow" Text=" World"/>
        </StackPanel>
        <Grid>
            <Grid.ColumnDefinitions>
                <ColumnDefinition Width="150"/>
                <ColumnDefinition Width="200"/>
            </Grid.ColumnDefinitions>
            <Grid.RowDefinitions>
                <RowDefinition Height="150"/>
                <RowDefinition Height="*"/>
            </Grid.RowDefinitions>
            <Button Grid.Row="0" Grid.Column="0">
                <TextBlock Text="Button"/>
            </Button>
            <Button Grid.Row="0" Grid.Column="1">
                <StackPanel>
                    <TextBlock Text="Other Button"/>
                    <TextBlock Text="hi"/>
                </StackPanel>
            </Button>
        </Grid>
```

```
        <TextBlock Text="Goodbye World"/>
    </StackPanel>
</Border>
</Grid>
```

Figure 5.1   Nested layout panels.

In the preceding example, the outermost element is a `Grid`. Inside that `Grid`, we've got a `Border`. Within that `Border` is a `StackPanel` with several child controls, including other `StackPanels`, another `Grid`, and a `TextBlock`. Figure 5.1 shows you how all those nested layout panels are measured and arranged to produce an output. It's also worth noting that you can set the content of a `Button` to a `StackPanel`, which can contain multiple child elements. As you progress throughout this book you'll see more tricks and incredible things you can do with Silverlight and XAML and controls, but for the purposes of this chapter, the important thing to note here is how the measure-and-arrange process is used on layout panels to produce output in a uniform, predictable fashion.

Summary

In this chapter I provided a brief introduction to the layout and rendering system used in Silverlight. Deliberately brief, this chapter provides just enough information to get you ready to start building full-featured Silverlight user interfaces. Knowing the recursive, hierarchical nature of Silverlight layout panels will go a long way toward helping you build amazing user interfaces in the future and as you read though this book.

6

From Xcode to Visual Studio

A tool is usually more simple than a machine; it is generally used with the hand,
whilst a machine is frequently moved by animal or steam power.

Charles Babbage

This chapter is all about tools. As much as we might like to think otherwise, developers can't produce applications without the aid of modern tools such as Xcode, Visual Studio, Eclipse, or any number of other IDEs.

This chapter covers the IDE used for developing iOS applications, Xcode, and the IDE used for building Windows Phone 7 applications, Visual Studio.

Developers need to know some basic things about Visual Studio so that they can move around within that environment smoothly and efficiently and write their applications without the tools getting in their way. In addition to a tour of Visual Studio 2010, I also provide a high-level overview of Xcode and its fundamentals.

Xcode and iOS Application Development

Xcode is the IDE used by developers for building Mac desktop applications as well as iOS applications. It is an incredibly configurable tool, allowing you to change everything from the window layout, whether it does all of its editing in a single window, the colors, and hundreds of other preferences.

The main output of an Xcode project can be found under the Targets folder. When you use Xcode to build an application, that application is a target. Each target is composed of a bunch of source code files, statically linked libraries, and Frameworks that are referenced as part of the project. For example, if you're going to build an iOS application that uses Core Data for persisting data on the phone, you'll have to add `CoreData.framework` to the Frameworks configuration of your Xcode project.

To further add power, functionality, and potential confusion for new developers, a single Xcode project can have multiple targets. Indeed, developers create targets for unit testing (I'll mention unit testing again in a later chapter), and a very common scenario is using a single Xcode project to produce different targets for iPhone and iPad. This is because the iPad's UI is so different from the iPhone's (and it includes controls that don't exist on the iPhone). Developers will build different UIs but share the same controller and back-end code within the same Xcode project.

The Xcode UI is much like any other IDE, such as Eclipse, MonoDevelop, or Visual Studio. In the layout (my personal preference) shown in Figure 6.1, the left side of the view is a navigation pane. This pane shows you the main node, the project root. Double-clicking this (called **FortuneBuilders** in the screenshot because that's the name of the project I was working on at the time) brings up the project settings dialog. Below the project node you have a bunch of folders, some of which are created for you by Xcode. One thing that iOS developers are familiar with is that the folder structure within Xcode does not necessarily match the folder structure on disk. Files sitting in the Classes folder are often sitting in the main project directory alongside the files sitting in the Controllers directory. This often confuses developers familiar with Visual Studio, which actually does have a 1:1 mapping between project folders and disk folders.

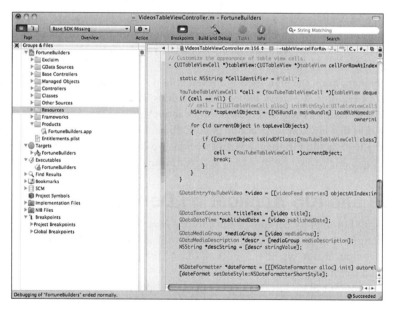

Figure 6.1   A typical Xcode screen in all-in-one mode.

The right side of the window shown in Figure 6.1 is the code editor. At the top of this window there is occasionally a separate navigation pane that I have hidden by using the Shift+Command+E macro. The color scheme is my own personal preference and not the Xcode default. Because developers are often very particular about the syntax highlighting colors in their IDE, I wanted you to see that Xcode can be made to mimic virtually any developer's favorite colors and fonts.

If you're curious, the code you're looking at in that screenshot is from a table view controller that displays a list of YouTube videos that were downloaded by accessing the Google Data feed for a particular YouTube user's uploaded videos. The code in the screenshot shows some of the code necessary to crack open the Google Data feed information and populate a custom table view cell that was loaded from an Interface Builder file. We'll talk about Interface Builder and Microsoft's Design tool, Expression Blend, in the next chapter.

When you want to run your application, you can select the environment in which you want the application to run. You can choose either Debug or Release mode, whether the application will run on the device or in the emulator, and even the particular base SDK under which to run the application. This gives you tremendous flexibility to quickly and easily run your application under all the possible environments you're planning to support. Figure 6.2 shows what it looks like when you run the application under the iOS 4.0 emulator.

Figure 6.2   The iOS 4 emulator running an iOS application.

Getting Started with Visual Studio 2010

The first thing you're going to need to start building Windows Phone 7 applications isn't the development tools—it's Windows.

It might seem strange to you Microsoft developers to include a reminder about this, but many iOS and Android developers might not even own a PC, and if they do, many Android developers might be running a variant of Linux rather than Windows.

Fortunately for Apple developers, through the use of tools such as VMWare Fusion and Parallels, you can run a fully functional (and licensed) copy of Windows on your Mac, allowing you to use both Xcode and Visual Studio side-by-side.

After you've got your copy of Windows and you're ready to download the Windows Phone 7 development tools, open a browser to http://create.msdn.com. This is the App Hub, Microsoft's version of Apple's iOS Dev Center that you can find at http://developer.apple.com/devcenter/ios.

This App Hub serves many purposes, including functioning as a starting point for documentation, blog rolls, videos, training, as well as entry to the Marketplace and other developer activities. To start downloading the tools, click the Download the Free Tools—Get Started Now link on the top left of the page.

The full installation package of the developer tools includes a free Express edition of Visual Studio 2010. This IDE includes everything you'll need to build Windows Phone 7 applications. If you already have a full version of Visual Studio because you've been doing other .NET development, downloading the full installation package just augments your existing Visual Studio installation with the WP7 tools.

Here's what you get in the free developer tools download:

- Visual Studio 2010 Express—This is the trimmed down, free version of Visual Studio 2010. It contains everything you need to write, edit, compile, debug, and package your WP7 applications.

- Windows Phone Emulator—This standalone tool allows you to debug WP7 applications, including the use of breakpoints, trace logs, and more.

- Silverlight (custom WP7 edition)—A special version of Silverlight is required to run the types of WP7 applications that we'll be building in this book.

- XNA Game Studio 4.0—If you plan to build graphically intensive applications, XNA Studio is your tool of choice. This is the same tool that developers use to build Xbox applications.

- Microsoft Expression Blend for Windows Phone—This is a Silverlight design tool that allows you to graphically design your user interfaces.

- .NET Framework v4.0—This is the underlying runtime that makes all the Windows Phone 7, Silverlight, and XNA magic possible.

After you've downloaded the tools, open up Visual Studio and poke around a bit to make sure it works. After you've familiarized yourself a little bit with the tools, go on to the next section and read more about Visual Studio 2010.

Introduction to Visual Studio 2010

Visual Studio has been around for quite some time; today, developers use it for building Windows Phone 7 applications, desktop applications in Windows Forms or Windows Presentation Foundation (WPF), web applications with ASP.NET or Silverlight, as well as bunch of other project types—even applications written in functional programming languages such as F#. In short, Visual Studio isn't just a WP7 development tool. It pretty much builds anything and can probably be configured to make your coffee in the morning if you want. (Unfortunately this is just a joke; my repeated attempts to get my compiler to also provide me with coffee have met with miserable failure.)

The upside to a tool like that is it can do everything, and it generally does everything exceptionally well. The downside to a tool like that is a tool that does everything can often be difficult to use or confusing. Hopefully, this section of the chapter will take some of the edge of confusion off Visual Studio and get you comfortable with the tool you're going to be using to build lots of incredible WP7 applications.

Figure 6.3 shows a typical Visual Studio screen that is probably close to what you might be looking at immediately after creating a Windows Phone 7 application from a template. It shows a split-screen XAML and design view, as well as the other parts of Visual Studio that will become very familiar to you by the time you finish this book.

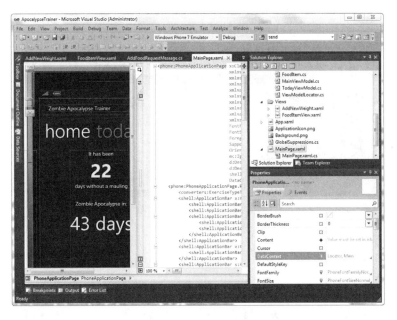

Figure 6.3   A Visual Studio screen.

As you look at the top left of Figure 6.3, you'll see a series of tabs with names, starting with one called `AddNewWeight.xaml`. These are all your open files, including C# files and

XAML files and anything else that Visual Studio can edit. If there are more open files than can be displayed in tabs (this happens to me usually within minutes of opening Visual Studio), a down-arrow appears at the top right of the code editor window. Clicking this brings up the full list of all your open files.

To the right of the code editor view is the Solution Explorer. This view is roughly analogous to the left side organizer tree shown in Xcode's UI in Figure 6.1. Here you can see all the projects in your solution and the files and folders within each solution. As I mentioned earlier, when you create a new folder within a project, it creates that folder on disk. This isn't always the case with Xcode.

Below the Solution Explorer is the Properties window. Sometimes this window manages to get closed, so to bring it back up again, click the View menu at the top and select Properties Window. If the Properties window is visible at the time you click this, it will make the window disappear.

If you look below the code editor window on the left, you'll see another series of tabs. These are docked windows that are currently hidden or collapsed. In the case of Figure 6.3, the hidden windows are Breakpoints, Output, and Error List. As you continue with development and learn to use more features of Visual Studio, you will see more windows appear in this area.

If you click one of the docked, collapsed windows, it will grow upward and cover some of the code editor window in the process, as shown in Figure 6.4.

Figure 6.4   Expanded Breakpoints window, covered code window.

Clicking the thumbtack icon in the top right of the window toggles whether the window automatically hides. Clicking it once in this case causes the window to move from the foreground to merge with the code editor window, pushing the code view up to make room for the docked Breakpoints window. You'll notice, as shown in Figure 6.5, that the Output window came along for the ride and is now a tab in the docked window for Breakpoints and Output, and the Error List window is still in auto-hide mode below.

Figure 6.5   Toggling auto-hide on the Breakpoints window.

Learning how to manage the windows within Visual Studio is essential to your ability to write code for long periods of time in this environment without losing your mind. The more windows you have and the more files you're working with, the more essential it becomes for you to stay organized and put the windows and files wherever you like.

Visual Studio is extremely configurable; in fact, it might be even more configurable than Xcode. For example, take a look at the screenshot in Figure 6.6 where I've moved the Solution Explorer to the left side, auto-hidden all the secondary windows and pushed them to the bottom, and provided for a very code-centric view. If I need any of the secondary windows, I can click their tab and the window pops out. If I then click the auto-hide button again, the window will re-merge with the main window.

Figure 6.6   Code-centric optimized layout.

Finally, if you click and hold the tab of any of the windows and start dragging, you will see the dock shortcut icons shown in Figure 6.7. These make it incredibly easy for you to figure out where you want your windows to appear and how you want them laid out for your own personal tastes. You can even drag a particular file's tab out of Visual Studio entirely and make it a standalone editing window.

Last but not least is the toolbar that sits on top of everything else. The most commonly used feature of this toolbar will more than likely be the Play button that you can see in Figure 6.7 right next to the deployment target of Windows Phone 7 Emulator and the build configuration of Debug. Here you can choose whether you are going to run your application on the device or on the emulator and whether you're going to run the application in Debug or Release mode. Clicking the Play button (or using the shortcut key of F5) starts a debugging session using these preferences.

At this point in a discussion of Visual Studio, I start to get into details and minutia that I think will only distract you from your ultimate goal of building Windows Phone 7 applications. If you want to know more about Visual Studio, I highly recommend that you pick up *Visual Studio 2010 Unleashed* by Mike Snell and Lars Powers. This book will give you everything you need to know (and then some!) about Visual Studio. If you don't want to read through it and don't want to slow down your WP7 learning, you can flip to the section of the book that interests you as you run into parts of Visual Studio you don't understand while building Windows Phone 7 applications.

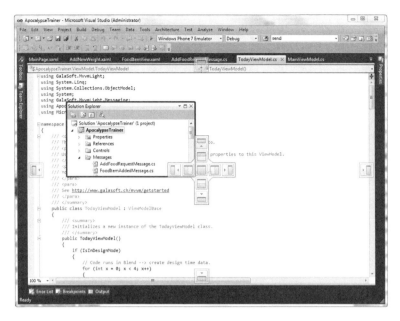

Figure 6.7   Docking target shortcut icons.

Summary

A developer's IDE is like a mechanic's toolbox. It isn't just a single wrench or a single screwdriver. It's everything needed to build applications. As a result, developers spend the vast majority of their development time sitting in front of that IDE.

Because of that, IDE creators spend an awful lot of time trying to make sure that their tools are fast, efficient, and—most important—easy to use. Visual Studio and Xcode are two of the most powerful IDEs available for building mobile applications today. In many ways they are similar, but there are also a lot of fundamental differences. The thing that I hope you take away from this chapter is that both of them are so configurable and so flexible that you should be able to make them lay out your environment in such a way that is comfortable to you, no matter how you like things set up.

Visual Studio will become your best friend as you progress throughout this book. You will use it for writing your XAML, for writing your C#, for debugging, for profiling, for running your application, for building your application, and even for getting it ready to be deployed to the marketplace. Taking the time now to step back from the code and familiarize yourself with this tool will go a long way toward making the rest of the book easier to plow through.

Introducing Expression Blend

I think design covers so much more than the aesthetic. Design is fundamentally more. Design is usability. It is Information Architecture. It is accessibility. This is all design.

Mark Boulton

This chapter provides you with an introduction to Microsoft's interaction design tool, Expression Blend. I start with an overview of Interface Builder, the application iOS developers often use to build their user interfaces. Next, I provide a walkthrough of Expression Blend—its purpose and key features and how it differs in form and function from that of Interface Builder.

In the previous chapter we walked through Visual Studio and its features that enable you to write code and compile and run applications. This chapter is all about design tools, how to use them, and more importantly, when you should use them.

Overview of Apple's Interface Builder

Interface Builder (IB) has been around for quite some time, and Mac developers have been using it to construct view hierarchies for desktop Cocoa applications for years. With the release of the original iPhone SDK, Interface Builder was tasked with giving developers a way to manipulate user interfaces in a near-WYSIWYG fashion.

Before diving into a description of how IB works, I think it's worth including a paragraph with a brief history lesson. Many people assume that the first release of the iPhone also came with the first release of the SDK. This isn't actually how it happened. When the iPhone 1.0 was first released, the "SDK" was Safari. There was no App Store, no Marketplace, and no Objective-C SDK. All developers could do was build web applications that used clever JavaScript, HTML, and CSS trickery to make those web applications look and feel like iPhone applications. To this day, many websites still have "iPhone-y" UIs that are presented when an iOS device browses to that site. *One year later*, the iPhone SDK was released. This SDK included Xcode and the capability to run applications on a simulator and upload applications to the App Store. However, this SDK did *not* include Interface Builder. Or rather, Interface Builder could not be used in conjunction with iPhone SDK projects. It wasn't until months later that a revision to the iPhone SDK included Interface Builder support. We should all count our blessings that Microsoft released not one but two designers with its *v1* product: Expression Blend and the VS2010-embedded designer, which share quite a bit of code.

Interface Builder is just as its name implies: a tool for building interfaces. As you can see in Figure 7.1, it does a fairly good job of giving you an estimate of the user interface that will be rendered when the application runs. Also keep in mind that older versions of Xcode and Interface Builder were separate tools, whereas with versions 4 and later, Xcode and the "visual designer formerly known as Interface Builder" are one and the same.

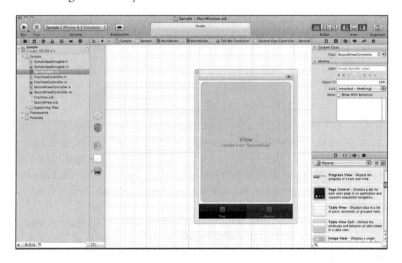

Figure 7.1   Building a UI with the Xcode 4 Designer.

The rub, of course, is that the UI that IB shows you at design time is just a rough estimate. For example, when you're working with a `TableViewController` and you are trying to set up a UI that will display a list of items using a custom cell, there's no way for IB to give you all of that merged into a single design surface. Take a look at Figure 7.2, which shows how a typical developer might use IB to rig up a `TableViewController` with a custom table view cell. You can't see what the cell is going to look like within the table; you can only look at one sell separately in a different window while IB provides a "simulated" UI for the table itself. As you'll see later in this book in Chapter 16, "Separating Your Concerns," not only can you see custom list boxes at design time in WP7 and Visual Studio, but you can even provide sample data to which you can bind your controls at design time to get a really good preview of the final rendering.

Figure 7.2   Working with a `TableViewController` in Xcode/Interface
Builder.

At its core, Interface Builder is taking a configuration of an object hierarchy (such as a view hierarchy including view controllers and subviews) and storing that information in a special file called a "nib" (although the more modern equivalent of this file is an XML file with the XIB extension, still called "nib" because it's much easier to pronounce).

By setting your main window's configuration through Interface Builder, you are indicating the state you would like that window to be in after the application has started up. When a reference for your main window is asked for by the application, it will take all the information contained in the XIB file and use it to create a fresh instance of a window object. This pattern continues throughout your application as UI objects are needed, including custom table view cells like the one shown in Figure 7.2.

This differs from the way designers work with Silverlight applications in that Interface Builder really just creates data files. These data files are written by Interface Builder and read by the application at runtime to generate instances of objects. Silverlight applications use XAML as a markup language to describe the instantiations that should occur. This is a subtle but important difference. XAML is an *instantiation language*. It uses XML to describe the objects that should be instantiated and the properties within those objects that should be set.

This is a subtle but important difference because there are some things that require a live, running application to render in iOS, which is why Interface Builder often supplies only "simulation" UI-like fake navigation bars, tab bars, and the like. The point at which iOS developers need to write pure Objective-C and where they need to build their UI in Interface Builder is often confusing, and the consequences for getting this split wrong can be immense. Some seasoned iPhone developers rarely use IB, and often use it only when there is no other alternative. Other iPhone developers have an IB-first approach in which they build everything in Interface Builder until they absolutely cannot get away without writing custom code in Objective-C. As you'll see later in Chapter 16 on MVVM (Model, View, ViewModel—a pattern for separating concerns when building user interfaces), because everything can be represented as XAML (even the objects to which your UI is bound), you can get an almost exact replica of your final UI inside either Expression Blend or Visual Studio without the need for mocked elements.

XAML is considered a first-class citizen in the Microsoft development environment. iOS developers never look at the serialization format used by IB; they either work in Objective-C or the point-and-click UI of the designer. Microsoft developers work in XAML all the time and, as you'll see in the screenshots in this book, many developers often type the XAML and watch the immediate effects of the markup on their UI.

Introduction to Expression Blend

When I first heard that Microsoft was working on an XAML design tool that would help developers build amazing UIs, guide them through building complex animations, and much more, I was a little skeptical. In fact, my reaction was something along the lines of, "Microsoft? Build a *design* tool? Inconceivable!"

However, over the years I've learned that first impressions (especially those clouded by prejudgment and simple ignorance, rather than those formed by an actual impression) are often wrong. I decided to give Expression Blend a try. As a somewhat relevant aside, I am not a designer. I have no digital design skills and prefer the comfort and form of a pencil to that of a mouse. I've never gotten along well with Photoshop, and I've always written my HTML in Notepad (or other text editors). I have also almost exclusively written my XAML in Visual Studio's text editor with the design surface actually removed, seeing the finished product only after running the application. I have been what you might consider the exact opposite of the target user for a design tool such as Blend. I fought it and resisted it like the plague. I was going to curmudgeonly refuse to adopt this shiny new tool no matter the cost. That was before I tried it.

At its core, all Blend does is provide you with a robust UI sitting on top of an XAML editor. All the fancy things you do with all the controls, widgets, knobs, trays, and panels eventually boil down to the manipulation of XAML (and occasionally C#) in your project. The interesting part is that, unlike my past experience with design tools that produce markup (yeah, I'm looking at you, FrontPage), Blend actually reduces the amount of time it takes you to build a UI, and—here's the shocking part—it actually produces clean XAML. If you want to take a few minutes and sift through some online tutorials to get you familiar with Expression Blend, I recommend you check out this URL: http://expression.microsoft.com/en-us/cc184874.aspx. If you want a full reference on building Silverlight 4 applications with Expression Blend (the vast majority of which will still apply to WP7 development), check out *Expression Blend 4 with Silverlight,* by Victor Gaudioso.

When you first see Expression Blend, like the screenshot shown in Figure 7.3, it can be a little overwhelming. Those of you who have used tools like Adobe Photoshop will almost immediately recognize all the core elements of a design tool. For developers like me, who tend to throw garlic and holy water at design tools like Photoshop, getting used to this application took a little time.

As I progress throughout this section and in the tutorial in this chapter, I might talk about visual controls and other things with which you aren't yet familiar. Don't worry about that and just go with the flow; everything that I do in this chapter with Blend will be explained in greater detail with C# and XAML in later chapters, including the stock controls, panels, building custom controls, and the animation system.

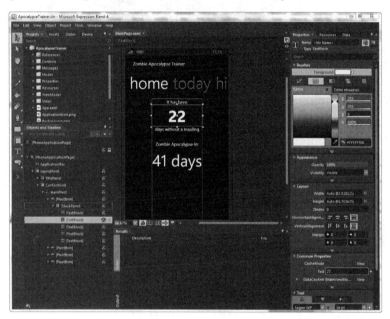

Figure 7.3   Expression Blend after opening a VS solution.

You can launch Expression Blend directly from your Start menu, or you can launch it already set to your current Visual Studio project by clicking Project, Open in Expression Blend from inside Visual Studio with an open WP7 application. On the left in the first panel you'll see a tab called Projects. This tree should look very similar to the Visual Studio Solution Explorer. This gives you a file system-based view of your solution. When you double-click an XAML file in this view, it will appear in the design view in the middle.

Below the first panel is an Objects and Timeline view. This gives you a hierarchical view of the objects discovered inside the current XAML file. As you can see in the screenshots in Figures 7.3 and 7.4, the root object is an instance of **PhoneApplicationPage**, which contains a **TitlePanel** and a **ContentGrid**, and inside that `ContentGrid` is a Pivot control named `mainPivot`. Items in this view show up as their data types when those elements haven't been assigned a name.

Figure 7.4   Editing different Pivot items directly in the designer.

Figure 7.4 shows how you can quickly and easily use the Objects and Timeline view to navigate directly to the item you want to edit. In this case, we are editing a `PivotItem` within a Pivot control. To do this in a pure-XAML text view, you would have to scroll down through all the XML content looking for the control you wanted to edit. The Objects and Timeline panel can be an incredible timesaver.

On the right side of the screen, as shown in either Figure 7.3 or 7.4, you can see a bunch of editing panels. The first is the Properties window, which allows you to edit the properties of a control. Notice that whenever a property can be set to a type of Brush, the Blend Properties window gives you a nice Brush editing tool. You can quickly use this tool to set backgrounds to be transparent, solid colors, or even gradients. Again, setting Brush properties using Blend is much easier than doing it by hand.

There are hundreds of different things you can do with the Properties window and with the selection tool. In Figure 7.4 you can see that there are little padlock icons on various key points in the selection highlight around my control. I can easily use those little padlocks to set how my control automatically resizes itself within a parent control, or I can set the height and width to fixed numbers. The possibilities are not infinite, but a developer or designer familiar with Expression Blend and its capabilities, and who has a bit of creativity, can truly create amazing user experiences.

Another feature I really like about Expression Blend is the capability to use annotations. Annotations give teams the capability to leave comments about particular UI elements so that other team members can see them and respond to them accordingly. For example, in Figure 7.5 I've left my team members a little sticky note directly in the Blend UI complaining about some UI elements that I don't like.

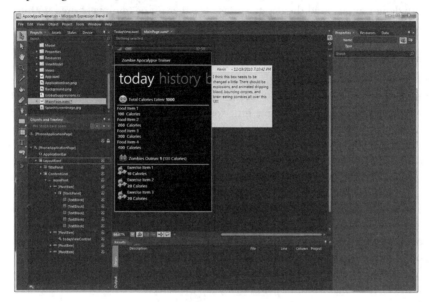

Figure 7.5   Using annotations to take notes and share with the team.

The presence of this annotation modifies the underlying XAML to include the following new XAML namespace:

```
xmlns:Anno="http://schemas.microsoft.com/expression/blend/extensions/annotations/
2008"
```

In addition, the annotation is added to whatever target control I was referencing at the time by adding an element as a dependency property, as shown in the following XAML that corresponds to the sticky note in Figure 7.5:

```
<Anno:AnnotationManager.Annotations>
    <Anno:Annotation AuthorInitials="K"
                     Author="Kevin" Left="496"
                     SerialNumber="1" Top="137"
                     Timestamp="12/20/2010 00:12:01"
                     Text="I think this box needs to be changed a
little. There should be explosions, and animated dripping blood,
bouncing corpses, and brain-eating zombies all over this UI!!"/>
</Anno:AnnotationManager.Annotations>
```

If another person on my team checked out the code (which includes the annotated XAML) from our source control repository, he would then be able to see my feedback and respond to it (hopefully without using foul language). One caveat here is that I have found that the presence of these annotations in a WP7 project can cause the built-in Visual Studio design surface to occasionally hiccup and be unable to render the UI. This has no effect on whether the application will run properly, but it can be annoying. I suggest not using annotations unless you and your team are planning to use Blend for your primary design surface, and the design surface is either off or minimally used within Visual Studio.

Blend Tutorial—Working with Visual States

In this section of the chapter I'm going to walk you through a simple Blend tutorial by starting fresh with a new WP7 application. This should give you some familiarity with the application and hopefully teach you a little something about an often underrated feature of Silverlight controls: the Visual State manager.

Visual states are, as the name implies, different states in which a control can be. These states are visual because the end user can visually tell the difference between those states. Stock controls come with their own built-in set of states, but you can also create your own states at the control- or even page-level.

For example, the standard Button control has several states already defined, including: Normal, MouseOver, Pressed, and Disabled. Don't worry about MouseOver, that's a holdover from the fact that WP7 is actually Silverlight under the hood, and the desktop version of Silverlight supports mouse movement. There is no finger gesture on a Windows Phone 7 device that can simulate the mouse-over movement because the device doesn't know where your finger is until you actually tap the screen.

The truly awesome thing about these visual states is that not only can you supply your own styles for each of these states, but you can also control the transition between these states. If you wanted to, you could make a button rotate between the Normal and Disabled states, making the button flip over and bounce a little and do a little "death" animation when it transitions into the Disabled state. Although there might not be much cause for this kind of thing, knowing that you can do it without writing your own custom Button control can come in quite handy.

In this tutorial, we're going to make a button that has a different style for the `Pressed` state. In a stock WP7 application, the button style is either white-on-black or black-on-white. When you press (tap) down on the button, it inverts this style. For example, if your UI is configured in "dark" mode, the normal button state is white-on-black and when you tap down on it, it flips to black-on-white. I want to make it so that tapping on my button switches to a green background color.

To get started, create a new WP7 project in Visual Studio. In Visual Studio, click the File menu item; then click New, Project. From here, click the Silverlight for Windows Phone category on the left and make sure Windows Phone Application is selected on the right. Type in a name for the project, and then click OK.

After the project has been created, click the Project > Open in Expression Blend menu item. If it takes a few seconds to load up Blend, don't worry. The first time you launch Blend might be slow, even on a powerful computer with a fast hard drive.

Next we need to add a button. Expand the Assets pane by clicking the right-facing chevron (it looks like two greater-than signs: >>) in the far left toolbar. Go to the Categories section on the left and click Panels. Click and hold on the `StackPanel` icon and then drag the mouse pointer to the Grid control named `ContentPanel`. When you let go, a `StackPanel` will have been added to the Grid. Next, create a button inside this Stack-Panel. To do this, make sure the StackPanel is highlighted and double-click the Button shortcut on the left toolbar. Make sure you give this Button a name by setting the name in the Properties pane on the right side of the editor.

Now right-click the Button (either in the Objects and Timeline pane or the visual button itself on the design surface) and choose Edit Template; then left-click Edit a Copy. Click OK when prompted to create a style resource. This will allow you to visually edit the control's template.

Now switch to the States tab in the top pane (the one that normally has the Projects tab selected). Inside the Objects and Timeline pane for the current control template, select `ButtonBackground`. You will then see all the prebuilt visual states for this control, as shown in Figure 7.6.

Figure 7.6   Changing visual states of stock controls.

Click the Pressed state and you'll see a message that Blend is now recording properties for the Pressed state. This means that while you are recording for this state, any property change made to the control or any of its nested properties will be saved as part of that visual state. We can now change the `Background` and `BorderBrush` properties of the button in this state without affecting those properties in the Normal or Disabled states.

At this point you can save your work and run the application by clicking Project, Run, or pressing the F5 key. Running the application will launch the Windows Phone 7 simulator. This simulator provides you with a very close representation of what your application might look like and how it might behave on an actual device.

The first time you launch an application after your computer starts up, it will take some time for the WP7 simulator to start. After it has done its initial startup, you can leave it running between debug sessions. This will cut down on the time it takes to start debugging your application.

After a few seconds of the simulator doing its initialization, your application will appear. Because the default Button control knows to put itself into the Pressed state when someone taps on the control, you don't need to do any of that plumbing yourself. Because we've just styled the visual state, our new button will now turn green with an orange border when someone taps it.

When you're done playing with this new button, take a look at the XAML inside MainPage.xaml (you can see this XAML by going back into Visual Studio and double-clicking the file) at the top in the newly created resource dictionary:

```xml
<Style x:Key="FancyButtonStyle" TargetType="Button">
<Setter Property="Background" Value="Transparent"/>
<Setter Property="BorderBrush"
  Value="{StaticResource PhoneForegroundBrush}"/>
<Setter Property="Foreground"
  Value="{StaticResource PhoneForegroundBrush}"/>
<Setter Property="BorderThickness"
  Value="{StaticResource PhoneBorderThickness}"/>
<Setter Property="FontFamily"
  Value="{StaticResource PhoneFontFamilySemiBold}"/>
<Setter Property="FontSize"
  Value="{StaticResource PhoneFontSizeMediumLarge}"/>
<Setter Property="Padding" Value="10,3,10,5"/>
<Setter Property="Template">
<Setter.Value>
<ControlTemplate TargetType="Button">
<Grid Background="Transparent">
<VisualStateManager.VisualStateGroups>
<VisualStateGroup x:Name="CommonStates">
        <VisualState x:Name="Normal"/>
        <VisualState x:Name="MouseOver"/>
<VisualState x:Name="Pressed">
<Storyboard>
        <ObjectAnimationUsingKeyFrames
        Storyboard.TargetProperty="Foreground"
        Storyboard.TargetName="ContentContainer">
            <DiscreteObjectKeyFrame KeyTime="0"
              Value="{StaticResource PhoneBackgroundBrush}"/>
```

```
      </ObjectAnimationUsingKeyFrames>
      <ColorAnimation Duration="0" To="#FF001BFF"
      Storyboard.TargetProperty=
        "(Border.BorderBrush).(SolidColorBrush.Color)"
      Storyboard.TargetName="ButtonBackground" d:IsOptimized="True"/>
      <ColorAnimation Duration="0" To="#FFFFC700"
        Storyboard.TargetProperty=
         "(Border.Background).(SolidColorBrush.Color)"
        Storyboard.TargetName="ButtonBackground" d:IsOptimized="True"/>
</Storyboard>
</VisualState>
<VisualState x:Name="Disabled">
      <Storyboard>
      <ObjectAnimationUsingKeyFrames
        Storyboard.TargetProperty="Foreground"
        Storyboard.TargetName="ContentContainer">
      <DiscreteObjectKeyFrame KeyTime="0"
        Value="{StaticResource PhoneDisabledBrush}"/>
      </ObjectAnimationUsingKeyFrames>
      </Storyboard>
</VisualState>
</VisualStateGroup>
</VisualStateManager.VisualStateGroups>
<Border x:Name="ButtonBackground"
   BorderThickness="{TemplateBinding BorderThickness}" CornerRadius="0"
   Margin="{StaticResource PhoneTouchTargetOverhang}" Background="Black">
<Border.BorderBrush>
      <SolidColorBrush Color="{StaticResource PhoneForegroundColor}"/>
</Border.BorderBrush>
<ContentControl x:Name="ContentContainer"
  ContentTemplate="{TemplateBinding ContentTemplate}"
  Content="{TemplateBinding Content}"
  Foreground="{TemplateBinding Foreground}"
  HorizontalContentAlignment=
   "{TemplateBinding HorizontalContentAlignment}"
  Padding="{TemplateBinding Padding}"
  VerticalContentAlignment="{TemplateBinding VerticalContentAlignment}"/>
</Border>
</Grid>
</ControlTemplate>
</Setter.Value>
</Setter>
```

If you scan through this XAML you can see all the visual states for the new button style, and you'll also see that we've modified the Pressed state. One thing especially worth noticing is that all the changes that occur to all the properties of the button occur within animation storyboards.

After developers spend a few seconds thinking about the fact that transitioning between different visual states is all done smoothly with animations, they start to see the power of this framework.

This means that when a Silverlight object transitions from one visual state to another, it does so with an animated storyboard. You can control how long it takes to switch to this new state and any special effects that occur as a result of this switch.

As curmudgeonly as I am about using visual design tools, I must admit that hand-typing in all the visual state management stuff, even for simple property changes, is going to get really old really fast. I am a firm believer in using the best tool for the job, and I know that working with visual states is absolutely best done in Blend.

Here's a little food for thought and an assignment to do some exploring on your own with Blend: Stock controls come with their own visual states, and different user interaction will switch a control between visual states. A page is just a different type of control. This means that a page can have visual states and you can create your own custom visual states.

One of the biggest pains when building UIs for the iPad and iPhone is dealing with rotation. Making sure that the user interface looks good when rotated between landscape and portrait is a difficult and time-consuming process, especially when you consider that you often need to hand-code property changes to your views when the user rotates the phone or the iPad. What if you were to assign names to your visual states such as "portrait" and "landscape" or "portraitup," and so on? Now all you need to do in Blend is rotate the design surface to the right orientation and, in that particular visual state's record mode, move and resize all your controls accordingly. Next, you need to programmatically transition your page's visual state every time the device changes orientation.

Here is some code you can override in your MainPage.xaml.cs that will programmatically transition the page from its current visual state to the new one, invoking any custom animations, layout changes, color changes, and whatever else you want done. Again, remember that all these changes can be done in a timed, animated storyboard.

```
protected override void OnOrientationChanged(OrientationChangedEventArgs e)
{
    // if you have 4 states instead of 2
    // PortraitUp, PortraitDown, LandscapeLeft, LandscapeDown
    // VisualStateManager.GoToState(this, e.Orientation.ToString(), true);

    // if you just have Portrait or Landscape
    string orientation = (e.Orientation & PageOrientation.Portrait) != 0
        ? "Portrait" : "Landscape";
    VisualStateManager.GoToState(this, orientation, true);

    base.OnOrientationChanged(e);
}
```

Take some time now to go back through the project you've been working on in Blend throughout this tutorial. Explore, click, and break things. Play around with all the panes, panels, and properties that you can find. I highly recommend poking around with things so much that you feel completely and utterly lost and overwhelmed. It's at that point where you can take a step back and go on with the rest of the chapters in this book. As you go through the subsequent chapters, all those foggy areas in your head and the questions you had about Blend, XAML, C#, and WP7 will eventually be answered, and lights will go on in your head. I've found that when learning new technology, having that initial experience of diving in and feeling completely lost helps guide my learning in the future. It makes the "light bulb" moments in the future that much more memorable, and I retain that information longer.

Summary

This chapter provided you with an overview of Apple's design tool for Xcode, Interface Builder. I then compared Interface Builder with Microsoft's design tool, Expression Blend. We went through the basics of how to operate Blend, how to use Blend to create a Windows Phone 7 application, and finally we walked through a tutorial of how to use visual states and the Visual State Manager from Blend and Visual Studio.

At this point you should have a good idea of what it will look and feel like to build WP7 applications using Expression Blend and Visual Studio. You probably have a lot of questions, and a lot of the controls used in this chapter might not make much sense. This is a good thing. Your curiosity will help keep you going throughout the rest of the book and will make the new information sink in deeper as you learn more about WP7 programming.

Using Basic UI Elements

The public is more familiar with bad design than good design.
It is, in effect, conditioned to prefer bad design, because that is what it lives with.
The new becomes threatening, the old reassuring.

Paul Rand

This chapter provides an overview of the basic UI building blocks that are available to Windows Phone 7 developers and relates them to the building blocks that iOS developers might already be familiar with. iOS developers should pay special attention to the section on layout and panels because things like flow panels and automatically adjusting grids simply do not exist in iOS and can save you a lot of hard work when used well.

When you have reached the end of this chapter, you should have a good idea of the basic arsenal of UI weaponry available to you to thwart your enemy (the empty design surface). You will learn about displaying and prompting for text, displaying buttons and reacting to button presses, layout panels, images, and even basic animation. This should provide you with a solid foundation on which to continue throughout the rest of the book as you make more compelling and complex applications.

Using the Basic Controls

This next section will take you on a tour through the basic building blocks of a Silverlight UI on Windows Phone 7. These primitive controls are all usable and quite powerful in their basic form but, as you will see in later chapters, the use of templates, inheritance, and other customizations can turn these building blocks into incredible controls that produce amazing user interfaces.

Try not to assume that because these controls are "primitive" that you should skip right past this section. iOS developers know the intrinsic value of primitive controls and how inheriting from them and customizing them can make the difference between a bland UI and an eye-popping UI that earns an app top billing in the App Store.

Using Text Blocks

One of the most common activities you will be doing when building your user interface is displaying text. Whether this text is data-bound and came from a web service, or whether it is static text displaying a greeting, the basic building block for rendering text is the TextBlock control.

Although I am aware that you can use Expression Blend to manipulate your UI and drag all these controls visually onto your design surface, I firmly believe in knowing the plumbing that makes everything work. As such, unless Expression Blend is specifically required or substantially simplifies a task, I will be showing you the XAML to build the control rather than screenshots of how to configure it in Expression Blend.

To get started, you can follow along by creating your own Windows Phone 7 project in Visual Studio 2010 and call it *BasicControls*. To create a Windows Phone 7 project, choose the Windows Phone Application project template from the Silverlight for Windows Phone template category.

> **Note**
>
> Whenever I refer to Visual Studio 2010 or simply Visual Studio, I am referring to either of the following: the full development version of Visual Studio 2010 that many developers might already have on their computers prior to downloading the WP7 SDK, *or* the WP7-specific "lite" version of Visual Studio 2010 that you receive when you install the WP7 SDK on a computer that had no previous installation of Visual Studio 2010. Throughout this book you can assume that any reference to Visual Studio can be applied equally to either product unless a difference is otherwise noted. For example, when it comes time to build service-oriented back-ends to support your WP7 application, you might need to install the full version of Visual Studio 2010 for some features.

After you have created your empty application, you'll see that inside the MainPage.xaml file are a couple of TextBlocks already created for you. I've just changed the text of these, as shown in Listing 8.1.

Listing 8.1 **Text Blocks in XAML**

```xaml
<TextBlock x:Name="ApplicationTitle"
           Text="SAMPLE APPLICATION"
           Style="{StaticResource PhoneTextNormalStyle}"/>
<TextBlock x:Name="PageTitle"
           Text="This is a test"
           Margin="9,-7,0,0"
           Style="{StaticResource PhoneTextTitle1Style}"/>
```

One thing that makes working with these controls declaratively so easy is that you can add an event handler to the control just by typing a few letters. Press Enter after the line of code that configures the Margin attribute for the PageTitle TextBlock. As soon as you start typing (type the letter M), you will see a drop-down box appear with a list of possible completions for whatever you're typing. The event you're looking for is `MouseLeftButtonUp`. Type the equal sign (=) after the word `MouseLeftButtonUp` and then press Tab. This automatically creates a piece of code in the code-behind for your XAML page that responds to the `MouseLeftButtonUp` (essentially the end of a single tap) event.

Press F7 to see the code-behind. Modify your code so that the `MainPage` class looks like the one defined in Listing 8.2.

Listing 8.2   **Responding to a Single Tap on a TextBlock**

```
namespace BasicControls
{
    public partial class MainPage : PhoneApplicationPage
    {
        // Constructor
        public MainPage()
        {
            InitializeComponent();
        }

        private void PageTitle_MouseLeftButtonUp(
          object sender, MouseButtonEventArgs e)
        {
            MessageBox.Show("You tapped the page title, " +
              (sender as TextBlock).Text);
        }
    }
}
```

The preceding code shows you how to create a simple event handler to allow your application to execute some code whenever the user taps on the page title. Just about every control is tappable, including controls that you might not think about, such as TextBlocks. We use the `as` keyword in C# to typecast the sender object to a TextBlock object so that we can access its `Text` property.

The `MessageBox` class is a static class that provides a few methods for displaying a modal box on top of other user interface elements. For iOS developers, a control with a nearly identical purpose is the UIAlertView control that you might invoke using the following code:

```
UIAlertView *alert = [[[UIAlertView alloc] initWithTitle:@"Alert"
    message:@"You tapped the page title."
```

```
    delegate:self
    cancelButtonTitle:@"Cancel"
    otherButtonTitles:nil] autorelease];
[alert show];
```

Then you might provide your own delegate code that responds to various button presses on your alert view. As you can see, for standard alert messages, the `MessageBox` class is easier and simpler to use.

Figure 8.1 illustrates what happens when you tap the title of this application.

Figure 8.1   A message box displayed in
response to tapping a TextBlock.

As you progress through the book, you will see a variety of things you can do with the seemingly basic and primitive TextBlock control. Remember that you can style virtually all aspects of any control, including the rendering color, and even create custom special effects that attach to any visual element.

Accepting User Input with TextBoxes

Most applications are not read-only displays. At some point you will probably have to break down and actually ask your users for some input, whether you like it or not. To do that, you're going to need a TextBox. As its name says, a TextBox is a box in which a user can supply text.

The user does this in one of two ways. The first, which is available on all Windows Phone 7 devices, is through the use of the onscreen soft keyboard. When a user taps inside the region of a TextBox, the keyboard will appear, allowing the user to enter text by tapping on the virtual keys. The second method is through an actual hard keyboard that is available only if the user has purchased a phone with a physical keyboard. At the time of the Windows Phone 7 launch, several manufacturers had slide-out keyboards, and one even had slide-out speakers (but only a touchscreen keyboard).

Whether a user is typing on a real keyboard or a virtual touch-screen keyboard, the TextBox control accepts the input the same and isolates the developer from having to write custom code to handle both situations.

Add the XAML code from Listing 8.3 below the last TextBlock from Listing 8.1 to create a new label and a text box for entering text.

Listing 8.3   **Adding a Label and TextBox**

```
<TextBlock x:Name="ApplicationTitle"
        Text="SAMPLE APPLICATION"
        Style="{StaticResource PhoneTextNormalStyle}"/>
<TextBlock x:Name="PageTitle"
        Text="This is a test"
        Margin="9,-7,0,0"
        MouseLeftButtonUp="PageTitle_MouseLeftButtonUp"
        Style="{StaticResource PhoneTextTitle1Style}"/>

<TextBlock x:Name="SampleLabel"
        Text="Enter some text:" />
<TextBox x:Name="SampleTextBox" />
```

Now change the code for the "single tap" event handler on the page title to the code shown in Listing 8.4 and the modal dialog box that appears will contain the text the user supplied in the text box rather than the fixed title of the page.

Listing 8.4   **Reading Text Property of a TextBox**

```
namespace BasicControls
{
    public partial class MainPage : PhoneApplicationPage
    {
        // Constructor
        public MainPage()
        {
            InitializeComponent();
        }

        private void PageTitle_MouseLeftButtonUp(object sender,
            MouseButtonEventArgs e)
        {
            MessageBox.Show("You tapped the page title, " +
```

```
            SampleTextBox.Text );
        }
    }
}
```

In the preceding code listing, we are accessing the `Text` property on the Sample-TextBox control that contains the text input into that control by the user, if any more. You can do a lot more with a text box, but this should whet your appetite for user input on the Windows Phone.

Run the sample project again and type something into the text box before you tap the page title. When you tap the page title you should see whatever text you entered in the box appear in the modal pop-up.

Working with Buttons

Buttons are an essential part of any user interface. They provide nice, easy-to-hit targets for your fingers. We use buttons to cause actions to occur. In general, you can think of a button as the user interface equivalent of a verb. When something needs to be done, you tap a button to get it done. Of course, this is just an example, and there are many examples of user interfaces where buttons are used more creatively or even not used at all.

If you don't already have it open, launch Visual Studio and bring up the project that we've been working on throughout this chapter. Open up the MainPage.xaml file and scroll down to the last control you added in Listing 8.3. Add the buttons shown in Listing 8.5.

Listing 8.5 **Adding Buttons to the Page**

```
<Button x:Name="TestButtonOne">
    <TextBlock Text="Zombies are your friends" />
</Button>
<Button x:Name="TestButtonTwo" Click="TestButtonTwo_Click">
    <Border BorderBrush="Yellow" BorderThickness="3" CornerRadius="15">
        <TextBlock Margin="5,5,5,5" Text="Some Text"></TextBlock>
    </Border>
</Button>
```

The first button is self-explanatory. It has a name and it has child content in the form of a TextBlock. This is your first example of a templated control, and you will see hundreds of these as you progress through this book. The child content of the button, no matter what it is, is wrapped up inside the functionality that makes a button a button—the capability to respond to a mouse click (or, in the case of WP7, a finger tap).

The next button (named TestButtonTwo) is a little more interesting. The first child element of this button is a Border control. A Border control does just what its name implies—it wraps whatever child content it contains with a configurable border. In our case, we wrapped the child content in a yellow border that is 3 points thick with a

15-degree corner radius, resulting in a yellow square with rounded edges. Within the border control is a TextBlock that displays the text "Some Text" (shown in Figure 8.2).

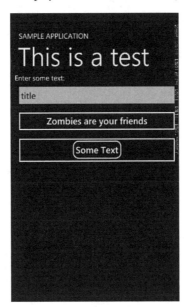

Figure 8.2   A few buttons added to the page.

nt handler for the second button's click event is shown in Listing king a special note of here is that the name of the event to which lick. You do *not* use the `MouseLeftButtonUp` event on buttons. The button has already done the work of listening for the mouse up and down events, leaving you with a much-easier-to-understand event: `Click`.

Listing 8.6   **Code Responding to a Button Click**

```
namespace BasicControls
{
    public partial class MainPage : PhoneApplicationPage
    {
        // Constructor
        public MainPage()
        {
            InitializeComponent();
        }

        private void PageTitle_MouseLeftButtonUp(object sender,
          MouseButtonEventArgs e)
        {
```

```
        MessageBox.Show("You tapped the page title, " +
            SampleTextBox.Text);
    }

    private void TestButtonTwo_Click(object sender,
        RoutedEventArgs e)
    {
        MessageBox.Show(
            "You tapped the button with nested controls!");
    }
  }
}
```

One thing worth pointing out is that the UIButton control in iOS has very similar functionality. Whereas the default behavior of a WP7 button is to appear as a square with a border around the child controls, the UIButton is more purpose-driven. It contains a property called `buttonType` that controls the button's core behavior and can be any of the following values: `UIButtonTypeCustom`, `UIButtonTypeRoundedRect`, `UIButtonTypeDetailDisclosure`, `UIButtonTypeInfoLight`, `UIButtonTypeInfoDark`, or `UIButtonTypeContactAdd`. The purposes of these different button types should be fairly self-explanatory to any iOS developer or even any well-versed iPhone user.

Philosophical Differences in SDK Design

The default implementation of buttons in WP7 and iOS is a classic example of how the SDK design philosophy differs between WP7 and iOS, and on a larger scale, the .NET Framework and Cocoa. The UI controls that come with the iOS SDK are all purpose-driven. They make accomplishing a certain task with a very iPhone-ish look and feel very easy. The main goal of the iOS SDK is to remove as many obstacles as possible between you and building an application that looks and behaves exactly like most of the stock applications. So, if you want a button with rounded edges or an info button with a light icon (both of which occur in copious quantities throughout the core OS), you have very little work to do. However, if you want to create a custom button in iOS with custom visuals inside the bounding frame, you have a lot of work to do.

Conversely, the goal of the .NET Framework and specifically Silverlight for Windows Phone 7 is to make any and all possible user interfaces equally available to you. It is a debate of breadth versus depth. iOS hides the complexity of customization behind a façade of extremely purpose-driven controls that will get you to the 80% point (in general) faster than you might in Silverlight. However, the last 20%, where customization and tweaking typically occurs, can be a frustrating, nail-biting, hair-removing experience in iOS, whereas the entire 100% of the development process in Silverlight typically requires the same level of effort.

Neither SDK design is the only right or wrong design, but both were clearly built for different audiences and different purposes. Silverlight makes doing amazing things with your UI just as easy as doing the mundane, whereas iOS makes the mundane nearly automatic and offloads that saved effort into the realm of customization.

Accepting Other Forms of User Input

Buttons and TextBoxes aren't the only way users can interact with your application using out-of-the-box controls that come with the WP7 SDK. This next section introduces you to a few new controls that provide richer and more flexible ways of accepting input from the user, such as the following:

- Checkbox—There is no functional native UIKit control in iOS for a check box.

- RadioButton—A UISegmentedControl often provides similar functionality in iOS.

- PasswordBox—A UITextField control with the `secureTextEntry` property set to `YES` provides nearly identical functionality in iOS.

- Slider—A UISlider control provides this functionality in iOS, although iOS sliders are hard to customize and always appear horizontally, whereas WP7 sliders can be easily customized and can be displayed vertically without customization.

- HyperlinkButton—The easiest way to produce this functionality in iOS is to create a tappable label that has been styled to look like a hyperlink (for example, blue, underlined text).

Open up the MainPage.xaml file that we've been working with throughout this chapter and add the code from Listing 8.7 to the page below the controls from the previous samples. I've deleted a couple of unnecessary controls to make room for the new UI elements (shown in Figure 8.3).

Listing 8.7   **Adding New User Input Elements**

```
<CheckBox x:Name="checkBoxOne"/>
<RadioButton x:Name="ChoiceOne" GroupName="DefaultGroup">
    <TextBlock Text="Radio One"/>
</RadioButton>
<RadioButton GroupName="DefaultGroup">
    <TextBlock Text="Radio Two" />
</RadioButton>
<Slider x:Name="SliderOne" Minimum="0" Maximum="100" Value="20"/>
<HyperlinkButton x:Name="hyperLinkButtonOne" Click="hyperLinkButtonOne_Click"
                 Content="hyperlink!!"/>
<PasswordBox x:Name="PasswordBox" />
```

The first control added is a check box, and these are pretty simple. They let users specify Boolean values, such as whether they want to enable a specific preference or whether a particular statement about some data is true.

The next controls added were two radio buttons. These allow a user to select between a finite set of available options. When a user selects one radio button in a group, the state of all the other buttons is cleared. To indicate which buttons belong to the same group, just assign them the same string for the `GroupName` property. In the preceding code we assigned the `GroupName` property of the two radio buttons the value of `DefaultGroup`.

You can have as many radio button groups on a screen at a time as you can fit (or as your sense of good taste and design might allow).

Next we added a slider, which allows a user to "slide" a value indicator between some arbitrary minimum and maximum. You can use a slider control to prompt the user to pick a volume level, allocate resources to a particular object in a strategy game, or even choose how much of something the user might want to buy. Despite its simplicity, the slider is a powerful and versatile control that can be used in a variety of situations.

Next is the HyperlinkButton. As its name implies, this control presents the user with some text that resembles a standard browser-clickable hyperlink. When the link is tapped, it can either navigate the user to a particular page (a Silverlight page, not a web page) using the `NavigateUri` property, or you can perform custom logic in the `Click` event.

Last, we have the PasswordBox control. This control functions identically to a TextBox control except that a moment after each character is typed into the box, it is replaced with a dot. This pattern and style should be familiar to users of web browsers, iPhones, and many other mobile devices, and users should have no problem recognizing the purpose of this control. However, don't mistake this control for built-in security. All this control does is obscure the display of the password; your code can still access the contents of this TextBox, and there is no automatic encryption. You will have to code your own security for passwords. Some tips and techniques for securing your WP7 application will be covered later in the book.

Figure 8.3   Some more user input elements.

Displaying Images

One of the easiest ways to spice up your application is through the use of images. Small, subtle images used judiciously throughout a UI, or even big images in the middle of a UI, can add a lot to your application and can often be the factor that sets your application above your competitors.

To use an image in iOS, developers typically use the `UIImageView` class. This class is derived from `UIView` and its sole purpose is for the display of images. Likewise, Windows Phone 7 developers have access to the Silverlight Image control, which is extremely easy to use both programmatically and through XAML markup.

The following code shows a basic image control configured completely through XAML.

```xaml
<Grid x:Name="myGrid" Width="150" Height="150" Background="White">
    <Image x:Name="myImage"
        Source="/images/SuperAwesomeScreen.jpg" Stretch="Fill" />
</Grid>
```

Don't worry about the Grid element; we'll be getting to that shortly. In the preceding code, the image control is configured to display a JPEG image called SuperAwesome-Screen.jpg with a Fill stretch mode.

The stretch mode of an image can be set to None, Fill, Uniform, or UniformToFill. No stretch means the image will be displayed exactly as it appears in the file. A stretch mode of Fill means that the image will be expanded to fill whatever layout container it resides within. In the preceding code the parent grid is 150x150, so the image will be scaled up to that size, regardless of whatever size it might be in its original file form. When using the Fill mode, the aspect ratio of the image is not maintained, so it can often warp the original image. To maintain the ratio between height and width even after scaling, use the Uniform stretch mode. This mode will stretch the image as close as it can get to the new size while still keeping the original aspect ratio. Finally, the UniformToFill stretch mode is like Uniform, except it has permission to cut some of the image away to get a better fit within the parent container. In addition to the `Stretch` property, you can control a variety of other aspects of the image, such as the `Width`, `Height`, and `Clip`, which can be used to give images a nonrectangular shape.

Add the following Image element above the first TextBlock control within the Stack-Panel in the same MainPage.xaml file that we have been working with throughout this chapter.

```xaml
<Image x:Name="sampleImage" />
```

That's it. The default mode for the `Stretch` property is Uniform, which is good enough for our purposes. Now go into the code-behind for the XAML and change the implementation of the hyperlink button's `Click` event to the following:

```
private void hyperLinkButtonOne_Click(object sender, RoutedEventArgs e)
{
    sampleImage.Source = new BitmapImage(
        new Uri("success.jpg", UriKind.RelativeOrAbsolute));
}
```

When this code executes, it is going to tell the Image control that it has a new source. This will cause the Image control to immediately redraw itself based on the new contents. The success.jpg file is included with the sample code that accompanies this chapter and can be seen in Figure 8.4.

Although this example might seem trivial, it is just the tip of the iceberg when it comes to the things that you can do with images. Knowing that the source and other properties of an image can be completely changed at runtime paves the way for all kinds of great functionality, such as downloading and caching images from the Internet or your application server, or even creating images on the fly, displaying them, and uploading them to an application server. Just about the only limitation on what you can do with images is your imagination.

Figure 8.4   Using an Image control.

Using a Basic List Box

So far we've been dealing with controls that deal with a single piece of information, such as a single image, an individual text box, or a single button. The list box control gives us the capability to define templates that will be used to render a list of items. This control comes built in with the capability to scroll through the items (including displaying a scrollbar at the appropriate times) and to respond to the selection of items, including changing their appearance when selected. Basically, it's everything you would expect from a list control.

To see this in action, right-click the Chapter 8 Basic Controls project and add a new portrait Windows Phone 7 page to the project; call it ListBoxPage.xaml. After the second TextBlock that is part of the default page, add the following code snippet to the page:

```xml
<ListBox x:Name="myList">
    <ListBox.ItemTemplate>
        <DataTemplate>
            <StackPanel Orientation="Horizontal">
                <Image Source="pistol_bullet.png"/>
                <TextBlock Height="30" Text="{Binding}"
                    Margin="10,10,10,10" />
            </StackPanel>
        </DataTemplate>
    </ListBox.ItemTemplate>
</ListBox>
```

There are a couple of new things in here. I'm actually showing you a little bit about data binding before I even get to that chapter!

At first we define a ListBox element and give it a name (myList). Next, we define an Item Template for the list box and place a data template within that. Templating and binding are topics covered later in the book, but for now you can think of a template as a piece of markup that is applied to each item as it is bound to a CLR object. We will also cover the StackPanel control in the next section of this chapter.

Open up the code-behind for this page and place the following code into the constructor:

```csharp
public partial class ListBoxPage : PhoneApplicationPage
{
    public ListBoxPage()
    {
        InitializeComponent();

        List<string> dummyData = new List<string>()
        {
            "Al",
            "Bob",
            "John",
            "Steve",
            "Ringo",
            "Zappo"
        };

        myList.ItemsSource = dummyData;
    }
}
```

This code creates a list of strings and then sets that as the ItemsSource of the list box. The list box will take this list of strings, merge that with the data template we provided, and produce a screen that looks something like what you see in Figure 8.5.

To get your application to display this page, modify the code for the hyperlink button's click event to navigate to the new page, as shown here:

```
private void hyperLinkButtonOne_Click(object sender, RoutedEventArgs e)
{
    sampleImage.Source = new BitmapImage(
      new Uri("success.jpg", UriKind.RelativeOrAbsolute));
    this.NavigationService.Navigate(
      new Uri("/ListBoxPage.xaml", UriKind.Relative));
}
```

Figure 8.5   Displaying the contents of a list box.

As you will see as we progress throughout the book, list boxes are far more powerful than just displaying simple lists of data. Through the use of templates and styles, you can create some amazing experiences using just a "simple" list box.

For example, one of my favorite demos to give at presentations is to illustrate turning a list box into a radar screen by turning the item container into a canvas and plotting the data-bound objects into the radar field with icons, all without creating a single custom control and using facilities available within just the list box control.

Performing Basic Animations

Although you can certainly create compelling user interfaces without any animation, today's typical smartphone users demand more from their apps. They want things to rotate, spin, bounce, jiggle, and do so in a smooth, subtle way that gives them animated feedback to let them know when the application is doing something, as well as to make the application look and feel good.

As you progress throughout this book you will see more animations and, if you want to dive into animations in depth, I suggest you pick up a copy of *Silverlight 4 Unleashed*, by Laurent Bugnion. Although some subtle differences exist in Silverlight versions between the full and mobile versions, this book will give you a great deal of information on how animation works.

To whet your appetite for animations, open up the ListBoxPage.xaml file you worked with in the previous section. Comment out the list box (highlight the control from begin tag to end tag and press Ctrl+K, and then Ctrl+C; this will wrap the entire block in HTML-style comments) and change the XAML so that it looks like the code in Listing 8.8.

Listing 8.8   **ListBoxPage.xaml, Modified for Animation**

```
<phone:PhoneApplicationPage
    x:Class="BasicControls.ListBoxPage"
    xmlns="http://schemas.microsoft.com/winfx/2006/xaml/presentation"
    xmlns:x="http://schemas.microsoft.com/winfx/2006/xaml"
    xmlns:phone=
"clr-namespace:Microsoft.Phone.Controls;assembly=Microsoft.Phone"
    xmlns:shell=
"clr-namespace:Microsoft.Phone.Shell;assembly=Microsoft.Phone"
    xmlns:d="http://schemas.microsoft.com/expression/blend/2008"
    xmlns:mc="http://schemas.openxmlformats.org/markup-compatibility/2006"
    FontFamily="{StaticResource PhoneFontFamilyNormal}"
    FontSize="{StaticResource PhoneFontSizeNormal}"
    Foreground="{StaticResource PhoneForegroundBrush}"
    SupportedOrientations="Portrait" Orientation="Portrait"
    mc:Ignorable="d" d:DesignHeight="768" d:DesignWidth="480"
    shell:SystemTray.IsVisible="True">
    <phone:PhoneApplicationPage.Resources>
        <Storyboard x:Name="buttonStoryboard">
            <DoubleAnimation Storyboard.TargetProperty="(Canvas.Top)"
                    Storyboard.TargetName="animateButton"
                    From="10" To="200" Duration="0:0:5"/>
            <DoubleAnimation Storyboard.TargetProperty="(Canvas.Left)"
                    Storyboard.TargetName="animateButton"
                    From="10" To="200" AutoReverse="true"
                    RepeatBehavior="Forever"
                    Duration="0:0:1"/>
```

```
        </Storyboard>
    </phone:PhoneApplicationPage.Resources>

    <Grid x:Name="LayoutRoot" Background="Transparent">
        <Grid.RowDefinitions>
            <RowDefinition Height="Auto"/>
            <RowDefinition Height="*"/>
        </Grid.RowDefinitions>

            <StackPanel
          x:Name="TitlePanel" Grid.Row="0" Margin="12,17,0,28">
            <TextBlock x:Name="ApplicationTitle"
Text="MY APPLICATION" Style="{StaticResource PhoneTextNormalStyle}"/>
            <TextBlock x:Name="PageTitle" Text="page name"
Margin="9,-7,0,0" Style="{StaticResource PhoneTextTitle1Style}"/>
            <!--<ListBox x:Name="myList">
            <ListBox.ItemTemplate>
                <DataTemplate>
                    <StackPanel Orientation="Horizontal">
                        <Image Source="pistol_bullet.png"/>
                        <TextBlock Height="30" Text="{Binding}"
                            Margin="10,10,10,10" />
                    </StackPanel>
                </DataTemplate>
            </ListBox.ItemTemplate>
        </ListBox>-->
            <Canvas Width="300" Height="500">
                <Button Canvas.Top="10"
                  Canvas.Left="10"
                  x:Name="animateButton"
                  Click="animateButton_Click">
                    <TextBlock Text="Click to Animate"/>
                </Button>
            </Canvas>
            <TextBlock x:Name="buttonPosition" Text="(none)"/>
        </StackPanel>

        <Grid x:Name="ContentPanel" Grid.Row="1"
            Margin="12,0,12,0"></Grid>
    </Grid>
</phone:PhoneApplicationPage>
```

At this point, your app won't compile, so resist the urge to click Build. We still need to write a few more lines of code.

I've highlighted in bold a Storyboard object that I added to the page's resource dictionary. Don't worry if this doesn't make much sense now, it will become clearer as you start writing more complex applications and progress through the book.

This storyboard contains two animations that will both start at the same time when the storyboard is started. If you are familiar with iOS and Cocoa development, you can think of the storyboard much like an animation context. For example, in iOS to perform a set of animations simultaneously, you first call the `beginAnimations:` method of the `UIView` class. After configuring all the animations you want to perform, as well as options like duration and easing curve, you call the `commitAnimations:` method of the `UIView` class.

For Windows Phone 7 Silverlight animations, the storyboard serves as the aggregator for related animations. In this case, we are going to animate the `Canvas.Top` property from 10 to 200 over the course of 5 seconds. At the same time, we animate the target button's `Canvas.Left` property from 10 to 200, but for this property we will reverse the animation and continue indefinitely. This will have the effect of moving the target button horizontally across the screen and back again forever.

After you've modified your XAML according to the code in Listing 8.8, add the following method to the ListBoxPage.xaml.cs file:

```
private void animateButton_Click(object sender, RoutedEventArgs e)
{
    if (buttonStoryboard.GetCurrentState() == ClockState.Stopped)
        buttonStoryboard.Begin();

    double top = (double)animateButton.GetValue(Canvas.TopProperty);
    double left = (double)animateButton.GetValue(Canvas.LeftProperty);

    buttonPosition.Text = string.Format("{0},{1}", top, left);
}
```

Dependency Properties

If you look carefully at how the Button is positioned within the Canvas, you'll see that it sets properties called `Canvas.Top` and `Canvas.Left`. The button itself does not have a `Top` or a `Left` property because those properties make sense only when the button is a child control of a Canvas. To keep controls from being littered with these situational properties (among many other reasons), dependency properties were created.

When you want to place a control somewhere within a Grid, you set the `Grid.Row` and `Grid.Column` properties on that control. These properties belong to the `Grid` class, but can be set on any object residing within a grid. These properties can also notify subscribers when they change and can be animated by Silverlight's animation sub-system. You see this when you look at the code that displays the current values of the `Canvas.Top` and `Canvas.Left` properties in the code for the animation button's `Click` event. Even though a background thread is constantly changing the value of the control's position within a Canvas, you can still read those values through the dependency property system.

> For more information on dependency properties and how they work, you can consult either *WPF Unleashed* or *Silverlight Unleashed*. Knowing how these work and how you can harness their power will make you an incredibly effective Silverlight developer for mobile devices and desktops alike.

Run the application now and navigate to the list box page. When you tap the button it will start moving. Keep tapping the button as it slowly descends down the page. Each time you tap the button while moving, it reports its current position within the parent canvas at the exact moment you tapped it, even though there is a completely separate background thread performing the animation.

Introduction to Layout in Silverlight

So far throughout this chapter you have seen several types of layout controls. This section of the chapter will provide a little more detail on the purpose of each type of layout control, how they work, and how you can use them in your applications.

Layout is an area in which Silverlight has a distinct advantage over iOS. iOS doesn't come with any low-level, flexible layout panel controls like the StackPanel or the Grid. The UIView itself functions like a WP7 Canvas—child views are placed at fixed positions within the parent view based on their coordinates. There is no Grid control in iOS either; the closest you can get to that would be creating a table view controller (we'll discuss various WP7 alternatives to Table View Controllers in later chapters as well) and subdividing custom cells. As an iOS developer, after you start working with Silverlight's advanced layout capabilities, there is a good chance you will quickly become addicted to having all that power available.

Painting on Canvas

As you might have guessed by now from the previous code samples, the Canvas control provides a fixed-position layout panel. Any child control within the panel has a fixed position within that Canvas as indicated by the `Canvas.Top` and `Canvas.Left` dependency properties.

You define a Canvas in XAML as follows:

```
<Canvas x:Name="myCanvas" Width="300" Height="400">
  <TextBlock Text="This is inside a Canvas"
     Canvas.Top="40" Canvas.Left="100" />
</Canvas>
```

As mentioned earlier in the chapter, you aren't limited to using plain old ordinary Canvases. You can nest a Canvas within other layout panels, and you can host other layout panels within a canvas. You can also do innovative things like change the layout panel of a list box from its default to a Canvas so that the list items are rendered in fixed, absolute positions.

Working with the StackPanel

As its name implies, the StackPanel is a layout panel that arranges child elements in stacks, either horizontally or vertically. You don't need to specify which controls appear in which order, nor do you have to specify any kind of coordinates.

The only thing you need to keep in mind is the order in which the child controls appear within the StackPanel. The first child element of the stack panel is the first one that will appear in the panel. Take a look at the following stack panel definition:

```
<StackPanel Orientation="Vertical">
    <Button>
        <TextBlock Text="Button 1"/>
    </Button>
    <Button>
        <TextBlock Text="Button 2"/>
    </Button>
    <Button>
        <TextBlock Text="Button 3"/>
    </Button>
    <Button>
        <TextBlock Text="Button 4"/>
    </Button>
</StackPanel>
```

By default, a StackPanel will render its children vertically with each new child element in the panel being placed below its preceding peer. To have the elements within a Stack-Panel rendered horizontally, change the `Orientation` property of the stack panel to `Horizontal`.

As with the Canvas, you can get some very nice and very powerful results by nesting multiple StackPanels within each other, within Canvases, or within Grids.

Using the Grid Control

The Grid control is an extremely powerful layout panel. I won't go into all the various details and nuances of a Grid here, because you can get excruciating detail online from Microsoft's MSDN documentation or your favorite Silverlight book. The following is a simple Grid definition:

```
<!--ContentPanel - place additional content here-->
<Grid x:Name="ContentPanel" Grid.Row="1" Margin="12,0,12,0"
 Background="AliceBlue">
    <Grid.ColumnDefinitions>
        <ColumnDefinition Width="200"/>
        <ColumnDefinition Width="200"/>
        <ColumnDefinition Width="55"/>
    </Grid.ColumnDefinitions>
    <Grid.RowDefinitions>
```

```xml
                <RowDefinition Height="60"/>
                <RowDefinition Height="75"/>
                <RowDefinition Height="75"/>
        </Grid.RowDefinitions>
        <Border Grid.Row="0" Grid.Column="0" BorderBrush="DarkGreen"
            BorderThickness="0,0,0,4" Background="BlanchedAlmond">
                <TextBlock TextAlignment="Center" VerticalAlignment="Center"
                        Foreground="DarkGreen" FontWeight="Bold"
                        Text="Account Number"/>
        </Border>
        <Border Grid.Row="0" Grid.Column="1" BorderBrush="DarkGreen"
            BorderThickness="0,0,0,4" Background="BlanchedAlmond">
                <TextBlock TextAlignment="Center" VerticalAlignment="Center"
                        Foreground="DarkGreen" FontWeight="Bold"
                        Text="Account Name"/>
        </Border>
        <Border Grid.Row="0" Grid.Column="2" BorderBrush="DarkGreen"
            BorderThickness="0,0,0,4" Background="BlanchedAlmond">
                <TextBlock TextAlignment="Center" VerticalAlignment="Center"
                        Foreground="DarkGreen" FontWeight="Bold"
                        Text="?"/>
        </Border>
        <!-- actual rows -->
        <Border Grid.Row="1" Grid.Column="0" BorderBrush="Black"
            BorderThickness="0,0,1,1">
                <TextBlock TextAlignment="Center" VerticalAlignment="Center"
                            Foreground="Black"
                            Text="ACT00001"/>
        </Border>
        <Border Grid.Row="1" Grid.Column="1" BorderBrush="Black"
            BorderThickness="0,0,1,1">
                <TextBlock TextAlignment="Center" VerticalAlignment="Center"
                            Foreground="Black"
                            Text="Account 1"/>
        </Border>
        <Border Grid.Row="1" Grid.Column="3" BorderBrush="Black"
            BorderThickness="0,0,1,1">
                <CheckBox IsChecked="True" Background="Transparent" />
        </Border>

        <Border Grid.Row="2" Grid.Column="0" BorderBrush="Black"
            BorderThickness="0,0,1,1">
                <TextBlock TextAlignment="Center" VerticalAlignment="Center"
                            Foreground="Black"
                            Text="ACT00002"/>
        </Border>
```

```
    <Border Grid.Row="2" Grid.Column="1" BorderBrush="Black"
        BorderThickness="0,0,1,1">
        <TextBlock TextAlignment="Center" VerticalAlignment="Center"
                   Foreground="Black"
                   Text="Account 2"/>
    </Border>
    <Border Grid.Row="2" Grid.Column="3" BorderBrush="Black"
        BorderThickness="0,0,1,1">
        <CheckBox IsChecked="False" Background="Transparent"/>
    </Border>
</Grid>
```

The preceding code produces a display that looks like the one shown in Figure 8.6.

Figure 8.6   Displaying controls in a grid.

Navigating to Test and Scratch Pages

As you have seen several times in this chapter, a common practice among Silverlight developers when doing rapid prototyping is to create a new blank page in which to experiment with something. They might use this new blank page to check out an idea for a control they want to write, a style they want to use, data binding templates, or anything else.

Earlier in this chapter you saw that we modified a hyperlink so that we could navigate to one of our experimental pages. Although this works for a book, it is often ugly and cumbersome in a real-world scenario. Here is what I like to do:

- First, create a new folder in your project and call it Playground. Create the new WP7 test pages in this folder. Now, instead of ruining your real UI by littering it with links to all your test pages, you can modify your application so that when it starts, it launches directly into your test page.

- Expand the Properties node below your project in Solution Explorer. Double-click the file WMAppManifest.xml. Look for an XML element called `DefaultTask`. Here you will see an attribute called `NavigationPage`. Change this from `MainPage.xaml` to `/Playground/Whatever.xaml`. The next time you launch your application, it will load directly to your test page and leave your real UI unscarred.

- When you are satisfied with the XAML markup from a page you've been working with in your Playground folder, you can copy and paste the markup into your real UI.

If you have worked with HTML tables before, you have a pretty good head start on figuring out how the Grid control works. It operates on the simple principle of columns and rows. You can add child elements that belong to individual columns, span multiple columns, span multiple rows within a single column, and so on.

The tricky part is that a Grid does not have a dynamic number of rows. In other words, if you have three row definitions and you try to add a control with a row value of 3 (remember, rows and columns both start at index 0) the control will not appear. You cannot add elements without an appropriate row definition.

This is an important distinction because developers new to Silverlight, and especially those familiar with the iOS UITableViewController (and the table view it controls), often expect the grid to be able to dynamically produce rows. Although you can programmatically manipulate a grid to add rows to it, this isn't the same as a list box, which expects to have an unknown number of rows to display at runtime. Strangely enough, for those looking for spreadsheet-style data displays, a trick often employed is to use a list box where *each row* produces a fixed-size grid.

Summary

This chapter gave you a whirlwind tour of the various primitive controls available to Windows Phone 7 developers and compared them with some similar offerings available to iOS developers. In some cases, such as with dynamic layout panels, we covered controls that are not available in iOS.

I deliberately avoided going into too much detail on any one control because the point of this chapter was to give you a big-picture view of the basic capabilities of the Windows Phone 7 SDK as accessed through Silverlight.

Using the text boxes, text blocks, buttons, layout panels, images, and even basic animation, you are already well on your way to writing powerful WP7 applications, and we have just barely scratched the surface of what you can do with this incredible SDK.

9

Using Advanced UI Elements

Form follows function—that has been misunderstood.
Form and function should be one, joined in a spiritual union.

Frank Lloyd Wright

This chapter focuses specifically on translating your knowledge of certain types of applications and application components from iOS to Windows Phone 7. Even if you aren't an iOS developer, you might learn a few things about how these various application components look on the iPhone.

When building iOS applications, you'll see a few types of application components reused over and over, to the point where these components are immediately recognizable in virtually any iOS app, no matter how much they have been customized.

The navigation bar is used in so many applications it is almost hard to find one that doesn't use it. Next, this chapter covers the use of tab bar applications and how you might migrate a tab bar application to have the same functionality but make use of native WP7 UI elements. Finally, this chapter covers what is arguably the single most used controller in the iOS SDK: the Table View Controller. This last section of the chapter covers the variety of options available to developers wanting to migrate Table View Controller apps to Windows Phone 7.

Migrating from Navigation Bars

Building iOS applications with navigation controllers is almost second nature to virtually any iOS developer. Not only does Xcode come with a built-in template for building a navigation application, but Interface Builder (or just Xcode in v4+) makes it incredibly easy to add a navigation controller to any interface.

The purpose of the navigation controller is to make navigating hierarchies of screens easy. The controller comes with built-in facilities for supplying each view with a title, back buttons, and even control "knobs" like edit buttons that can inform other parts of the UI to switch from a read-only mode to a view mode.

As I have said multiple times so far in this book, the iOS SDK is purpose-driven. The navigation controller is a clear example of that. Apple wanted to make the experience of navigating through screens smooth and, more importantly, consistent. Anyone who has used an iPhone is aware of this consistency because the ubiquitous nature of the navigation controller coupled with its consistent look and feel make the act of going back (or "up" a hierarchy), drilling down, or changing screen state almost instinctive.

There is no direct correlation for a navigation controller in the Windows Phone 7 SDK, but a couple of controls and a complete navigation subsystem make rolling your own navigable UI quite easy. First we'll take a look at the Silverlight navigation system (available both in regular and WP7 versions of Silverlight), and then we'll take a look at some possible ways we can put a nice easy UI on top of this system, and even consider a few scenarios when we wouldn't want a navigation UI.

Figure 9.1 is a screenshot of the FB Investor iPhone App that follows the activity of the folks on the FortuneBuilders team. At the top of this screenshot you can see a navigation controller. These controllers typically have a view that manifests itself as this top bar. The middle of the bar is reserved for the title of the current view in the hierarchy, and the left side stays empty until there is a view that you can navigate back to, as shown in Figure 9.2.

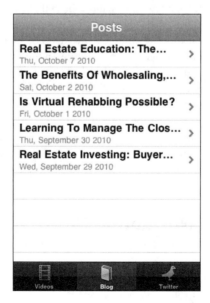

Figure 9.1   An iOS navigation controller at the
top of a hierarchy.

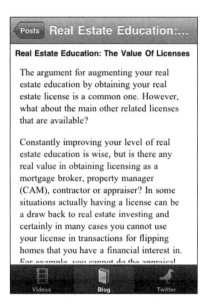

Figure 9.2   An iOS navigation controller in the middle of a hierarchy.

Figure 9.2 shows an iOS navigation controller that is at least one level deep in a view tree or hierarchy. You can see by the title of the back button that tapping it will take you back to a view titled Posts, and the current view is one that displays the contents of a blog post.

The next few sections will show you how to produce this kind of functionality (although not quite the same UI) on Windows Phone 7 using Silverlight.

Using the Silverlight Navigation System

The Silverlight navigation system is an API exposed through a single object, the `NavigationService` object that is a property of the `Page` object. It maintains a basic navigation trail as the user moves through an application.

The `CanGoForward` and `CanGoBackward` properties provide developers with a basic way of interrogating the user's navigation history. If either of these properties are true, the `GoForward()` and `GoBack()` methods can be invoked, respectively. If you attempt to invoke either of these methods when navigation in that direction is not possible, an exception will be thrown. To be safe and to avoid throwing unnecessary exceptions, always check the values of these properties before performing the actual navigation. To move the user from one page to another, use the `Navigate()` method.

Although this might seem like a simple concept, it helps to see it in action to see how everything works. To do this, create a new Windows Phone application, which will create a portrait-based main page. On the MainPage.xaml, add a new button called `navigateButton`. The following code snippet shows the `Click` event handler for this button:

```
private void navigateButton_Click(object sender, RoutedEventArgs e)
{
    NavigationService.Navigate(new Uri("/Page1.xaml", UriKind.Relative));
}
```

This code navigates the user from MainPage.xaml to Page1.xaml instantly. The fact that the user originated on MainPage.xaml will be stored in the navigation system. When the user lands on the Page1.xaml page, the `CanGoBack` Boolean property of `NavigationSystem` will be true. In addition, when the NavigationSystem object's `GoBack()` method is invoked from Page1.xaml, the user will be sent back to MainPage.xaml.

You can see this in action by adding a new portrait page to the project (leave the default name of Page1). On that page, add a button and set its `Click` handler to the following:

```
private void backButton_Click(object sender, RoutedEventArgs e)
{
    if (NavigationService.CanGoBack)
        NavigationService.GoBack();
}
```

Note how we checked to see whether backward navigation was possible before calling the `GoBack()` method. You can also use the Boolean properties `CanGoBack` and `CanGoForward` to activate or deactivate various pieces of your own navigation bar control.

No Forward Movement for WP7

No matter when you try or how you try, you will never be able to move forward through a navigation hierarchy on Windows Phone 7. Although WP7's version of Silverlight might be nearly identical to that of the desktop version, some differences still exist, and this is one of them. The desktop version of Silverlight allows users to go forward and back, whereas on WP7, the `CanGoForward` property will never be true and the `GoForward()` method will always throw an exception.

The actual navigation is just a small part of the system. The real work comes in the pages themselves and how they respond to construction, navigation, and activation. In an iOS application, the developer typically has explicit control over the instantiation of the view controller to which the user will navigate next. This means that the developer also has explicit control over the lifespan of that object.

Using the Silverlight navigation system, the lifespan and activation cycle of these pages might not be immediately obvious. You need to know when and where you can place code that will be executed when pages are first created, when they are loaded, and when a user navigates to the pages. Failure to pay attention to these could cause anything from performance problems to memory issues or worse—your application crashing.

Using the Page Constructor

Every page object is still just a C# object and, as such, has a regular constructor. When you create a new page object for a WP7 application, it comes with a constructor that invokes the `InitializeComponent()` method. It looks like the code in the following snippet:

```
public partial class Page1 : PhoneApplicationPage
{
    public Page1()
    {
        InitializeComponent();
    }
}
```

The `InitializeComponent()` method invokes all the generated code produced by the XAML markup that configures everything according to the markup you see on the design surface. Without delving into too much detail about what goes on inside that method, the key thing to remember is that no objects defined in your user interface will be available for you to use until after this method has been invoked. In short, do not ever create any initialization code in your constructor before the `InitializeComponent()` method has been called.

The tricky part about page constructors is that they are called only at very specific times. The constructor of the default (first) landing page of an application is called when the application starts up. The constructor of other pages are not called unless you manually instantiate the page or the user navigates to the page through a call to `Navigate()` on the `NavigationService` object.

It is possible that at some point during the course of the application's running, the page will be removed from memory. I will get into the topics of tombstoning and multitasking in later chapters, but for now, keep in mind that it is possible that a page will not remain in memory forever after its constructor has been called, and that its constructor may be called multiple times if the application is "awoken" from a previous suspension.

The reason I bring this up is because people often get into lazy habits of assuming that constructors are absolute, so they use them to fetch whatever data they need and then they assume that data will be around forever.

Using the Page Loaded Event

One of the problems with relying on the constructor for your initialization code is that the constructor is called very infrequently and often in unpredictable times. The Page's `Loaded` event is called, appropriately enough, whenever the page is loaded.

The `Loaded` event is a low-level event that you will find on most of the UI elements within Silverlight including shapes, buttons, borders, text blocks, and more. You should think of the fact that the page's `Loaded` event is called during a navigation as a side effect. Even though you might see a 1:1 correlation between loading and navigation, do not treat them the same. There are more ways than just navigation to load a page, and so there might be unexpected times when the `Loaded` event is fired on your page. As a result, don't put initialization code in here unless you are guarding against that or you are specifically taking advantage of that fact.

To utilize the `Loaded` event, you need to subscribe to it in the Page's constructor (after the call to `InitializeComponent`!), as shown here:

```
public Page1()
{
    InitializeComponent();
    this.Loaded += new RoutedEventHandler(Page1_Loaded);
}

void Page1_Loaded(object sender, RoutedEventArgs e)
{
    // do something important.
    Debug.WriteLine("Page1 was loaded.");
}
```

Experiment with this code in the existing navigation sample. Watch when the phrase "Page1 was loaded." appears in the debug output window. You will see it appear every time you navigate to the page (even if you land on the page using the back button). The small caveat here is that every once in a while, your code might be doing something tricky enough to cause the `Loaded` event to fire when you don't expect it.

Using the `OnNavigatedTo` Method

When you really want to associate your code with the navigation event, the best thing to do is override the `OnNavigatedTo` method. This method is a part of the WP7 Page object, so you don't need to subscribe to an event; all you have to do is override the method and place your code inside. Additionally, there is an `OnNavigatedFrom` method and an `OnNavigatingFrom` method. The following table describes when each of these methods is invoked.

Method	Description
`OnNavigatedTo`	When a page has been navigated to. Keep in mind that this is invoked BEFORE the destination page's `Loaded` event is fired.
`OnNavigatedFrom`	This is called after the user has left the current page in favor of another.
`OnNavigatingFrom`	This is called after the user triggers the navigation action away from the current page but BEFORE the user has actually navigated to the new target.

Add the following override methods to the Page1.xaml.cs file and run the application, navigating back and forth between MainPage.xaml and Page1.xaml. Pay close attention to the Debug output window and when each of these methods is called.

```
protected override void OnNavigatedTo(
System.Windows.Navigation.NavigationEventArgs e)
{
    System.Diagnostics.Debug.WriteLine("Navigated to page1.");
}

protected override void OnNavigatingFrom(
    System.Windows.Navigation.NavigatingCancelEventArgs e)
{
    System.Diagnostics.Debug.WriteLine("NavigatING from page1.");
}

protected override void OnNavigatedFrom(
    System.Windows.Navigation.NavigationEventArgs e)
{
    System.Diagnostics.Debug.WriteLine("Navigated From page1.");
}
```

Spicing Up Navigation Events with Animation

One of the many things that you get "for free" from the iOS navigation controller and all its moving parts is just that—moving parts. When you "push" another controller onto a navigation controller, the entire UI will slide away to the left, revealing the new controller's view hierarchy as it slides in from the right.

As you know, the iOS SDK makes utilizing the default look and feel incredibly easy and everything else slightly more difficult. With Windows Phone 7, we have easy access to virtually any kind of animation effect you want, and we can tie those into the navigation events to create our own animated transitions.

To see what kinds of animations we can rig up to our navigation events, I'm going to modify the MainPage class so that when you navigate to Page1, the page's entire UI swings toward you like a door opening, revealing the UI of Page1 underneath. When the user navigates back to MainPage, that same door will swing "shut," again hiding the Page1 UI underneath. This particular style makes for an excellent transition between master and detail views. After you're done following along with this sample, experiment with the timing and other options like the grid transparency and even the rotation angle—the possibilities are endless.

Listing 9.1 shows the modified MainPage.xaml. Pay special attention to the new storyboards and a new addition to the Grid control, the PlaneTransform element that belongs to the Grid.Transform element. This highlights Silverlight's unique capability to provide 3D transformations of 2D elements without requiring the developer to render his entire UI in a 3D engine.

Listing 9.1   **MainPage.xaml—Animated Page Transitions**

```xml
<phone:PhoneApplicationPage
    x:Class="NavigationBars.MainPage"
    xmlns="http://schemas.microsoft.com/winfx/2006/xaml/presentation"
    xmlns:x="http://schemas.microsoft.com/winfx/2006/xaml"
    xmlns:phone=
      "clr-namespace:Microsoft.Phone.Controls;assembly=Microsoft.Phone"
    xmlns:shell=
      "clr-namespace:Microsoft.Phone.Shell;assembly=Microsoft.Phone"
    xmlns:d="http://schemas.microsoft.com/expression/blend/2008"
    xmlns:mc="http://schemas.openxmlformats.org/markup-compatibility/2006"
    mc:Ignorable="d" d:DesignWidth="480" d:DesignHeight="768"
    FontFamily="{StaticResource PhoneFontFamilyNormal}"
    FontSize="{StaticResource PhoneFontSizeNormal}"
    Foreground="{StaticResource PhoneForegroundBrush}"
    SupportedOrientations="Portrait" Orientation="Portrait"
    shell:SystemTray.IsVisible="True">
    <phone:PhoneApplicationPage.Resources>
        <Storyboard x:Name="openDoorStoryBoard">
            <DoubleAnimation Storyboard.TargetName="gridPlaneProjection"
                            Storyboard.TargetProperty="RotationY"
                            From="0"
                            To="90"
                            Duration="0:0:1"/>
        </Storyboard>
        <Storyboard x:Name="closeDoorStoryBoard">
            <DoubleAnimation Storyboard.TargetName="gridPlaneProjection"
                            Storyboard.TargetProperty="RotationY"
                            From="90"
                            To="0"
                            Duration="0:0:1"/>
        </Storyboard>
    </phone:PhoneApplicationPage.Resources>

    <!--LayoutRoot is the root grid where all page content is placed-->
    <Grid x:Name="LayoutRoot" Background="Transparent">
        <Grid.Projection>
            <PlaneProjection
                x:Name="gridPlaneProjection" CenterOfRotationX="0.0"/>
        </Grid.Projection>
        <Grid.RowDefinitions>
            <RowDefinition Height="Auto"/>
            <RowDefinition Height="*"/>
        </Grid.RowDefinitions>

        <StackPanel x:Name="TitlePanel" Grid.Row="0" Margin="12,17,0,28">
```

```
            <TextBlock x:Name="ApplicationTitle"
               Text="MY APPLICATION"
               Style="{StaticResource PhoneTextNormalStyle}"/>
            <TextBlock x:Name="PageTitle"
               Text="Main Page"
               Margin="9,-7,0,0"
               Style="{StaticResource PhoneTextTitle1Style}"/>
        </StackPanel>

        <!--ContentPanel - place additional content here-->
        <Grid x:Name="ContentPanel" Grid.Row="1" Margin="12,0,12,0">
            <StackPanel>
                <Button
                    x:Name="navigateButton"
                    Click="navigateButton_Click" Height="75">
                     <TextBlock Text="Click to Navigate to Page 1" />
                </Button>
            </StackPanel>
        </Grid>
    </Grid>
</phone:PhoneApplicationPage>
```

Now modify MainPage.xaml.cs so that it looks like the code shown in Listing 9.2.

Listing 9.2   **MainPage.xaml.cs—Animated Page Transitions**

```
public partial class MainPage : PhoneApplicationPage
{
    // Constructor
    public MainPage()
    {
        InitializeComponent();
    }

    private void navigateButton_Click(object sender, RoutedEventArgs e)
    {
        openDoorStoryBoard.Completed +=
          (s, ev) =>
            {
              NavigationService.Navigate(
                new Uri("/Page1.xaml", UriKind.Relative));
            };
        openDoorStoryBoard.Begin();
    }

    protected override void OnNavigatedTo(
      System.Windows.Navigation.NavigationEventArgs e)
```

```
    {
        // if the door isn't "open", don't shut it.
        if (gridPlaneProjection.RotationY == 90)
            closeDoorStoryBoard.Begin();
    }
}
```

Try the application out now and watch how the grid from MainPage.xaml swings out of the way and then, when done swinging away, navigates to Page1. The animation is allowed to complete because we don't perform the actual navigation until the animation is finished by subscribing an anonymous delegate to the `Completed` event. Anonymous delegates used this way with the lambda (=>) syntax are analogous to the use of Blocks in Cocoa for the Mac and in newer versions of the iOS SDK. The syntax should actually look somewhat familiar if you've used some of the new Blocks-based method calls in the iOS SDK.

Before moving on to the next section, play around with the configuration of the 3D perspective transform to change the way the UI appears and reappears. The `CenterOfRotationX`, `CenterOfRotationY`, and `CenterOfRotationZ` properties of the `PlaneTransform` all start off with default values of 0.5, placing the rotation in the center of the UI element. By shifting the `CenterOfRotationX` value to 0.0, when the animation spins the UI element around the X axis, it does so on the far left of the object. If we set the same center of rotation to 1.0, the rotation would occur on the far right side of the object (and we'd have to change the rotation angles to maintain the appearance of a door opening).

A Note on Storyboards and Double Animations

Long before the folks at Disney or Pixar or any other animation company sit down and start churning out smooth, fluid animations, they need to produce what is commonly called a *storyboard*.

A storyboard, in the traditional sense, is a big board stuck up on a wall where the animators and other crew sketch out how all the characters in the movie are going to act. It often looks like a comic book, showing the various key frames that illustrate the flow of animation. Another important point to remember about storyboards is that at any given time, multiple characters and objects can be moving in many directions. Rarely will you ever see a (well made) cartoon where everything in the scene stands absolutely still while one character moves.

In the Silverlight and Windows Phone 7 sense, a storyboard is a collection of animations that will all start in parallel. I say "start" because it is possible (and actually quite regular) that the animations started by a storyboard do not finish at the same time.

Think of the various UI elements in your XAML as characters or actors in a scene. In this scene, your actors are going to move in such a way that they produce a pleasing and informative motion clip for your viewers (the people using your application).

The storyboard lets you plot out exactly which elements will be moving, how fast they are moving, where they are moving, and so on.

The animations contained within a storyboard can be anything from simple animations that change one property from a source value to a target value to complex animations, such as key frame animations, where you indicate what a property's value should be at specific time markers.

The animations I used in the preceding example are double animations, which animate a property of type `double` from a source value to a target value over a specific period of time.

Migrating from Tab Bar Applications

In iOS applications, the tab bar control is an extremely common control that shows up in thousands of applications in the App Store. The purpose of this control is to segment an application into categories or provide quick, shortcut-style access to particular pieces of the application's functionality. When there are more tabs than can be displayed on a single bar, a More button appears, which brings the user to a table view displaying the list of the remaining tabs. Tapping on any of the tabs launches the view controller associated with that particular tab.

Although Windows Phone 7 doesn't have its own exact replica of the Tab Bar control, WP7 developers have plenty of options for building UIs that serve the same purpose as the Tab Bar control. These include the Pivot control, the Panorama control, and finally the Application Bar control. The following sections cover each of these controls respectively and how they support "tab bar-like" functionality.

Using the Pivot Control

The Pivot control is an incredibly powerful control but also just as easy to use. A Pivot has a title and then a series of PivotItem child controls. Each of these PivotItem controls contains a XAML hierarchy of visual elements that can be anything from list boxes to buttons to whatever you like.

When the Pivot control first appears, the first pivot item is visible, and the title of the second pivot item is visible at the top of the Pivot control next to the first. Tapping the title of the second pivot item will pivot or slide the focus from the first pivot item to the second. This continues until you reach the last pivot item where the title of the first pivot item appears, allowing you to continuously move through the items without having to worry about using the back button.

One of the places you will see the Pivot control used extensively is Outlook for WP7. You can "pivot" between different views of your mail and, when used in your application, you can pivot between different categories of information or different areas of functionality within your application.

To see the Pivot control in action, you can make use of the ready-made Pivot Application WP7 template. Open up Visual Studio and create a new project. Choose the Pivot Application template and then run it. You should see a screen that looks like the one in Figure 9.3.

Figure 9.3   Using the Pivot control.

Tap the word "second" to see the Pivot control slide so that the contents of the first pivot item move away and the contents of the second pivot item slide into view. Listing 9.3 shows the XAML for the Pivot control. As you can see, it is fairly straightforward, and the Pivot control is doing a great deal of work on your behalf.

Listing 9.3   **MainPage.xaml from the Pivot Control Application Template**

```
<controls:Pivot Title="MY APPLICATION">
    <!--Pivot item one-->
    <controls:PivotItem Header="first">
        <!--Double line list with text wrapping-->
        <ListBox x:Name="FirstListBox" Margin="0,0,-12,0"
            ItemsSource="{Binding Items}">
            <ListBox.ItemTemplate>
                <DataTemplate>
                    <StackPanel Margin="0,0,0,17" Width="432">
```

```
                <TextBlock Text="{Binding LineOne}"
            TextWrapping="Wrap"
            Style="{StaticResource PhoneTextExtraLargeStyle}"/>
                <TextBlock Text="{Binding LineTwo}"
            TextWrapping="Wrap" Margin="12,-6,12,0"
            Style="{StaticResource PhoneTextSubtleStyle}"/>
                </StackPanel>
            </DataTemplate>
        </ListBox.ItemTemplate>
    </ListBox>
</controls:PivotItem>
<!--Pivot item two-->
<controls:PivotItem Header="second">
    <!--Triple line list no text wrapping-->
        <ListBox x:Name="SecondListBox"
            Margin="0,0,-12,0" ItemsSource="{Binding Items}">
            <ListBox.ItemTemplate>
                <DataTemplate>
                    <StackPanel Margin="0,0,0,17">
                        <TextBlock Text="{Binding LineOne}"
                    TextWrapping="NoWrap" Margin="12,0,0,0"
                    Style="{StaticResource PhoneTextExtraLargeStyle}"/>
                        <TextBlock Text="{Binding LineThree}"
                    TextWrapping="NoWrap" Margin="12,-6,0,0"
                    Style="{StaticResource PhoneTextSubtleStyle}"/>
                    </StackPanel>
                </DataTemplate>
            </ListBox.ItemTemplate>
        </ListBox>
    </controls:PivotItem>
</controls:Pivot>
```

It is surprisingly easy to use this control. Just create a new Pivot control and then define the panels through which you want your user to be able to pivot. Pivots can be used for everything from a complicated line of business applications to social applications, and even for casual gaming scenarios.

Experiment with this control and see what kinds of compelling UIs you can produce using just a Pivot control and the primitive Silverlight controls discussed in the previous chapter. You might be surprised by how much you can accomplish.

Using a Panorama Application

Where the Pivot control slides items out of your way and new items into view atop a fixed background, the Panorama control is a much more fluid control. Rather than tapping the title of nearby items, you simply swipe to bring the nearby items into view. This creates a nice parallax scrolling effect where the user sees the background shift and the new items come into view.

In many cases you can use either a Panorama or a Pivot to provide the same functionality in your application; there are a few differentiating factors between the two controls. In a Pivot control, you tap the item names to bring the item content into view, and the Panorama requires a swiping gesture to bring the next item into view. The Pivot control is more often used when the UI structure of each element is somewhat similar to its peers. A Panorama control, as you can see when you flip through various hubs on a WP7 phone (especially the music area), gives the user a much looser, more fluid experience. You can use the Panorama to flip between data-driven views, rich graphical content, or anything else the phone provides.

The key differentiating factor to remember is that a Pivot control can be used to switch between completely unrelated areas of application functionality without it feeling awkward to the user. When using a Panorama control, users have the impression as they swipe that they are expanding the original view, perusing through more and more content all with a similar purpose or logical relation. This is why Panoramas are used for the "hub" UI pattern throughout the phone.

In other words, if you used a tab bar to separate completely disparate areas of functionality in your application, the Pivot control is the logical choice. On the other hand, if you used a tab bar to provide visual segmentation of logically related functionality, the Panorama is the natural choice for your UI.

To see the Panorama control in action, open up Visual Studio and create a new WP7 application, choosing the Panorama Application template. This will create a default implementation of a Panorama with a nice background image, a title, and two items that you can swipe between. Remember that if you swipe past the last item, the Panorama wraps around and the first item will come into view.

Figure 9.4 shows what it looks like when you run an application created by the stock Panorama Application project template.

Like the Pivot control, the Panorama control's content is split up into separate child items, each one providing a piece of the virtual panorama experience. The code in Listing 9.4 shows the default XAML from the stock project template for the Panorama application.

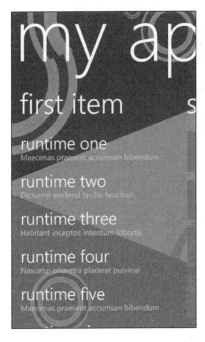

Figure 9.4   Using a Panorama control.

Listing 9.4   **MainPage.xaml for the Panorama Application**

```
<controls:Panorama Title="my application">
<controls:Panorama.Background>
    <ImageBrush ImageSource="PanoramaBackground.png"/>
</controls:Panorama.Background>
<!--Panorama item one-->
<controls:PanoramaItem Header="first item">
    <!--Double line list with text wrapping-->
    <ListBox Margin="0,0,-12,0" ItemsSource="{Binding Items}">
        <ListBox.ItemTemplate>
            <DataTemplate>
                <StackPanel Margin="0,0,0,17" Width="432">
                <TextBlock Text="{Binding LineOne}"
                  TextWrapping="Wrap"
                  Style="{StaticResource PhoneTextExtraLargeStyle}"/>
                <TextBlock Text="{Binding LineTwo}"
                  TextWrapping="Wrap" Margin="12,-6,12,0"
                  Style="{StaticResource PhoneTextSubtleStyle}"/>
                </StackPanel>
            </DataTemplate>
        </ListBox.ItemTemplate>
    </ListBox>
```

```
        </ListBox>
    </controls:PanoramaItem>
    <!--Panorama item two-->
    <!--Use 'Orientation="Horizontal"' to enable a panel that lays out
     horizontally-->
    <controls:PanoramaItem Header="second item">
        <!--Double line list with image placeholder and text wrapping-->
        <ListBox Margin="0,0,-12,0" ItemsSource="{Binding Items}">
            <ListBox.ItemTemplate>
                <DataTemplate>
                    <StackPanel Orientation="Horizontal" Margin="0,0,0,17">
                        <!--Replace rectangle with image-->
                        <Rectangle Height="100" Width="100"
                            Fill="#FFE5001b" Margin="12,0,9,0"/>
                        <StackPanel Width="311">
                        <TextBlock Text="{Binding LineOne}"
                            TextWrapping="Wrap"
                            Style="{StaticResource PhoneTextExtraLargeStyle}"/>
                        <TextBlock Text="{Binding LineTwo}"
                            TextWrapping="Wrap" Margin="12,-6,12,0"
                            Style="{StaticResource PhoneTextSubtleStyle}"/>
                        </StackPanel>
                    </StackPanel>
                </DataTemplate>
            </ListBox.ItemTemplate>
        </ListBox>
    </controls:PanoramaItem>
</controls:Panorama>
```

Like you did with the Pivot control, take this stock application template and experiment with it. Create a bunch of panorama items with all kinds of varying UIs and see how it looks and reacts to user swipes. Play around with the background image to see what kinds of experiences you can create just by using an interesting background image. The key is to tinker with this until you feel very comfortable with the Pivot and the Panorama controls, because they are two of the main ways iOS developers migrate tab bar functionality from the iPhone to Windows Phone 7.

Using the Application Bar

Another control at your disposal as a Windows Phone 7 developer is the application bar. At first, when you see this control, you might think that its purpose maps directly to that of the tab bar, but be careful, the application bar is much more than just a tab bar alternative.

An application bar sits at the bottom (or side, depending on the phone orientation) of the UI and provides a few icons that can be tapped to perform some task. In addition, when there are more items than can be displayed on the screen at a given time, an ellipsis option will appear. When you tap this, it brings up additional menu items. Sounds kind of like a tab bar so far, right? Not quite.

You can have global application bars that show up on the bottom of every page or you can have a specific application bar for every page in your application. Better still, you can dynamically change the active application bar at runtime based on any number of factors. With iOS, you are pretty much limited to the tab bar that you configured either at application start up or at design time. The tab bar has a very parental, controlling role in the iOS UI, whereas the application bar in WP7 works almost like a context menu that, if configured a certain way, can provide "tab bar-like" functionality. The key is to remember that the application bar is incredibly powerful and far more flexible than the iOS tab bar.

To see what an application bar looks like in action, add the following lines of XAML to the bottom of whichever MainPage.xaml you feel like working with (except Panorama or Pivot, both of which specifically should not be combined with application bars).

```
<phone:PhoneApplicationPage.ApplicationBar>
    <shell:ApplicationBar IsVisible="True" IsMenuEnabled="True">
        <shell:ApplicationBarIconButton
    IconUri="/Images/appbar.feature.email.rest.png"
    Text="Button 1"/>
        <shell:ApplicationBarIconButton
    IconUri="/Images/appbar.feature.search.rest.png"
    Text="Button 2"/>
        <shell:ApplicationBarIconButton
    IconUri="/Images/appbar.feature.settings.rest.png"
    Text="Button 2"/>
        <shell:ApplicationBarIconButton
    IconUri="/Images/appbar.feature.video.rest.png"
    Text="Button 2"/>
        <shell:ApplicationBar.MenuItems>
            <shell:ApplicationBarMenuItem Text="MenuItem 1"/>
            <shell:ApplicationBarMenuItem Text="MenuItem 2"/>
        </shell:ApplicationBar.MenuItems>
    </shell:ApplicationBar>
</phone:PhoneApplicationPage.ApplicationBar>
```

The application bar in the preceding code defines four different icon buttons with caption labels and two additional menu items. As the screenshots in Figures 9.5 and 9.6 show, these menu items appear when you tap the ellipsis and expand the application bar.

Figure 9.5   Application bar in its default state.

Figure 9.6   Application bar with menu items expanded.

Each of the buttons and menu items can have an event handler attached to its `Click` event, allowing you to perform whatever logic you need to perform or even navigate to different pages.

Every page also has an `ApplicationBar` property that you can set at any time. This lets you programmatically swap application bars in and out based on context or any other activity within your application. This gives you far more power and flexibility than a standard iOS Tab Bar control.

Summary

One of the hardest tasks in adopting a new platform is mapping all your existing skills to the new environment. You need to learn new languages, new terminology, new patterns, new practices, and develop new habits.

This chapter provided you with that basic mapping of iOS skills with some of the most common UI patterns: navigation bars and tab bars. These user interface elements show up in a vast majority of the applications available in the App Store.

Using the information in this chapter, you should now have a very good idea of how you can take the skills you have in building navigation and tab bar applications for iOS and map that to building new and compelling Pivot and Panorama applications with powerful controls like the application bar on Windows Phone 7.

Using Hardware and Device Services

It's hardware that makes a machine fast. It's software that makes a fast machine slow.

Craig Bruce

This chapter provides an overview of the device and overall system capabilities of Windows Phone 7. Up to this point you've seen how to create your own user interfaces and learned some of the basic techniques for building simple Windows Phone 7 applications.

One of the biggest reasons developers like to build smartphone applications and the main reason people like to own smartphones is because they're, quite simply, *smart*. Without the capability to make phone calls, store contacts, open web pages, play videos, or listen to music, a smartphone has very little appeal, and applications on those devices have even less appeal.

This chapter takes you through the various system capabilities of iOS devices and provides you with a walkthrough of similar (or even entirely new) functionality on Windows Phone 7 devices. By the time you're done with this chapter, you will know how to take advantage of all the shared services, launchers, choosers, and device sensors available to you as a WP7 developer. Armed with the information you've read up to this point and with this new information, you will be well on your way toward making incredible WP7 applications.

Review of Device Capabilities

When the iPhone first came out, it was the first device of its kind in many respects. However, it was certainly not the first nor the most powerful smartphone. Some might argue that it was the easiest to use or the most universally appealing, but the physical capabilities of the device (aside from multitouch) have been in smartphones for a while now.

Because of the incredible popularity of the iPhone, Android devices, Blackberries, and even Windows Mobile (not to be confused with Windows Phone 7) devices, consumer demand for features on those phones has reached an all-time high. Devices that don't take pictures now are often considered broken or "crippled." Smartphone consumers scoff at the idea of owning a phone that doesn't play video, music, run apps, and do a handful of other things that even just a few years ago would have been considered the stuff of science fiction.

The following list describes the capabilities and services offered by modern smartphones. As I address each item, I will point out areas where the iPhone or Windows Phone 7 differ, where they are similar, and where the access to those features by developers might differ. For example, some smartphones might have a feature but might not allow developers to access it. Others might allow developers to access it but only in the form of a launcher (a system application is launched with no low-level API interference from the developer). Finally, some system features might be exposed as rich APIs that the developers can manipulate directly.

- Address Book/Contacts—iOS has exposed access to the underlying Contacts list through an API. Windows Phone 7 allows users to select contact emails and phone numbers with a chooser, as well as save emails and phone numbers to new or existing contacts.

- Text Messaging—Both the iPhone and Windows Phone 7 devices have very rich SMS capabilities, including the capability to send and receive pictures attached to those messages. Programmatic access to sending text messages is available to developers on both platforms.

- Phone Calls—Obviously, both platforms have the capability to make phone calls. To initiate a new phone call on the iPhone, you instruct the application to open a URL with the "tel:" prefix. We will cover how to initiate phone calls in Windows Phone 7 later in this chapter.

- Location/GPS—Both the iPhone and Windows Phone 7 devices have the capability to receive GPS signals. These days, a smartphone without a GPS isn't considered very smart at all. This is evidenced by the sheer number of location-aware applications, ranging from augmented reality to apps that help you find the best plate of cheese fries within two miles of your current location.

- Accelerometer—Accelerometers in smartphones measure the current amount of acceleration on three different axes. These sensors can be used for everything from turning your phone into a steering wheel for a video game to letting you shake the phone to roll the dice in your favorite board game. Both the iPhone and Windows Phone 7 are equipped with accelerometers with very high sampling rates, allowing for all kinds of applications.

- Multimedia—When it comes to multimedia, no one can deny the market domination of iTunes, so it is only natural that the iPhone would contain a rich multimedia experience. Building on the work Microsoft started with the Zune and later the Zune HD, Microsoft has also built in rich media playback capabilities in its OS.

- Messaging (email)—Both devices have rich email capabilities, although the list of features available in Microsoft's Exchange for Windows Phone 7 builds on Microsoft's history of building enterprise mail servers.

- Photos—Picture-taking capabilities vary by device. Older iPhones have cameras with less resolution; newer iPhones have the capability to take videos, and camera resolution and capabilities vary by manufacturer and model for WP7 phones.

- Maps—iOS devices make use of Google Maps and its underlying APIs to provide map services and integrate them with the onboard GPS device. Windows Phone 7 utilizes, unsurprisingly, the Bing Maps service and its APIs.

- Calendar—iOS exposes access to the underlying Calendars through a robust API. At the time of the writing of this book, the Windows Phone 7 SDK offers no such access to calendar events stored on the phone.

- Search (web, local, and news)—On an iOS device you can slide the springboard out of the way (swipe to the right on the first page), and this reveals a search box, allowing you to search through applications, data, emails, and contacts. Windows Phone 7 takes this one step further by allowing you to use the same interface to search the phone, search locally (via a combination of Bing search and the phone's GPS), search the web, and search news. You can programmatically bring up the WP7 search interface.

- Web Browsing—A mobile version of Safari (which is built on the open source browser framework called WebKit) provides the user interface to the web on iOS devices, whereas a mobile version of Internet Explorer (a hybrid of IE9 and custom features) fills this role on Windows Phone 7 devices. Both browsers on both platforms can be activated programmatically by applications.

Using Launchers

With all the power available in devices that fit in the palm of our hands comes a great deal of responsibility. If the device manufacturers or the OS creators gave us developers unfettered access to all of the minute details of the device and its hardware, invariably we would create applications that could wreak all kinds of havoc on a cellular network. In an effort to safeguard the network integrity of the cellular providers and to ensure that all applications play as nicely together as possible, sometimes developers are given only partial access to system resources.

In these cases, one option we have is to use launchers. Launchers give us the capability to invoke various system-level functions, but to do so using vendor-controlled UI and in a tamper-proof fashion. For example, instead of giving developers the ability to directly manipulate outbound calls (which would create a giant candy-filled piñata of hackery for malicious developers), we must instead use a launcher. We can seed that launcher with a phone number or contact that we would like to dial, but in the end the phone has the ultimate authority as to whom and when it dials.

Using the Save Phone Number Task

Although some launchers allow applications to start various system processes, others allow applications to save data to systemwide resources such as Contacts. One such launcher is the `SavePhoneNumber` task. With this task, you can tell it that you would like to save a phone number, and the phone will then bring up a dialog asking the user to select a contact (or create a new one) to which the phone number will be assigned.

The following code creates an instance of the `SavePhoneNumber` task and calls the `Show` method to bring up the dialog that will then guide the user through the process of completing (or canceling) the act of saving a phone number to a contact.

```
SavePhoneNumberTask phoneSave = new SavePhoneNumberTask();
phoneSave.PhoneNumber = "8675309";
phoneSave.Completed += (s, e) =>
    { MessageBox.Show("Phone number task complete."); };
phoneSave.Show();
```

Figure 10.1 shows the screen prompting the user for a new phone number, and Figure 10.2 shows the screen after a new contact has been created with this phone number.

Figure 10.1   The `SavePhoneNumber` task, prompting the user to enter a number.

Figure 10.2 New Contact, after being created
via the `SavePhoneNumberTask`.

Using the Save Email Address Task

Much like the `SavePhoneNumber` task, the `SaveEmailAddress` task allows your application to trigger a dialog that prompts users to add an email address to a contact or create a new one.

You can see that the following code attempts to save the email address "big.moe@somedomain.com" to one of the phone's contacts. If the task succeeds (as indicated by the `TaskResult.OK` enumerated value), the application can handle that event. Likewise, the application can detect when the user pressed cancel or the task failed for some other reason.

```
SaveEmailAddressTask saveEmail = new SaveEmailAddressTask();
saveEmail.Email = "big.moe@somedomain.com";
saveEmail.Completed += (s, e) =>
    {
        if (e.TaskResult == TaskResult.OK)
        {
            MessageBox.Show("Email Address Saved.");
        }
        else
            MessageBox.Show("Email Address Not Saved.");
    };
saveEmail.Show();
```

Using the Search Task

Windows Phone 7 has a multipurpose search dialog that allows you to search data on your phone, the web at large, the web within your area, and news. To launch this dialog, create a new instance of the `SearchTask` class with the search parameter you want, as shown in the following code.

```
SearchTask search = new SearchTask();
search.SearchQuery = "kevin hoffman";
search.Show();
```

Figure 10.3 shows a prompt where the search task asks the user for permission to use their location. One of the features that distinguishes WP7 from other systems is the unique, integrated search that incorporates web searches with localized searches.

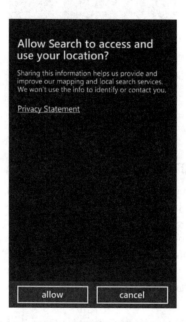

Figure 10.3   Search task prompting for permission to use location data.

Figure 10.4 shows the results of a WP7 search task using my name.

Figure 10.4   The WP7 Search task.

Launching a Web Browser

If your application provides links to web content, you might want to offer your users the capability to view that content by launching a web browser with the `WebBrowserTask`, as shown next.

```
WebBrowserTask browserTask = new WebBrowserTask();
browserTask.URL = "http://www.kotancode.com";
browserTask.Show();
```

Launching the Media Player

Launching a media player is just as easy as the other launchers. You can launch an instance of the media player to play content distributed with your application or content available online, as shown in the following code sample.

```
MediaPlayerLauncher mediaLauncher = new MediaPlayerLauncher();
mediaLauncher.Controls = MediaPlaybackControls.FastForward |
                         MediaPlaybackControls.Pause |
                         MediaPlaybackControls.Stop;
mediaLauncher.Location = MediaLocationType.Install;
mediaLauncher.Media = new Uri("Media/Bear.wmv", UriKind.Relative);
mediaLauncher.Show();
```

Launching the Phone Application

As mentioned at the beginning of this section, Windows Phone 7 will not allow any application you write to have direct access to the phone features. This is to keep the cellular network (and the people using it) from being abused. A compromise is to allow your applications to suggest to the phone a phone call that it would like to make. This then brings up a dialog that a user must confirm in order to place the call, as shown in Figure 10.5.

```
PhoneCallTask phoneCall = new PhoneCallTask();
phoneCall.DisplayName = "Jenny";
phoneCall.PhoneNumber = "8675309";
phoneCall.Show();
```

Figure 10.5   Placing a call with the
PhoneCallTask.

Sending a Text Message

The same reasoning behind limiting direct access to phone functionality prevents us from being able to directly send text messages. If you want your users to be able to send an SMS from your application, you can utilize the SmsComposeTask as shown in the following code (see Figure 10.6). The iPhone allows applications to send text messages through the use of an MFMessageComposeViewController that works in a nearly identical fashion.

```
SmsComposeTask newSms = new SmsComposeTask();
newSms.To = "Jenny Jenny";
newSms.Body = "Who can I turn to?";
newSms.Show();
```

Figure 10.6   Sending a text message with the
`SmsComposeTask`.

Composing an Email Message

If the Windows Phone 7 device has at least one configured mail account, emails can be created programmatically. Again, because you are accessing system-level services, the user must provide final confirmation before sending the email.

To create a new email message from your application, use the `EmailComposeTask` as shown next.

```
EmailComposeTask newEmail = new EmailComposeTask();
newEmail.To = "Jenny Jenny";
newEmail.Subject = "I got it";
newEmail.Body =
@"For a good time, for a good time call....";
newEmail.Show();
```

Using Choosers

For the same reason that devices cannot allow developers to directly manipulate data and system-level services, developers are often prevented from querying or reading detailed, low-level information. This is for the protection of the consumer as much as it is for the protection of the device manufacturer and cellular carrier. To be able to guarantee consumers, carriers, and device manufacturers that rules and legal obligations with regard to data security and isolation have been met, Windows Phone 7 (and iOS) cannot allow developers to crack open the system databases and browse freely.

The compromise is the use of choosers. Whenever an application wants to allow the user to locate information of a certain kind on the system, the chooser provides a standard user interface that is designed to require the confirmation of the end user before the information is made available to the application. This section will take you on a quick tour through some of the choosers available in Windows Phone 7.

Using the Phone Number Chooser Task

The phone number chooser task, as its name implies, allows your users to select a phone number from among the phone's stored contacts. This might be used in conjunction with the launcher that will allow a user to initiate a phone call. Your application might occasionally need to prompt the user to select a phone number from one of the contacts stored on the phone and this chooser task provides that functionality.

To do this, make use of the `PhoneNumberChooserTask` as shown next:

```
PhoneNumberChooserTask phoneChooser = new PhoneNumberChooserTask();
phoneChooser.Completed += (s, e) =>
    {
        if (e.TaskResult == TaskResult.OK)
        {
            MessageBox.Show("You picked " + e.PhoneNumber);
        }
        else
            MessageBox.Show("You didn't pick anyone");
    };
phoneChooser.Show();
```

Using the Email Address Chooser Task

To prompt the user to select an email address (which is returned to your application in the form of a string) from an existing contact, you use the `EmailAddressChooserTask` as shown next:

```
EmailAddressChooserTask emailChooser = new EmailAddressChooserTask();
emailChooser.Completed += (s, e) =>
    {
        if (e.TaskResult == TaskResult.OK)
        {
            MessageBox.Show("You picked email: " + e.Email);
        }
        else
```

```
            MessageBox.Show("You didn't pick anyone.");
    };
emailChooser.Show();
```

Choosing or Capturing Photos on the Device

To prompt the user to select a picture from the phone's photo library, you can use the
PhotoChooserTask. This task comes with an option called ShowCamera, which gives the
user the option to take a picture when prompted by your application for a photo. For
example, an expense report application might prompt the user for a photo, and the user
can either pull up a previously taken picture of a receipt or take a new photo. Regardless
of the original source of the image, the picture the user selects is made available to the
application in the ChosenPhoto property of the event arguments.

```
PhotoChooserTask photoChooser = new PhotoChooserTask();
photoChooser.ShowCamera = true;
photoChooser.Completed += (s, e) =>
    {
        if (e.TaskResult == TaskResult.OK)
        {
            BitmapImage bmp = new BitmapImage();
            bmp.SetSource(e.ChosenPhoto);
            targetImage.Source = bmp;
        }
    };
photoChooser.Show();
```

The previous code converts the ChosenPhoto property (which is a stream) into a
BitmapImage, which can then be set as the source of an Image control (declared in
XAML as <Image/>). Figure 10.7 shows a sample screen the user might see when being
prompted to choose a picture from the camera's media library. At the bottom of this
image you can see an icon of a camera. Tapping this will bring up a capture screen for the
phone's embedded camera.

Figure 10.7　Selecting a photo with a chooser.

Using Hardware Services and Sensors

So far, you've seen how to use "soft" services such as choosers and launchers. These facilities allow your application to interact with system-level data and services in a safe way that never allows your application to do, see, or modify anything without the explicit consent of the user.

This next section takes you through using some actual hardware services, such as the accelerometer, the phone vibration controller, using an FM radio tuner, and of course, using the GPS.

Controlling Vibration

Windows Phone 7 devices have the capability to vibrate. Most modern cell phones have the option of vibrating instead of playing an audible ringtone to make the devices less obtrusive in public places. This has become a blessing in recent years as the people who have cell phones vastly outnumber those who do not.

A nice feature in the Windows Phone 7 SDK is the capability for your application to start and stop vibration on the phone. This gives you the capability to vibrate the phone when something important happens, like a message arriving or a player scoring a point in a game.

To utilize this functionality, you need to make sure your project has a reference to the `Microsoft.Devices` assembly. If it doesn't already have this reference, right-click the References node in the project explorer, click Add Reference, and choose the Microsoft. Devices library. Then add the following line of code to the top of whatever page you want to vibrate:

```
using Microsoft.Devices;
```

Now add the following code to start vibration (and continue vibrating for a set amount of time):

```
VibrateController.Default.Start(TimeSpan.FromSeconds(1));
```

If you want to force vibration to stop at any time, call the `Stop` method, as shown here:

```
VibrateController.Default.Stop();
```

Accessing a Radio Tuner

In this age of Internet radio, satellite radio, and hundreds of other ways to stream music to your mobile device over cellular data networks or Wi-Fi, you might be thinking, "FM radio? What's that?"

Whether you agree with the decision or not, Windows Phone 7 devices have the capability to support an FM radio tuner, and the Windows Phone 7 SDK has the capability to control this tuner.

The following bit of code will turn the radio on, tune it to 96.5, and report the radio signal strength in RSSI units. If you have tried out no other code sample in this chapter, I highly recommend you try this one out in the simulator. If you're expecting the simulator to report that the FM radio is disabled on this device, that's all the more reason for you to run this sample on your own. Seriously, go type this in and run it. The book will still be here when you get back.

Remember that your project will need a reference to the `Microsoft.Devices` assembly for the following code to work:

```
try
{
    FMRadio radio = Microsoft.Devices.Radio.FMRadio.Instance;
    radio.Frequency = 96.5;
    radio.PowerMode = RadioPowerMode.On;
    Debug.WriteLine("Radio signal strength : {0}", radio.SignalStrength);
}
catch (RadioDisabledException rde)
{
    MessageBox.Show("the radio is not available on this device.");
}
```

A Note on Try/Catch

If you were looking at the FM radio code sample and the use of the keywords `try` and `catch` looked a little unfamiliar, don't worry. This is C#'s exception-handling system. The code within the `try` block attempts to execute. If something happens that the runtime didn't expect (an exception), the code inside the `catch` block executes, allowing you to safely handle the error without crashing the application.

The important thing to remember is that if your code fails to "catch" an exception that occurs, the application's only resort is to crash. If this happens in a production application that someone paid good money for, the customer will not be happy.

Putting code inside a try/catch block incurs a slight performance penalty in exchange for guarding that code against unexpected failures. As a general rule, you should use `if` statements and other tests to check for user input mistakes, edge cases, and other predictable failures. You should use try/catch blocks only as last-ditch guards against your application crashing.

Using the Accelerometer

Only a handful of modern smartphones come equipped with accelerometers. An accelerometer measures the force of acceleration in any of three directions: X, Y, and Z. These correspond to the "normal," or the direction pointing downward into the center of the earth (the direction of the pull of gravity, more commonly known as "down"), left/right acceleration, and forward/back acceleration. The directions of left, right, forward, and back are all determined relative to the normal (remember, that's "down" for us nonphysics types).

Accelerometers can be used for silly tricks, such as allowing you to use your phone to slowly empty a glass; interesting things, such as providing a "shake" motion to shuffle cards; fully immersive joystick–like controls (such as steering a car by moving your phone like a steering wheel); or even high-end uses, such as putting your phone in your car, stomping on the gas, and recording your 0-60 time. From personal experience, this last use is quite possibly my favorite use of an accelerometer so far.

The accelerometer reports the force of acceleration in any of three directions through three properties on an accelerometer monitor: X, Y, and Z. How you interpret these values is beyond the scope of this book because these things typically require smoothing and aggregation and varying sampling rates to produce the desired results. However, to obtain these values and activate the accelerometer, you can create an XAML page in your Windows Phone 7 application as follows. (You can create a button and a few text blocks to store the values, as you'll see in Listing 10.1.)

Listing 10.1   MainPage.xaml.cs, Using the Accelerometer Sensor

```
using System;
using System.Collections.Generic;
using System.Linq;
using System.Net;
```

```csharp
using System.Windows;
using System.Windows.Controls;
using System.Windows.Documents;
using System.Windows.Input;
using System.Windows.Media;
using System.Windows.Media.Animation;
using System.Windows.Shapes;
using Microsoft.Phone.Controls;
using Microsoft.Devices.Sensors;

namespace AccelerometerDemo
{
public partial class MainPage : PhoneApplicationPage
{
    private Accelerometer accel;

    // Constructor
    public MainPage()
    {
        InitializeComponent();
    }

    private void startAccelButton_Click(object sender, RoutedEventArgs e)
    {
        if (accel == null)
        {
            accel = new Accelerometer();
            accel.ReadingChanged +=
              new EventHandler<AccelerometerReadingEventArgs>(
              accel_ReadingChanged);
            try
            {
                accelerometerStatusText.Text = "Accelerometer starting.";
                accel.Start();
            }
            catch (AccelerometerFailedException ex)
            {
                accelerometerStatusText.Text = "Accelerometer error.";
            }
        }
        else
        {
            try
            {
                accel.Stop();
                accel = null;
```

```
                  accelerometerStatusText.Text = "Accelerometer Stopped.";
            }
            catch (AccelerometerFailedException ex)
            {
                accelerometerStatusText.Text =
                  "Error stopping Accelerometer.";
            }
        }
    }

    void accel_ReadingChanged(object sender,
      AccelerometerReadingEventArgs e)
    {
        Deployment.Current.Dispatcher.BeginInvoke(
          () => HandleNewReading(e));
    }

    void HandleNewReading(AccelerometerReadingEventArgs e)
    {
        xText.Text = e.X.ToString();
        yText.Text = e.Y.ToString();
        zText.Text = e.Z.ToString();
    }
}
}
```

Before discussing the code, I should point out here that this application will not compile unless you add a reference to the **Microsoft.Devices.Sensors** assembly.

A couple of things might appear new to you if you haven't written code in C#, Silverlight, or WPF. There is a button declared in MainPage.xaml called **startAccelButton**.
When you tap this button the first time, it starts the accelerometer monitoring. When you
tap it a second time, it stops the monitor.

Every time the monitor reports a change (this happens according to its sampling rate,
which is a set number of times per second), the **accel_ReadingChanged** method is called.

This is where we're doing something slightly different. We're calling the **BeginInvoke**
method on the Deployment.Current.Dispatcher object. The reason is that this event is
being fired in the background by a background thread. Only code on the foreground
(primary) thread can make changes to UI objects. In other words, if we were to try to
directly set the Text properties of the three text blocks from the background thread, an
exception would be thrown and the text would never change.

To get around this, we need to execute the code that changes the text blocks on the
foreground thread. iOS developers should be intimately familiar with this concept, and in
fact, Silverlight and WPF developers also regularly run into this problem.

Were we to forward this change to the foreground thread in an iOS application, our code might look like the following:

```
[self performSelectorOnMainThread:@selector(handleNewReading)
        withObject:e
        waitUntilDone:false];
```

Keep in mind that in situations where you would use `performSelectorOnMainThread:withObject:waitUntilDone:`. In an iOS application, you need to use `Deployment.Current.Dispatcher.BeginInvoke( ... )` on Windows Phone 7.

Using the GPS

Location-aware applications are incredibly popular. They can be used for everything from being able to "check in" at your current location, see where your friends are, and find nearby restaurants or gas stations; all the way to advanced uses such as maps, turn-by-turn directions, and hobbyist activities like geocaching.

GPS works by triangulating the position of your device using incredibly accurate clocks, timing, a set of satellites, and some math. Thankfully, however, developers don't need to worry too much about how GPS coordinates are obtained—only that those coordinates are available. GPS coordinates give a device's position anywhere on the planet using latitude, longitude, and altitude.

To see how this works, create a new application that has a page with a button to start and stop GPS monitoring, as well as a few text blocks to report the latitude, longitude, and altitude. Make sure you add a reference to the `System.Device` assembly from this project.

Modify your MainPage.xaml.cs so that it looks like the one shown in Listing 10.2.

Listing 10.2   **MainPage.xaml.cs, Using the Location Monitoring API**

```
using System;
using System.Collections.Generic;
using System.Linq;
using System.Net;
using System.Windows;
using System.Windows.Controls;
using System.Windows.Documents;
using System.Windows.Input;
using System.Windows.Media;
using System.Windows.Media.Animation;
using System.Windows.Shapes;
using Microsoft.Phone.Controls;
using System.Device.Location;


namespace Location
```

```csharp
{
    public partial class MainPage : PhoneApplicationPage
    {
        GeoCoordinateWatcher watcher;

        // Constructor
        public MainPage()
        {
            InitializeComponent();

            stopLocationButton.IsEnabled = false;
        }

        private void startLocationButton_Click(object sender,
            RoutedEventArgs e)
        {
            if (watcher == null)
            {
                watcher =
                  new GeoCoordinateWatcher(GeoPositionAccuracy.High);
                watcher.MovementThreshold = 20; // compensate for noise
                watcher.StatusChanged +=
                  new EventHandler<GeoPositionStatusChangedEventArgs>(
                                    watcher_StatusChanged);
                watcher.PositionChanged +=
                  new EventHandler<
                    GeoPositionChangedEventArgs<GeoCoordinate>>(
                                    watcher_PositionChanged);
                watcher.Start();
            }
        }

        void watcher_PositionChanged(object sender,
          GeoPositionChangedEventArgs<GeoCoordinate> e)
        {
            latitudeText.Text =
              e.Position.Location.Latitude.ToString("0.000");
            longitudeText.Text =
              e.Position.Location.Longitude.ToString("0.000");
            altitudeText.Text =
              e.Position.Location.Altitude.ToString("00000.00");
        }

        void watcher_StatusChanged(object sender,
          GeoPositionStatusChangedEventArgs e)
        {
            switch (e.Status)
```

```
        {
            case GeoPositionStatus.Disabled:
                if (watcher.Permission ==
                    GeoPositionPermission.Denied)
                {
                    watcherStatus.Text =
                "Application is not allowed to use location services.";
                }
                else
                {
                    watcherStatus.Text =
                    "Location services not working properly.";
                }
                break;
            case GeoPositionStatus.Initializing:
                startLocationButton.IsEnabled = false;
                watcherStatus.Text = "Initializing...";
                break;
            case GeoPositionStatus.NoData:
                stopLocationButton.IsEnabled = true;
                watcherStatus.Text = "Active, but no location data.";
                break;
            case GeoPositionStatus.Ready:
                watcherStatus.Text = "Location data is available.";
                stopLocationButton.IsEnabled = true;
                break;
        }
    }

    private void stopLocationButton_Click(object sender,
        RoutedEventArgs e)
    {
        watcher.Stop();
        watcherStatus.Text = "(not monitoring GPS)";
    }
  }
}
```

If you run this in the emulator, you won't get any useful information, although it will still report that the GPS monitor is active when you tap the start button. To see this in action, you need to run this on an application with a clear GPS signal. (Hint: Don't try this from underground bomb shelters, bunkers, or sealed basements.)

Summary

This chapter started off with an overview of common system services that are provided by most modern smartphones, including the iPhone and Windows Phone 7. Following that, we took a tour through the choosers and launchers that are available to Windows Phone 7 applications. Finally, we closed out the chapter by exploring some of the hardware services available to our applications, such as the accelerometer, the GPS, and even an FM radio tuner.

If you have been reading the book straight through up to this point, you should now have a very good understanding of the capabilities and power available to Windows Phone 7 applications, how to harness those capabilities, and how to present them to users with WP7 Silverlight user interface elements.

Introduction to Application Tiles

Imagination is more important than knowledge. For knowledge is limited, whereas imagination embraces the entire world, stimulating progress, giving birth to evolution.

Albert Einstein

This chapter, although short, provides a useful introduction to programming application tiles for Windows Phone 7. No direct correlation exists between the concept of a Windows Phone 7 application tile and some concept on an iPhone or an iPad. As you read this chapter, you will see what role the application tiles fill, how they encompass multiple areas of functionality that exist in iOS, and how they provide some features that don't exist in iOS.

This chapter also provides an overview of how to manipulate these tiles without push notifications, the subject of the next chapter. Finally, at the end of this chapter I will show you how to do some fancy tricks on a server to get around some of the limitations of tiles and create incredibly compelling tiles without sending a single push notification.

What Is a Tile?

After you slide away your home screen when you unlock or turn on your Windows Phone 7 device, the first thing you see is a collection of tiles. This collection is scrollable and should, in general, contain your most frequently used applications. As shown in Figure 11.1, Microsoft gives you some tiles out of the box for dealing with things like the phone, people (including social networks like Facebook), messaging, email, pictures, gaming (Xbox Live), and Internet Explorer.

Figure 11.1   A home screen filled with
application tiles.

These tiles have two main purposes. The first is to provide you with an easy target to tap to launch your most popular applications. You can think of this as the mobile equivalent of having a shortcut to an application on your desktop or in your system tray (or your Dock on Mac OS X). Second, these tiles provide meaningful summary information that you can use to decide whether you want to launch the application.

For example, the phone tile displays how many calls you have missed or voicemails you have waiting. The messaging tile tells you how many unread text messages you have. The Outlook tile tells you how many unread emails you have. If the information on these tiles changes, you can use the easy-to-read tile surface to make a decision about whether you want to launch the application. Another sample might be a weather tile that displays the current temperature on top of a background image representing the current weather conditions. This gives you the most important information you might need about the weather, and if you want details, you can tap the tile to launch the full weather application.

What you don't see in Figure 11.1 is that application tiles written by non-Microsoft developers (that's probably you) can have a background image and a numeric badge that appears superimposed on the background image. This gives your tile the capability to notify users that items within your application might need their attention. This next section shows you how to create your own tiles and discusses some of the limitations and quirks about working with them.

Creating Your First Tile

Tiles are easy to create. In fact, the developer doesn't have to do anything to create them, because the act of creating a tile is entirely up to the end user. All the developer has to do is tell the application manifest which background image and title text should be used in case a user creates a tile for the developer's application.

To see how this works, create a new Windows Phone 7 application. Right-click the project in the Solution Explorer and choose Properties. Scan down the property page to the last few items, and you will see where the application's tile properties are defined. You can choose the background image (one is supplied for you by the default WP7 application template) and the tile's title text. The text you supply here has to be short enough to display on the bottom of a tile. Change the text to whatever you like, and then run the application.

With the application running in the emulator, hit the Start (the flying window) button. Now go to the applications list (the right-arrow at the top right of the screen). Left-click *and hold* on the title of the application you just created. You will be presented with two options, as shown in Figure 11.2: Pin to Start and Uninstall.

Figure 11.2   Holding finger/button down
on an application.

If you choose Pin to Start when prompted, the emulator takes you back to the home screen, and there you will see your tile. If you do not have any other tiles installed, your screen might look something like the one in Figure 11.3.

Figure 11.3   Home screen after a tile has been added.

Now when users unlocks their device, they will see a nice big tile for your application. They can tap this tile to launch the application or launch the application manually by using the right arrow and clicking the application's title in the list that appears.

The default background that comes with the new application template is a 173x173 24-bit PNG file. When creating your own background images for your applications, you must stick to this convention. Home screen tiles (at least those created by regular non-Microsoft developers) are always the same size and must never exceed 80KB in size.

Working with Tile Schedules

Many applications will be satisfied using the tile surface as nothing more than a large icon; a place for branding and a super-large hit target for fingers to tap. However, depending on the type of application you're writing, you might want to do more than that. You might want to make your application tile *somewhat* dynamic. Note that I say *somewhat* here, because we'll talk about how to make your tile much more dynamic in the next chapter when I talk about push notifications.

Tile schedules are at the mercy of the phone itself. You can create an instance of a tile schedule that will cause your application tile to update once, every week, every day, or every hour. You can also set a maximum number of occurrences. This allows you to update your application tile once every day for three days and other interesting combinations.

To update your application tile every day until the application is removed, you can create a schedule as follows:

```
ShellTileSchedule schedule = new ShellTileSchedule();
schedule.Interval = UpdateInterval.EveryDay;
schedule.Recurrence = UpdateRecurrence.Interval;
schedule.RemoteImageUri = new
    Uri(//www.myserver.com/myapp/tile.png");
schedule.Start();
```

The preceding code will change the application's background tile to whatever the image is that resides at www.myserver.com/myapp/tile.png every day. When during that day is up to the phone. If the phone is locked or the screen is off when the update should occur, the update will occur immediately whenever the phone screen is activated next.

The next thing that you should pay attention to is the `RemoteImageUri` property. This property doesn't use the word "remote" just for the heck of it. You cannot specify the URI of an image that was deployed within your Application's XAP file (iPhone developers should think of XAP files as functionally equivalent to Bundles). In short, if you plan to update your application tile's background image, no matter how you plan to update that image, you're going to need to store that image on a publicly available server.

You might think that the restrictions on these background images are a little too severe. However, keep in mind that a nearly unlimited number of developers will have applications that can be pinned as tiles. If these tiles are allowed to update as fast as the developer wants them to, not only will the overall user experience of the tile screen degrade to the point of utter chaos, but the phone's resources (including battery life!) will be sucked dry attempting to keep up with these rapidly refreshing tiles. By enforcing these fixed interval types and requiring that the tile images be reachable over the public Internet, Microsoft is ensuring that everybody's tiles will be able to play nice with all the other tiles.

Even with these restrictions in place, you can still do some creative things with tile update schedules. For instance, you can use an immediate schedule change in response to a button click to allow users to personalize the background image for their tile.

Suppose you have written a game for the phone. In this game, through player actions, the player can become good or evil. To indicate whether the player is currently good or evil on the application's tile, you can create a schedule that runs immediately and changes the background image to either a good or an evil background.

The following bit of code shows how two different run-once, immediate schedules can be created that will change the background image of the application tile:

```
private void buttonGood_Click(object sender, RoutedEventArgs e)
{
    ShellTileSchedule schedule = new ShellTileSchedule();
```

```
    schedule.Recurrence = UpdateRecurrence.Onetime;
    schedule.StartTime = DateTime.Now.AddMinutes(1);
    schedule.RemoteImageUri = new Uri(//localhost/good.png");
    schedule.Start();
}

private void buttonEvil_Click(object sender, RoutedEventArgs e)
{
    ShellTileSchedule schedule = new ShellTileSchedule();
    schedule.Recurrence = UpdateRecurrence.Onetime;
    schedule.StartTime = DateTime.Now.AddMinutes(1);
    schedule.RemoteImageUri = new Uri(//localhost/evil.png");
    schedule.Start();
}
```

This code block doesn't show the using statements, but it is worth pointing out that the ShellTileSchedule class is part of the Microsoft.Phone.Shell namespace, and the preceding code won't compile without that using statement at the top of the file. If you're using the code downloads and not typing as you go, you don't have to worry about this.

After the schedule executes in due time, the application tile will change to reflect the current alignment of the player toward good or evil. Figure 11.4 shows the application tile after I've clicked the "I am evil" button within the application and then exited the application.

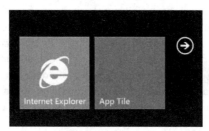

Figure 11.4   Application tile after being modified
by a tile schedule.

A Caveat About Tile Schedules

One thing that you need to remember as you work with tiles and their schedules is that the schedules are not precise. To prevent the phone from consuming too many resources while updating the background images of the tiles, there is a one-hour timer in charge of executing the schedules. This means that even if your schedule is set to run immediately, it could take up to 60 minutes before it actually runs, even in the emulator. If you absolutely need your tile to update more frequently than every hour, you will need to use push notifications, which are explained in the next chapter. To debug your schedule changes, you are going to spend a lot of time sitting around waiting. Make sure you have some coffee and something else fun to do nearby before testing your schedules.

Using Remote Background Images

Up to this point, you might still be complaining (or worse, I know how programmers get) that you don't have enough control over the tile image. From what we've seen so far, the only way you can add any kind of dynamic nature to the tile background image is through the use of a tile schedule. Even when you have a tile schedule, the background images are limited to static images that are located out on the Internet somewhere—or are they?

As a famous, anonymous cat-hater once said, "There's more than one way to skin a cat." The key concept is that although the URI pointing to the image for the tile background might need to be fixed at the time the schedule executes, the actual *content* of that image can be generated on-demand by the server.

To see how this might work, let's take a few examples of how to "beat the system." In other words, how you can create dynamic application tile backgrounds even though the Windows Phone 7 SDK won't let you do so directly on the phone.

One of the simplest examples might be a weather application. When you run the full weather application, you get all kinds of animated content, including radar maps and wind speed and direction. But, for the weather application's tile, you want to display the current temperature on top of a background that shows the type of weather conditions. If you have seen the Windows 7 desktop weather widget or even the weather widget for the OS X Dashboard, this concept should be fairly familiar to you.

Because the URI pointing to the remote image background cannot change (unless you discard the old update schedule and update it with a new one, as in the earlier good versus evil example), one way around this might be to use a URI that indicates the ZIP Code of the user. For example, you might point the remote URI to http://www.myapp.com/weather/90210.png. The server, whether ASP.NET, PHP, Ruby, Java, or any other framework, can then extract the ZIP Code from the URI and use that to dynamically render an image containing the current temperature and weather conditions.

Another option more closely related to what might be on my Windows Phone would be a zombie apocalypse monitor. Let's say the zombie apocalypse has begun and you, the digitally connected consumer that you are, need to keep tabs on who is winning the war. To do this, you've downloaded and installed an application that has a tile that updates every hour. Every hour the image changes and shows the current world population of humans and the world population of zombies. To make this happen, all you really need is a single URL (such as http://www.myapp.com/us_vs_them.png) that is generated periodically on the server, and a cached version of that image is served up to every mobile device that requests it.

As you can see, all it takes is a little creativity and some knowledge of server-side programming, and you can create dynamic, compelling, visually appealing tile images. Although you can't achieve the custom, animated effects that you see in the People and Xbox Live tiles that ship with the phones, you can get pretty close with clever use of schedules (or push notifications) and server-generated images.

Summary

iOS doesn't have a concept equivalent to application tiles. Application icons in iOS have a badge count that displays a little white-on-red number superimposed on top of an application icon. This functionality is similar to the way that application tiles can have counts appear over top of the image (you'll see how to do this in the next chapter).

This is where the similarity between iOS application icons and Windows Phone 7 application tiles ends. Windows Phone 7 tiles can have their background images updated on a schedule or in response to push notifications. These schedules are incredibly flexible and can be everything from once per hour to once every week for a six-week period.

This chapter provided you with a basic overview of how users create these tiles by pinning applications to the start area. In addition, I took you on a tour through using and manipulating tile schedules. Finally, I discussed a few server-side techniques that you can use to get around some of the limitations to the dynamic nature of application tiles. This chapter provided you with a good foundation so that you can extend your knowledge of application tiles in the next chapter by learning how to manipulate those tiles with push notifications.

12

Using Push Notifications

The single biggest problem in communication is the illusion that it has taken place.

George Bernard Shaw

This chapter provides you with an introduction to push notifications and their implementation on Windows Phone 7 devices. *Push notifications* are a facility that allow servers hosted publicly on the Internet (or "in the cloud" as people like to call it these days) to send messages directly to applications installed on mobile devices, oftentimes even when those applications are not currently running or active.

The underlying implementation of push notifications between Microsoft and Apple differs greatly in the details, but the overall goals are the same. Push notifications allow your application to be kept up to date on information that is changing in the cloud without having your application waste a bunch of bandwidth and other resources by constantly polling a remote URL and asking the question, "Is there anything new yet?" This type of behavior is as annoying to a server as the kids in the back seat constantly yelling "Are we there yet?" are to a driver. Sometimes the server just wants to shout, "I'll tell you when we get there!" Push notifications allow the server to do just that, and a happy server is a good server.

This chapter provides you with all the information you need to start delivering push notifications to your Windows Phone 7 applications, as well as information to allow you to compare and contrast the experience with Apple's Push Notification Service (APNS).

Review of Apple Push Notification Services (APNS)

When push notifications were originally made available to iPhone developers, they were hailed as the answer to the fact that multitasking was not available on the phone. Even though iOS 4 introduced a form of multitasking, push notifications are no less important, and not just for creating the illusion of multitasking or background processing. Push notifications are used for everything from letting you know when important activity occurs in your Facebook account, to informing you when your bank balance gets too low, or letting you know that someone just sunk your battleship.

APNS works through a combination of sending raw binary data over HTTP and securing those communications with tokens and certificates. When an iOS application launches, it can request a token from the push notification system. Apple takes care of the plumbing that goes out and fetches this token.

With this token in hand, an iOS application then sends the token to a third-party service, usually a service in the cloud run by the people who developed the application. Sending this token to the service effectively registers a unique installation of an application on a specific device as a possible target for notifications.

Next, when this service decides that it needs to send a notification to one or more tokens (remember, a token is an abstraction that represents a unique installation of an application on a single device), it needs to talk to Apple.

To talk to Apple, the service verifies the notification message with a certificate that a developer generated using the Apple iOS developer portal. So at this point we have two certificates: the certificate that validates the application installed on the device, and the certificate that validates the service as an authorized sender of notification messages.

Using a fairly complex (though this complexity can be overcome once by writing a wrapper layer or downloading one of the many publicly available APNS utilities) system of converting a message payload into an array of bytes to be sent over HTTP, the service sends a notification message to Apple. To add to this complexity, Apple prefers that the service keep open a live HTTP session to send multiple notifications in a single batch session.

Apple then sends the notification message to the appropriate device. After the notification is on the device, the device then displays the message and can optionally "wake up" the target application to respond to the message. If the token that identifies the target of the message doesn't exist or doesn't respond to Apple, the message is not delivered. It is the responsibility of the service developer to periodically poll Apple for the list of "dead tokens" (undeliverable notifications). This list of dead tokens is then used to cull the list of notification subscriptions from the application vendor's notification service.

For example, every time a device is wiped and then restored, the applications on that device will obtain new notification services tokens the next time they are started. This means that the tokens previously used by the apps on that device will be "dead," and notifications sent to those tokens will never be delivered. To keep Apple from wasting valuable resources and bandwidth in attempts to deliver notifications to dead tokens, your service needs to use the dead token list to remove those tokens from notification delivery lists.

Apple push notifications can carry different kinds of information, including the name of a sound to play, a badge count that will change the number appearing over the top-right corner of the application's icon, and some text to display in the dialog box that appears when the notification is delivered.

As a side note that is particularly important to developers, push notifications do not work in the iOS simulator. In other words, you cannot test push notifications without provisioning a test device.

WP7 Push Notifications Overview

For Windows Phone 7 development, the process of registering for, sending, and receiving push notifications is significantly easier. The main reason for this is the lack of certificates. Anyone who has done a fair amount of work with certificates, especially if he works on multiple machines, probably has far less hair today than before he started working with those certificates.

When your WP7 application starts, it talks to Microsoft's notification back-end to get what Microsoft calls a notification channel. This notification channel has a unique URI. Every application on every WP7 device talking to the notification back-end gets a unique notification channel URI. When your service (yes, you still need a service on the Internet that is capable of sending notifications to devices) sends a notification, it delivers it directly to the URI given to your application when it acquired a notification channel. Microsoft code listening on this URI then sends the push notification down to the device securely.

One of the many things that I like about this method of sending push notifications is that Microsoft has been able to secure all aspects of the transmission of notifications without requiring developers to hand-code certificate loading and signature methods into their applications. There are certificates and secure transmissions involved, but they're done by Microsoft on your behalf. The other thing that I like about WP7 push notifications is that *they work in the emulator.* This means you can debug, test, and refine your push notification code without ever having to tether a device or provision certificates from a web portal. This also means that I can get push notifications working in my application and then hand the code to another member of my team to test on a different machine, and things will work without me having to export private keys between team workstations.

Figure 12.1 shows a high-level overview of the push notifications system. This figure is from the online Microsoft documentation on WP7 push notifications and can be found at http://msdn.microsoft.com/en-us/library/ff402558(v=VS.92).aspx.

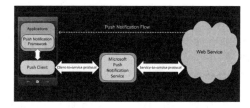

Figure 12.1   Push notifications overview diagram
(Microsoft).

Using Toast Notifications

Throughout the rest of this chapter I will be using a sample premise for an application that requires push notification functionality. Hypothetically, let's assume that the zombie apocalypse has indeed arrived. You need to keep informed on who is winning the war against the walking dead, and so you have downloaded the "Us Versus Them" application for your phone. Now you can be kept up to date when we retake cities from the undead or, unfortunately, as human cities fall to the zombie scourge.

There are three types of push notifications that you can use for your WP7 applications: toast, tile, and raw. In this section I show you how to send toast notifications. I will be building the "Us Versus Them" application, a web service that I will be using to represent the server run by the IT department of the human resistance, and a Windows Presentation Foundation (WPF) application that we will use as a console to send out notifications to simulate ones that might be sent automatically by a full-fledged Zombie Apocalypse Planning Program (ZAPP for short, of course). Don't worry if you don't know anything about writing web services or WPF applications; I'll keep that code to a minimum so we can concentrate on what you need to do on the device to prepare for and respond to push notifications.

To get started, let's create a new WP7 application project called Us_vs_Them in a solution that I called Chapter12. Before we do anything else, expand the Properties node in Solution Explorer underneath the project. Double-click the WMAppManifest.xml file. Inside the **App** element, make sure that you supply a meaningful value for both the **Publisher** and **Author** attributes. You cannot send push notifications of any kind without these in place.

To prep your application for push notifications, the first thing it needs to do is talk to the Microsoft server and obtain a notification channel. This notification channel has a unique URI that will be used by your cloud application (in our case, a WPF test harness) on which to send notifications.

After your application has a notification channel, it can then bind that channel to different types of notifications. It will always be able to respond to raw notifications, but you need to write a few lines of code to bind the channel to toast and tile notifications. For the purposes of this section of the chapter, we are not going to bind the channel to a tile yet.

First, open up App.xaml.cs and add the following lines of code below the declaration for the **RootFrame** property. If you press Ctrl+period (.) after typing **HttpNotificationChannel**, Visual Studio automatically adds the corresponding using statement to the top of the file:

```
public HttpNotificationChannel NotificationChannel
   { get; private set; }
private const string NOTIFY_CHANNEL_NAME = "us_vs_them_channel";
private const string NOTIFY_SERVICE_NAME =
   "www.usversusthemsampleapp.com";
```

Next, after the call to `InitializePhoneApplication()` that you see in every WP7 application, add your own call to `InitializeNotifications`. The code for `InitializeNotifications` and all the methods on which it relies is shown in Listing 12.1.

Listing 12.1   **Preparing App.xaml for Push Notifications**

```
private void InitializeNotifications()
{
    NotificationChannel =
      HttpNotificationChannel.Find(NOTIFY_CHANNEL_NAME);

    if (NotificationChannel == null)
    {
        NotificationChannel = new
          HttpNotificationChannel(NOTIFY_CHANNEL_NAME,
                                  NOTIFY_SERVICE_NAME);
        SetupDelegates();

        NotificationChannel.Open();
    }
    else
    {
        SetupDelegates();

        Debug.WriteLine("Found existing channel at {0}",
          NotificationChannel.ChannelUri.ToString());
    }


    SubscribeToNotifications();
    if (NotificationChannel.ChannelUri != null)
    {
        RegisterNotificationChannelWithService(
          NotificationChannel.ChannelUri.ToString());
    }
}

private void SubscribeToNotifications()
{
    // Cannot receive toasts without binding our notification channel
    // to toasts. If we receive a toast and we have not bound our channel
    // to those toasts, a very hard to debug exception will occur.
    if (NotificationChannel.IsShellToastBound == true)
    {
        Debug.WriteLine("Already bound to Toast notification");
    }
    else
    {
```

```csharp
            Debug.WriteLine("Registering to Toast Notifications");
            NotificationChannel.BindToShellToast();
        }
    }

    private void SetupDelegates()
    {
        NotificationChannel.ChannelUriUpdated +=
          new EventHandler<NotificationChannelUriEventArgs>(
          NotificationChannel_ChannelUriUpdated);
        NotificationChannel.HttpNotificationReceived +=
          new EventHandler<HttpNotificationEventArgs>(
          NotificationChannel_HttpNotificationReceived);
        NotificationChannel.ShellToastNotificationReceived +=
          new EventHandler<NotificationEventArgs>(
          NotificationChannel_ShellToastNotificationReceived);
        NotificationChannel.ErrorOccurred +=
          new EventHandler<NotificationChannelErrorEventArgs>(
          NotificationChannel_ErrorOccurred);
    }

    void NotificationChannel_ErrorOccurred(object sender,
        NotificationChannelErrorEventArgs e)
    {
        throw new NotImplementedException();
    }

    void NotificationChannel_ShellToastNotificationReceived(object sender,
        NotificationEventArgs e)
    {
        throw new NotImplementedException();
    }

    void NotificationChannel_HttpNotificationReceived(object sender,
        HttpNotificationEventArgs e)
    {
        throw new NotImplementedException();
    }

    void NotificationChannel_ChannelUriUpdated(object sender,
        NotificationChannelUriEventArgs e)
    {
        Debug.WriteLine("Channel URI updated " + e.ChannelUri.ToString());
        RegisterNotificationChannelWithService(e.ChannelUri.ToString());
    }

    private void RegisterNotificationChannelWithService(string channelUri)
    {
```

```
    // proxy to my home-grown channel URI registration service
    NotificationService.NotificationsClient client =
      new NotificationService.NotificationsClient();
    client.RegisterChannelAsync(channelUri);
    client.RegisterChannelCompleted +=
      new EventHandler<System.ComponentModel.AsyncCompletedEventArgs>(
      client_RegisterChannelCompleted);
}

void client_RegisterChannelCompleted(object sender,
    System.ComponentModel.AsyncCompletedEventArgs e)
{
    if (e.Error == null)
    {
        Debug.WriteLine(
          "Registered channel URI with notification service.");
    }
}
```

In the preceding code, the `NotificationService.NotificationsClient` class is created by adding a service reference to the WCF service I've written as part of this project. All of this is taken care of for you in the downloadable code sample, but it is helpful to know where all these components come from.

The first thing the application needs to do is look to see whether there is already a notification channel registered by the name we gave it for our application. The `HttpNotificationChannel.Find()` method performs this task and hides from us the complexity of how Microsoft is keeping track internally of all the notification channels for all the apps.

If the application doesn't find an existing channel, it creates a new one using the `HttpNotificationChannel` constructor and then opens this new channel. At this point the code knows that, whether new or previously created, the `NotificationChannel` property we've created now holds a valid instance of a notification channel.

Next, we make a call to the `SetupDelegates()` method. This method attaches a bunch of event handlers to various events, such as `ChannelUriUpdated`, `HttpNotificationReceived`, `ShellToastNotificationReceived`, and `ErrorOccurred`.

With the event handlers in place, we can perform the final task in setting the application up to receive toasts: binding. Binding associates a particular notification channel with any of the delivery mechanisms, such as toast notifications or tile notifications. In our case, for this first version of the application, the `SubscribeToNotifications` method binds only to toast notifications.

At this point the application has all of the following:

- A valid `HttpNotificationChannel` instance with a valid `ChannelUri`
- Event handlers assigned to all of the important events on the channel
- Bindings between the notification channel and notification types like toast or tile

The application is now ready to receive push notifications. The tricky part, of course, is actually *sending* them. From personal experience, having written several applications for the iPhone that receive push notifications and from talking to many developers of push-enabled applications, I can tell you that this part is usually where the iOS developers start cringing. Their blood pressure goes up, the stress level rises, and they start eating antacid drops like they were candy. Needless to say, getting push notifications sent to an iPhone is a very brittle process. It isn't necessarily difficult, but there are hundreds of tiny little moving parts, and if any of them are not in exactly the right place, nothing works.

Thankfully, the process is a bit easier on Windows Phone 7. An application that you've written that resides in the cloud can send a push notification to a specific device using the channel URI that is part of the `HttpNotificationChannel` instance returned either through construction or the `Find` static method. This URL will look something like the one that follows:

```
http://sn1.notify.live.net/throttledthirdparty/01.00/
AAEMRpKul9RqTZiGRgBVQpKvAgAAAAADAQAAAAQUZm52OjIzOEQ2NDJDRkI5MEVFMEQ
```

After you have this URL, you can send an HTTP POST to this URL from your application or service. The XML payload that gets sent to this URL for a toast notification looks like this:

```xml
<?xml version="1.0" encoding="utf-8"?>
<wp:Notification xmlns:wp="WPNotification">
        <wp:Toast>
                <wp:Text1>Toast message 1</wp:Text1>
                <wp:Text2>Toast message 2</wp:Text2>
        </wp:Toast>
</wp:Notification>
```

There is plenty of documentation on how to create these XML messages—what custom headers your service needs to send to deliver toast, tile, or raw notifications. For details on how to deliver a push notification (using C#), see the MSDN documentation at http://msdn.microsoft.com/en-us/library/ff402545(v=VS.92).aspx.

The code that accompanies this chapter includes a full solution that has a WPF test harness application. Using this harness (called `UsVsThemConsole`), you can send a toast notification to the sample application like the one shown in Figure 12.2.

This is a decent start but, with the code we have at the moment, the application will not properly handle toast notifications that are sent when the application is running in the foreground. To make sure that we handle that case, change the `ShellToastNotificationReceived` event handler to the following code:

```csharp
void NotificationChannel_ShellToastNotificationReceived(
    object sender, NotificationEventArgs e)
{
    string title = e.Collection.Values.First();
    string message =
```

```
    e.Collection.Values.Skip(1).FirstOrDefault() ?? string.Empty;
  Deployment.Current.Dispatcher.BeginInvoke(
    () => MessageBox.Show(message, title, MessageBoxButton.OK));
}
```

Figure 12.2   Receiving a sample toast
notification.

This code cracks open the incoming toast notification and then displays a message box with the contents. Note again that we're using the `BeginInvoke` method of the current deployment dispatcher. This is because we need to forward any UI changes that occur as a result of background thread changes onto the foreground UI thread. Figure 12.3 shows what a sample message box looks like in response to a delivered toast notification.

Figure 12.3   Getting a toast notification with
application running.

Using Raw Notifications

Raw notifications sent to WP7 applications are just that—raw. When a server or service sends a raw notification, it sends a blob of binary data. This data doesn't need to conform to any specific shape or size, so long as both the server sending the data and the WP7 application receiving the data can agree on that shape. This is an ideal situation for C# binary serialization. As you'll see in the code sample, no XML serialization is available for Silverlight on WP7, so we're left with using binary serialization using the WCF `DataContractSerializer` class as the easiest option for going from raw data to something usable by the application.

Before looking at the code, another thing worth pointing out is that raw notifications can be sent only to applications currently running in the foreground. When you send a toast notification, it is delivered to the start screen if the application isn't running. If the application is running, the toast notification is delivered directly to the application using an event handler. If a raw notification is sent to an application that is not currently running in the foreground, the notification is discarded as if it never happened.

For this reason, a very common design pattern in push notifications is to tell the registry service when the application is running and when the application shuts down. This lets the registry service know when the app can receive raw notifications versus receiving tile updates and toasts, which can be received at any time.

The following code handles the reception of a raw HTTP notification:

```
void NotificationChannel_HttpNotificationReceived(object sender,
    HttpNotificationEventArgs e)
{
    if (e.Notification.Body != null && e.Notification.Headers != null)
    {
        // Thanks to Daniel Vaughn (WP7 Unleashed by SAMS Press)
        // for this tidbit on having to remove nulls from the serialized
        // data contract sent from the push app/service
        using (BinaryReader reader =
         new BinaryReader(e.Notification.Body))
        {
            byte[] bodyBytes =
              reader.ReadBytes((int)e.Notification.Body.Length);

            int lengthWithoutNulls = bodyBytes.Length;
            for (int i = bodyBytes.Length - 1;
              i >= 0 && bodyBytes[i] == '\0';
              i-, lengthWithoutNulls-)
            {
                /* Intentionally left blank. */
            }

            byte[] cleanedBytes = new byte[lengthWithoutNulls];
            Array.Copy(bodyBytes, cleanedBytes, lengthWithoutNulls);
```

```
DataContractSerializer ser =
  new DataContractSerializer(typeof(ZombiePopulationPayload));
using (MemoryStream stream = new MemoryStream(cleanedBytes))
{
    ZombiePopulationPayload zombiePopulation =
      (ZombiePopulationPayload)ser.ReadObject(stream);
    Deployment.Current.Dispatcher.BeginInvoke(
        () =>
            MessageBox.Show(
              string.Format("Us:{0} Them:{1}",
              zombiePopulation.Humans,
              zombiePopulation.Zombies),
            "Population Update", MessageBoxButton.OK)
        );
    }
  }
}
}
```

When we run the code and send a raw notification, the response to that notification looks similar to the dialog in Figure 12.4. (The full notification sample, including the registry service and push notification simulator, is available in the Chapter 12 solution in the code accompanying this book.)

Figure 12.4   Receiving a raw notification with custom data.

The first thing the code does is open up the stream contained in e.Notification.Body. The binary sent by the notification tool (which takes the place of a server in the cloud) is padded by the WP7 push notification infrastructure with a pile of nulls at the end, so the next thing we need to do is strip off all those excess nulls before attempting to deserialize the binary into a C# class. Daniel Vaughan, author of *WP7 Unleashed,* by Sams Publishing, recently published a blog post illustrating this phenomenon.

After the binary has been prepped and stripped of excess nulls, it can be converted into a class using the DataContractSerializer class. Finally, with an intact instance of the ZombiePopulationPayload class, we can use the Dispatcher to forward a request for a MessageBox display onto the foreground thread.

In case you're curious about the server-side aspect of all of this, the following code will send a raw notification to Microsoft's push notification infrastructure (this code is also included with the chapter):

```
private void sendRawButton_Click(object sender, RoutedEventArgs e)
{
    ZombiePopulationPayload zombiePopulation =
      new ZombiePopulationPayload() { Humans = 5.25m, Zombies = 8.23m };
    DataContractSerializer ser =
      new DataContractSerializer(typeof(ZombiePopulationPayload));
    MemoryStream ms = new MemoryStream();
    ser.WriteObject(ms, zombiePopulation);
    ms.Seek(0, SeekOrigin.Begin);
    byte[] zombieBytes = ms.GetBuffer();

    // instantiate proxy to our custom notification registry svc
    NotificationService.NotificationsClient client =
      new NotificationService.NotificationsClient();
    string[] uris = client.GetRegisteredChannels();

    Console.WriteLine("About to send raw data to the following URIs:");

    foreach (string uri in uris)
    {
        HttpWebRequest sendNotificationRequest =
          (HttpWebRequest)WebRequest.Create(uri);

        sendNotificationRequest.Method = "POST";
        sendNotificationRequest.Headers.Add("X-NotificationClass", "3");

        sendNotificationRequest.ContentLength = zombieBytes.Length;

        using (Stream requestStream =
          sendNotificationRequest.GetRequestStream())
        {
            requestStream.Write(zombieBytes, 0, zombieBytes.Length);
        }

        HttpWebResponse response =
          (HttpWebResponse)sendNotificationRequest.GetResponse();
        // Troubleshooting information returned by WP7 push server
        string notificationStatus =
          response.Headers["X-NotificationStatus"];
        string notificationChannelStatus =
          response.Headers["X-SubscriptionStatus"];
```

```
        string deviceConnectionStatus =
            response.Headers["X-DeviceConnectionStatus"];
    }
}
```

Using Tile Notifications

The last of the three types of notifications is probably the easiest to deal with—the tile notification. It is the easiest because your application does not have any code that responds to the arrival of a tile notification. Tile notifications are handled directly by WP7, and WP7 doesn't explicitly tell your application that a tile notification has been sent.

As you saw in the previous chapter, WP7 application tiles consist of three main ingredients: a background image, title text, and a count.

The background image is fairly self-explanatory. This image is the image that appears on the start screen after a user has "pinned" your application. The application title is the text that appears (typically in white) at the bottom of the tile. The count is a number that appears in a dark circle at the top-right corner of the tile. Many applications, including some weather applications, use custom-generated images so they can avoid the default look and feel of the application title and badge count.

Whether changed by tile schedule as shown in the previous chapter or changed by push notification, these tiles serve as a quick glance area to give users the information they need to decide whether to open your application.

As I mentioned, you don't need to write any code whatsoever to receive a tile notification. However, you still need to write code that will bind your `HttpNotificationChannel` to tile notifications. Without this, tile notifications sent to your application will be dropped. When you bind the channel to tile notifications, you can choose to either allow images contained within your application's `.xap` file to be used as backgrounds, or you can specify a list of allowable URLs from which updated tile images can originate.

The following code shows how to bind an `HttpNotificationChannel` to tile notifications from application-local images:

```
if (NotificationChannel.IsShellTileBound == true)
{
    Debug.WriteLine("Already bound to tile");
}
else
{
    Debug.WriteLine("Registering to Tile Notification.");
    NotificationChannel.BindToShellTile();
}
```

The following code sends an XML payload to a registered notification channel URL that changes an application's tile image, badge count, and title text:

```
private void SendTile(string[] uriTargets, string backgroundImage,
    int count, string title)
{
    Console.WriteLine("About to send tile to the following URIs:");

    foreach (string uri in uriTargets)
    {
        Console.WriteLine(uri);
        HttpWebRequest sendNotificationRequest =
         (HttpWebRequest)WebRequest.Create(uri);

        sendNotificationRequest.Method = "POST";
        sendNotificationRequest.ContentType = "text/xml";
        sendNotificationRequest.Headers.Add("X-WindowsPhone-Target",
          "token");
        sendNotificationRequest.Headers.Add("X-NotificationClass", "1");

        string payloadString =
         string.Format("<?xml version=\"1.0\" encoding=\"utf-8\"?>" +
            "<wp:Notification xmlns:wp=\"WPNotification\">" +
            "<wp:Tile>" +
                "<wp:BackgroundImage>{0}</wp:BackgroundImage>" +
                "<wp:Count>{1}</wp:Count>" +
                "<wp:Title>{2}</wp:Title>" +
            "</wp:Tile>" +
            "</wp:Notification>", backgroundImage,
            count.ToString(), title);

        byte[] notificationMessage =
         System.Text.UTF8Encoding.UTF8.GetBytes(payloadString);
        sendNotificationRequest.ContentLength =
          notificationMessage.Length;

        using (Stream requestStream =
           sendNotificationRequest.GetRequestStream())
        {
            requestStream.Write(notificationMessage, 0,
              notificationMessage.Length);
        }

        // Sends the notification and gets the response.
        HttpWebResponse response =
           (HttpWebResponse)sendNotificationRequest.GetResponse();
        string notificationStatus =
```

```
            response.Headers["X-NotificationStatus"];
        string notificationChannelStatus =
            response.Headers["X-SubscriptionStatus"];
        string deviceConnectionStatus =
            response.Headers["X-DeviceConnectionStatus"];
    }
}
```

There is one last point to make about push notifications that is more of a design pattern than anything else. If you have been paying close attention to the samples (or you've looked at the code download already), you might have noticed that whenever the application starts, it sends its notification channel URL to the registry service. This information is sent without any other identifying information. This means that the service won't know the difference between new registrations and duplicate registrations. Additionally, if your application requires that different applications be sent different notifications, in contrast to a single mass broadcast, the model shown so far in this chapter won't work.

In this case, I recommend creating an application ID the first time the application starts. This ID will remain constant and persist with the application for the rest of the time the application is installed on the user's device. Every time the application gets a notification channel URI from Microsoft's push notification infrastructure, it then sends that URI plus the application's constant ID to the registry server. This not only prevents the same application from registering multiple notification channel URIs, but it also allows for single applications to be the target of specific push notifications. Later in the book, you will see how to store application configuration, settings, and user data (such as an application GUID) in something called isolated storage. Until then, remember that the service registry shown in this chapter was only complex enough to support the demonstration code and is by no means a design you should mimic in your production application.

Summary

In today's age of smartphones, typical users want to spend as little time as possible actually using the phone, unless they are playing a game, reading a book, and so on. Users have grown so accustomed to tailored alerts that they expect their phone to tell them when something important enough to warrant their attention has happened—whether that means they got an email, a friend wrote on their wall on their favorite social network, or the zombies have taken over a nearby town during the apocalypse.

This chapter provided you with the information, tools, and sample code to get you going building your own applications that can support push notifications in the form of tile changes, toasts, or even sending arbitrary, raw binary payloads that contain application-specific data such as stock price updates or changes in zombie population.

As you progress throughout the rest of the book, you will build on this knowledge and have push notifications in your tool belt filled with techniques for building powerful, compelling, highly engaging applications.

13

The Phone Execution Model

Intellectual growth should commence at birth and cease only at death.

Albert Einstein

This chapter provides an overview of the Windows Phone Execution model and explains how the iPhone and Windows Phone 7 deal with multitasking, or at least as close as either platform can get to true multitasking. The first part of this chapter provides a review of the various multitasking capabilities of the iPhone and to what extent developers are allowed to participate in those features.

The rest of this chapter deals with the application life cycle of Windows Phone applications, also known as the *Windows Phone Execution Model*. You will learn how to take advantage of transient and persistent application state, application activation, tombstoning, and much more.

Multitasking on iOS 4

With the release of the fourth generation of the iPhone and iOS 4 came the long-awaited "multitasking." The reason that I put the word "multitasking" in quotes is because regardless of whatever the hype might say, it isn't quite the kind of multitasking to which desktop application developers have become accustomed.

There are certainly features of the phone that are truly multitasking, but the extent to which everyday iPhone developers are allowed access to multitasking and background functionality is still limited.

The following is a brief list of the ways in which users and developers alike experience multitasking on the iPhone 4:

- Background audio—Users were already familiar with the experience of having music playing in the background while they performed other tasks. iPhone 4 extends this capability to non-Apple applications, allowing your application to continue to play audio even after the user has exited the application.

- VoIP—Along the same lines as background audio, Voice-over-IP (VoIP) applications can receive calls while the user is in another application. In fact, users can even receive VoIP calls if the phone is locked and no applications are running in the foreground.

- Location/GPS—Whether on the iPhone or Windows Phone 7, getting a decent GPS coordinate from the hardware can sometimes take a while. The iPhone 4 lets applications continue to monitor location in the background.

- Push notifications—The previous chapter provided an in-depth look at how push notifications work on Windows Phone 7. Push notifications provide an elegant means of keeping users informed of important events without requiring the application to be running in the foreground all the time.

- Local notifications—iPhone 4 now allows for the scheduling of events and alarms for specific applications rather than just the alarm clock functionality. Although not true multitasking, this also provides an elegant way of delivering certain kinds of solutions without requiring an application to be running constantly in the background.

- Fast app switching—iPhone 4 allows for fast application switching, which allows users to leave an application and come right back to the spot they were when they left without having to reload the app. As you'll see later in this chapter, a similar facility is used extensively on Windows Phone 7.

- Task completion—If your iPhone application is in the middle of doing something that shouldn't be interrupted for fear of data loss or corruption, iOS 4 now allows an application to finish up the important task in the background as the user exits the application.

As you can see, although there are an awful lot of clever and efficient ways to get work done without consuming battery or running applications constantly in the background, developers have very little access to what desktop programmers would consider true multitasking. However, if you spend a little time thinking about the design of your application, you can create some very compelling features without needing "real" multitasking.

Introducing the Phone Execution Model

When you are using your desktop computer, you can interact with application processes in a variety of ways. Typically, you launch an application process, interact with the application, and then shut the application down. With today's modern computers and operating systems, people usually launch multiple applications and leave them all running until they shut the computer down. On today's laptops, many people don't even bother shutting their computer down anymore—they just close the lid and open the lid again the next time they want to resume their work. They expect everything to appear as it last was when they shut the lid.

The idea that all your applications are running on your computer and are available by clicking the window or using a hot key (such as Alt+Tab on Windows) is nothing new. In fact, it is so prevalent that people expect applications to look exactly as they left them when they lost focus.

This particular model doesn't work on mobile phones. Mobile devices have limited memory and CPU resources and cannot leave a bunch of applications running at the same time. In fact, Windows Phone 7 allows only a single application to be running at any given time.

Just because the phone is limited to one active application at a time doesn't mean the user can't get a rich experience in which applications remember what they were doing at the time the user launched a different application. Applications can save transient state, such as what a user had typed into a textbox when a new application was launched, and they can save persistent state that, as the name implies, persists between multiple launches.

This is where the application life cycle comes in. Windows Phone 7 applications are given fair warning when pages are about to be navigated away from, when the application was launched as a fresh instance, or when it was reactivated from a previously suspended (*tombstoned*) instance, when an application is going to be deactivated as a result of some other application (such as a phone call) moving to the foreground.

This next section takes you on a tour of all the various stages and events in the life cycle of a Windows Phone 7 application. When you are done reading this section, you should have a thorough understanding of how WP7 compensates for the one-application limitation and how, if your application is written properly, end users will never even notice this limitation.

Application Life Cycle Walkthrough

Unlike desktop applications that can be started only by launching a brand new instance, Windows Phone 7 applications have multiple entry and exit points, and each of those implies a different impact on the application, its running state, and the data the application is holding in memory. The following sections describe the various stages in the lifetime of a Windows Phone 7 application and how users typically get into and out of those stages. Figure 13.1 shows an example of transitions between the various stages of the WP7 application life cycle.

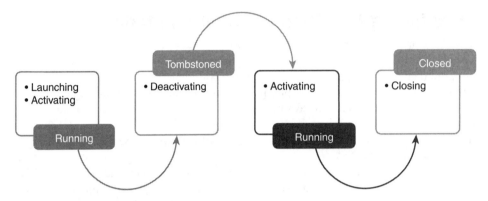

Figure 13.1   Sample application states and transitions.

The following is a list of terms you'll need to be familiar with to understand the phone's execution model:

- Navigating backward—Backward and forward navigation isn't just built in to the web browser model, it is built into how users navigate through the Windows phone. When users tap the back button, they go to the previous page within an application. Tapping the back button while on an application's home page exits the application. Tapping back again takes the user to the last page of the previous application, and so on. Keep in mind, however, that there is no forward button on a WP7 device; only back, home, and search.

- Tombstoning—This refers to when your application process has been terminated because a user navigated away from your application. State information about your application is maintained by the operating system (for a period of time determined by the operating system) and will be handed back to your application when it is resumed (or "dug up," if you prefer to continue the tombstone analogy).

- Page state—This refers to the visual state of a specific page within an application.

- Application state—This refers to the current, in-memory state of an application. This state is not associated with a specific page.

- Transient state—This refers to state data that has occurred since the application was activated last. This could be information recently downloaded from a web service or other information changed as a result of user interaction.

- Persistent data—This is data that is shared by all instances of an application, whether created by a launch or an activation. Classic examples are application settings and data created by users when using the application that they expect to be permanent.

Launching

When an application is started through any other means than a user pressing the back button to resume a previously running instance, the application is considered to be in the "launched" state. This can happen when the user taps the application's tile or the icon or name in the installed applications list. Additionally, if the user taps an active toast notification, it will cause the application to launch.

Regardless of how an application is launched, a brand new instance of the application is created when it is launched. This means that it won't have any transient state left over from previous instances of the application. The `Launching` event is fired during this phase, allowing you to write custom code that is executed during this phase.

This custom code should *not* access isolated storage during this event because the UI has not been displayed to the user at this point, and reading files from isolated storage can further delay the UI from appearing and can give the user an impression of poor or sluggish performance. Finally, every application only has 10 seconds to finish the launching stage. If the application doesn't become responsive within 10 seconds, WP7 terminates the process.

Even if some leftover state might be available from a previously running instance that might have been stored somewhere and made available for the application, it should not be used after a launch. Launching implies a new instance of the application, and users should expect a new instance from every application they launch, regardless of manufacturer.

Running

After an application has finished the launching phase and whatever custom code you've written in the `Launching` event has completed, the application is in the running stage. This is what most developers are used to when they think of application states. There is a process running; variables developers have stored in memory are safe and accessible.

While running, if an application needs to make data persist to be available for future instances, it can store that data in isolated storage, preferably during times when the application is idle to avoid creating a sluggish UI when storing large amounts of data. Another option is to progressively store small chunks of data into isolated storage rather than making a single giant write operation.

Activating

When a user returns to a previously tombstoned application, either through the back button or because something else (like a launcher, chooser, phone call, and so on) took over the ground, that application is reactivated.

When an application is awakened from a tombstoned state, the `Activated` event is fired. This event is special in that it provides the application with access to previously stored state data. If, during the deactivation process, application code stored serializable objects in a special state dictionary, that same dictionary is made available to the application upon activation. If handled properly, the user will never even know that the application's process was shut down in the interim.

In the `Activated` event, the application code can access the `State` property of the `PhoneApplicationService` class to restore the data saved during the deactivation process.

Just like with the `Launching` event handler, applications should not make network calls or make prolonged read operations from isolated storage, because doing so during the

`Activated` event handler could prolong application start time, make the UI take too long to appear, and if it takes longer than 10 seconds, prevent the application from loading altogether.

Deactivating

When an application is running in the foreground and it is replaced by another application (because only one application can be running in the foreground at a time), the original application is deactivated. Applications can be deactivated when a user presses the start button, when a launcher or chooser takes over the foreground, and when an idle timeout causes the lock screen to engage.

When an application is being deactivated, the `Deactivated` event is fired. This is an extremely important event for developers to be aware of and to have their applications handle properly. During this event, your application can store transient data in the `State` property of the `PhoneApplicationService` class. This might be the most recent results of a web service query or some other information that was created or downloaded since the application launched. In addition to storing transient data in the state dictionary so that it can be retrieved during a subsequent activation, you also want to make sure that you store any persistent data in isolated storage. Just because an application is deactivated doesn't mean it will always be reactivated. If resource limits are reached, or too many applications are sitting on the stack waiting to be activated again, your application could be closed and all transient state for it will be cleared.

There is also a small chance that your application might be deactivated without being tombstoned. This could happen if a user presses the start button to deactivate the application and then quickly taps the back button to reactivate the application before the operating system has a chance to terminate the original process. For this reason, you will want to avoid destroying any data or wiping out any potentially important in-memory data during the `Deactivated` event.

Closing

If an application is terminated without another application taking its place in the foreground, such as when a user taps the back button enough to leave the home page of an application, the application is in the closing state and the `Closing` event is fired.

During the `Closing` event, an application should save any persistent data to isolated storage. There is no need to store transient information in the `State` dictionary because the application is being terminated, not deactivated or tombstoned. The next time the application becomes active, regardless of how, it will be a result of a launch of a fresh instance and there will be no transient state to restore.

Tombstoned

So far in this chapter, you've seen me use the term "tombstoned" a lot; I wanted to make sure that the tombstoned application state had its own special mention here.

As you already know, an application that loses its place in the foreground becomes deactivated. This deactivated application has a chance to save transient state in a dictionary. There is a (typically short) period of time during which an application has been deactivated but it has not yet been tombstoned. If an application is not reactivated quickly after deactivation, it will then be tombstoned. This means that the application process will be terminated but the transient state of that application, as well as some other information about the original process, will remain behind (the tombstone, as it were).

When a tombstoned application is reactivated, a new instance of the application process is created, but instead of having the `Launching` event raised, the `Activated` event is raised, and the information originally left behind on the tombstone is used to restore the application to the state in which it was before deactivation.

Managing Application and Page State

In this section of the chapter we're going to put the information we've been discussing so far about activation, deactivation, tombstoning, and launching to good use. We'll use that information to build an application that plays nicely with the Phone Execution Model to provide a seamless user experience. This sample application is very basic and just stores the date and time of the last application exit in the `PhoneApplicationService`'s state dictionary. From now on, throughout the rest of the book, I will refer to this state dictionary as "tombstone state" because the latter is easier to read and easier to say aloud than the former.

Despite the simplicity of the application, a few things there might teach some very valuable lessons. The first is that rather than putting the code that reads to and writes from tombstone state in the App.xaml.cs global `Activated` and `Deactivated` events, I've put the tombstone state code in the `OnNavigatedTo` and `OnNavigatedFrom` events in an individual page.

I like this for a number of reasons. The first is that if all your transient state "load and restore" code exists at the application level, you don't really know what's in scope and what isn't. Why would you need to try to save transient state for a page that hasn't even been instantiated? The other is if you want to affect your GUI as a result of restoring from tombstone state, it's much easier if these updates are done as close to the GUI as possible, by the page that will be affected by the state restore.

The choice is yours, and cases can be made for both options. Deciding how and when to utilize tombstone state is an architectural decision that will be different for each application you write; there is no single cookie-cutter recipe that will tell you what you should do. However, your application must abide by some rules.

At first you might be tempted to shove an entire view model object (which in many cases is a deeply nested object hierarchy) into the tombstone state dictionary. As much as you might like to do this, not only is it not possible, it's not a good idea. You can only store primitive data types in the state dictionary. Even if you could store complex graphs in the state dictionary, you wouldn't want to. That isn't what the tombstone state is for. Use the following guidelines to determine whether you should be storing a value in tombstone state:

Is the value you want to store in tombstone state one that takes a considerable amount of time to generate but can be stored as a primitive data type? Is the value you want to store in tombstone state one that cannot be stored permanently on disk for design purposes but can be stored as just a few primitive data types? If the answer is yes to either of these, there's a good chance your application might benefit from using tombstone state.

Quite possibly, one of the best examples I can think of for when you *should* use tombstone state is that of a location-aware application. When the application starts up, it uses the phone's GPS to gather the current position. Then it centers a Bing Maps control on that position. Without using tombstone state, when a user briefly exits the application and then comes back, the application will reacquire the GPS location, which can take a long time. You can provide the user with a better experience by caching the current longitude and latitude values in the tombstone state dictionary. This way, when your application is `Activated`, you can center the Bing map on the cached location rather than re-acquiring it.

To create this sample, create a new WP7 application called ExecutionModelTest and add a single text box control to the main page. Change the code-behind of MainPage.xaml.cs to read like the code shown in Listing 13.1.

Listing 13.1   **Using Tombstone State During Activation and Deactivation**

```
using System;
using System.Collections.Generic;
using System.Linq;
using System.Net;
using System.Windows;
using System.Windows.Controls;
using System.Windows.Documents;
using System.Windows.Input;
using System.Windows.Media;
using System.Windows.Media.Animation;
using System.Windows.Shapes;
using Microsoft.Phone.Controls;
using System.Threading;
using Microsoft.Phone.Shell;
using System.Diagnostics;

namespace ExecutionModelTest
{
public partial class MainPage : PhoneApplicationPage
{
```

```
private ViewModel vm;

// Constructor
public MainPage()
{
    InitializeComponent();

    vm = new ViewModel();
    this.DataContext = vm;
}

protected override void OnNavigatedTo(
    System.Windows.Navigation.NavigationEventArgs e)
{
    base.OnNavigatedTo(e);

    if (PhoneApplicationService.Current.StartupMode ==
        StartupMode.Activate)
    {
        IDictionary<string, object> state =
            PhoneApplicationService.Current.State;

        if (state.ContainsKey("LastLaunchDate"))
        {
            Deployment.Current.Dispatcher.BeginInvoke(() =>
                {
                vm.LastLaunchDate =
                 (DateTime)state["LastLaunchDate"];
                });
        }
    }
    else
    {
        Deployment.Current.Dispatcher.BeginInvoke(() =>
        {
            vm.LastLaunchDate = DateTime.MinValue;
        });
    }
}

protected override void OnNavigatedFrom(
  System.Windows.Navigation.NavigationEventArgs e)
{
    base.OnNavigatedFrom(e);

    IDictionary<string, object> state =
      PhoneApplicationService.Current.State;
```

```
            Debug.WriteLine(
              "storing value in tombstone state.");
            state["LastLaunchDate"] = DateTime.Now;
        }
    }
}
```

The `ViewModel` class referenced in the preceding code is a simple class that holds a sin-gle property. When this property changes, it fires the `PropertyChanged` event, which in turn notifies the databound WP7 Silverlight GUI that a value has changed. This data-bound GUI contains the text box mentioned earlier, which is bound to the `LastLaunchDate` property in the following view model:

```csharp
using System;
using System.Net;
using System.Windows;
using System.Windows.Controls;
using System.Windows.Documents;
using System.Windows.Ink;
using System.Windows.Input;
using System.Windows.Media;
using System.Windows.Media.Animation;
using System.Windows.Shapes;
using System.ComponentModel;

namespace ExecutionModelTest
{
    public class ViewModel : INotifyPropertyChanged
    {
        private DateTime lastLaunchDate;

        public DateTime LastLaunchDate
        {
            get
            {
                return lastLaunchDate;
            }
            set
            {
                lastLaunchDate = value;
                NotifyPropertyChanged("LastLaunchDate");
            }
        }


        private void NotifyPropertyChanged(string propName)
```

```
        {
            if (PropertyChanged != null)
                PropertyChanged(this,
                    new PropertyChangedEventArgs(propName));
        }
        public event PropertyChangedEventHandler PropertyChanged;
    }
}
```

After you have the code typed in (or you are executing the code that comes with the book), launch the application. Notice that when you first launch the application, the value in the text box is equivalent to `DateTime.MinValue`. Click the Start button on the emulator and then a second later hit the Back button. If all goes well, you will briefly see a screen that says Resuming. This screen appears when an application has been tombstoned and is being reactivated. Thankfully, this is exactly the scenario we wanted to test. After the Resuming screen disappears, the application will reappear. This time, instead of displaying `DateTime.MinValue`, the application displays the date and time as the emulator knew it at the time the application last exited.

The last thing you should know about working with tombstone state is that it is incredibly difficult to debug. If your code executes as the application is activated and something goes wrong when attempting to read values out of the tombstone state dictionary, there's a very good chance that your debug session will simply stop and the emulator will be stuck on the Resuming screen. The next time you start your application, the emulator might even require a full OS reboot because of the previous crash. In short, test your tombstone state manipulation code outside of the activation/deactivation handlers (or better yet, as a Unit Test, which I cover later in the book) so you can be sure it works before you put it in the hard-to-debug event handlers.

Summary

This chapter took you on a tour through the Phone Execution Model. Multitasking is something that most desktop users take for granted. In fact, we take it for granted so much that phone manufacturers have gone out of their way to make their applications look as though they are multitasking, even if all they're doing is faking it in a productive manner.

This is how both the iPhone and Windows Phone 7 devices multitask. Although there are a few things that the iPhone can do in the background that, at least at the time of this writing, Windows Phone 7 doesn't do, multitasking on either device is very similar. This chapter showed you how WP7 applications work and walked you through the various events and important stages in the lifetime of a WP7 application. You learned about activation, deactivation, launching, closing, and what "tombstoning" means.

Armed with this knowledge of what's really going on under the hood when your users tap the start button, the back button, or launch your application from a tile or menu, you will be better able to produce applications that have a smooth, seamless user experience that performs the way WP7 users expect.

Local Storage on the Phone

Data is a precious thing that will last longer than the systems themselves.

Tim Berners-Lee

In this chapter, you learn about Windows Phone 7's capability to store and retrieve local, isolated data. We start by taking a look at the equivalent capability on the iPhone, Core Data, and discuss why WP7 doesn't need this framework. Throughout the chapter you will see examples of how to use isolated storage to work with persistent data and see a real-world example of an application that maintains its own data.

Core Data on the iPhone

Core Data has long been a valuable part of the Apple developer's toolbox, existing long before the first iPhone was ever sold. Core Data is a broad framework that provides more than a façade in front of a database.

Core Data provides a nice logical abstraction of data storage. As the developer, you define entities, attributes that belong to those entities, and you define relationships between other entities. Unlike other low-level data modeling tools, you don't create foreign keys and map the ID column of some table to the ID column of another table. The design surface of Core Data, as shown in Figure 14.1, allows for modeling at a higher (and many believe, far easier and better) level.

As you can see from the figure, Core Data supports a robust array of features, including object inheritance, many-to-many relationships, many-to-one, lookups, and so on. One thing many developers really like about Core Data is that you don't see any primary keys in the preceding diagram, nor do you see any internal IDs that might be required to establish the "sightings" relationship between Monsters and instances of the Sighting entity.

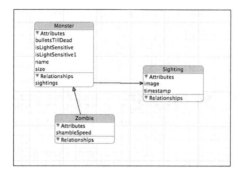

Figure 14.1   The Core Data design surface.

Another feature of Core Data is the capability to generate Objective-C classes that serve as the intermediary layer between the underlying database (sqlite on the iPhone; can be mySQL or others on the Mac), as shown in Figure 14.2.

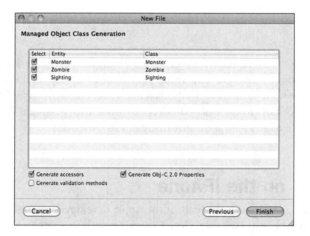

Figure 14.2   Generating Objective-C classes from a
Core Data model.

Listing 14.1 shows some of the classes (.h and .m files) that are generated by a Core Data model.

Listing 14.1   **Core Data-Generated Objective-C Classes**

```
//
//  Monster.h
//  SampleCoreData
//
//  Created by Kevin Hoffman on 11/17/10.
```

```
//  Copyright 2010 Kevin Hoffman. All rights reserved.
//

#import <CoreData/CoreData.h>

@class Sighting;

@interface Monster : NSManagedObject
{
}

@property (nonatomic, retain) NSNumber * size;
@property (nonatomic, retain) NSNumber * bulletsTillDead;
@property (nonatomic, retain) NSNumber * isLightSensitive;
@property (nonatomic, retain) NSString * name;
@property (nonatomic, retain) Sighting * sightings;

@end

//
//  Monster.m
//  SampleCoreData
//
//  Created by Kevin Hoffman on 11/17/10.
//  Copyright 2010 Kevin Hoffman. All rights reserved.
//

#import "Monster.h"

#import "Sighting.h"

@implementation Monster

@dynamic size;
@dynamic bulletsTillDead;
@dynamic isLightSensitive;
@dynamic name;
@dynamic sightings;

@end

//
//  Zombie.h
//  SampleCoreData
//
//  Created by Kevin Hoffman on 11/17/10.
```

```
//  Copyright 2010 Kevin Hoffman. All rights reserved.
//

#import <CoreData/CoreData.h>
#import "Monster.h"


@interface Zombie :  Monster
{
}

@property (nonatomic, retain) UNKNOWN_TYPE shambleSpeed;
@end
```

Why am I showing you all of this great stuff about Core Data? Mostly because, on a personal level, I am a huge fan of Core Data and have used it extensively for applications that I have published in the App Store.

There is no direct equivalent to Core Data on Windows Phone 7. Upon first hearing this, my initial reaction was to jump out a window and end it all right there, but after coming to my senses, I took stock of some of the tools developers have at their disposal when developing Windows Phone 7 applications:

- WCF's Data Contract Serializer—Hydrate and dehydrate entire C# object graphs quickly and easily and in a file-friendly format.
- LINQ—A rich, language-integrated query engine that makes many of Core Data's ORM (object-relational mapping) features unnecessary in WP7.
- Isolated storage—A powerful, secure, sandboxed region of reusable storage allocated to every application that gives developers access to a lightweight file store.

With this in mind, the rest of this chapter is dedicated to illustrating how you can store and retrieve data on the phone as well as discussing several reasons why you might *not* want to use local data; we'll also discuss hybrid approaches like smart clients, which are covered in the next chapter. Hopefully by the time you reach the end of this chapter, you will come to the same conclusion that I did: As good as Core Data is, WP7 doesn't need an equivalent because the tools are already available do the job quite nicely on their own.

Reading and Writing Local Data with WP7

In this next section, I'll cover the basics of isolated storage and then walk you through a sample that uses isolated storage to persist data between executions of an application. Regardless of how much data you're storing, you should always be aware of the fact that interacting with isolated storage is a relatively slow process. As a result, you should try to time your I/O operations so that they have a minimal impact on the overall user experience. Additionally, you might want to avoid using a single file and a single "one class to rule them all" approach to your data. Although it might make things a little easier for you, it has the side effect of writing a whole bunch of data unnecessarily every time a change is made. To compensate for this, one technique is to use one file and one object graph (hierarchy of object instances) for each logical area of your application. This way, when you write data to disk, you're writing only the data that has changed recently.

Isolated Storage 101

Isolated storage is a quota-enforced, isolated sandbox environment that allows applications to create files without introducing risk to the operating system. It does this by ensuring that these files are accessible only via API, and not directly, and that the physical storage of these files is done securely, preventing applications from accessing the isolated storage areas of other applications.

The primary class for interacting with isolated storage is the `IsolatedStorageFile` class. Despite ending in "file," it is actually a container capable of holding and providing access to both files and directories. It is an interface through which you can find files, open files, create files, and so on. The following are some of the more important properties and methods of this class:

- **AvailableFreeSpace**— This property represents the amount of free space available in isolated storage as seen by the current application.

- **Quota**— This property indicates the maximum amount of space that can be consumed by the application in isolated storage.

- **CreateDirectory**— This method creates a directory within the isolated store.

- **CreateFile**— Creates a new file in the isolated store.

- **DeleteDirectory**— Removes a directory and its contents.

- **DirectoryExists**— Returns a Boolean indicating whether a particular directory (or subdirectory) exists.

- **FileExists**— Returns a Boolean value indicating whether a given filename exists in the isolated store.

- **GetDirectoryNames**— Returns a list of directory names in the isolated store.

- **GetFileNames**— Returns a list of filenames in the root of the isolated store or in a given subdirectory.

- **GetUserStoreForApplication**— One of the most frequently called methods, this method returns a user-scoped isolated storage instance.

- **OpenFile**— Opens a file from isolated storage. You can configure the mode and access levels of the file being opened.

- **Remove**— Removes the entire isolated storage scope and all its contents.

Rather than giving out instances of low-level, unfiltered file streams, isolated storage API calls give out instances of `IsolatedStorageFileStream` objects. An `IsolatedStorageFileStream` object inherits from `FileStream`, which in turn inherits from `Stream`. In other words, if you know how to work with streams, you know how to work with isolated storage streams.

Building a Storage-Backed Databound Application

Before we get into the building of the actual application, I know that there are a couple of tasks related to isolated storage that I will be performing over and over again and even across multiple applications. As a result, the first thing I'm going to do is wrap that functionality in a helper class that you can use in your projects and that I use in many of my own.

This class, shown in Listing 14.2, exposes a couple of useful helper methods:

- **WriteGraphToFile**— This method takes an instance of an object that has been decorated with the DataContract attribute and stores it in the given filename in isolated storage.

- **ReadGraphFromFile**— This method uses isolated storage to open the given filename and then deserialize its contents into a fully functioning C# object.

- **ReadGraphFromFile (overload)**— This version of the ReadGraphFromFile method does the same as the other, but it also allows the developer to supply a block of code that acts as a seed. If the given filename was not found, this method executes the seed block to return a default instance of the object. This is useful if you want your application to load its default data from a resource to "seed" the data model with starter data.

As a reader exercise to continue building your own isolated storage skills, try to extend the `IsoStoreHelper` class (Listing 14.2) to include methods that allow you to read and write C# objects in directories as well as just the root directory of the isolated store.

Listing 14.2   **The `IsoStoreHelper` Class**

```
using System;
using System.Net;
using System.Windows;
using System.Windows.Controls;
using System.Windows.Documents;
using System.Windows.Ink;
using System.Windows.Input;
using System.Windows.Media;
using System.Windows.Media.Animation;
using System.Windows.Shapes;
using System.IO.IsolatedStorage;
using System.IO;
```

```
using System.Runtime.Serialization;

namespace IsolatedStorageDemo
{
    public static class IsoStoreHelper
    {

        public static void WriteGraphToFile<T>(string filename,
          T sourceObject)
        {
            using (IsolatedStorageFile isf =
                IsolatedStorageFile.GetUserStoreForApplication())
            {
                using (IsolatedStorageFileStream stream =
                  new IsolatedStorageFileStream(filename,
                    FileMode.Create, isf))
                {
                    DataContractSerializer dcs =
                      new DataContractSerializer(typeof(T));
                    dcs.WriteObject(stream, sourceObject);
                    stream.Close();
                }
            }
        }

        public static T ReadGraphFromFile<T>(string filename)
          where T:class
        {
            T result = null;
            using (IsolatedStorageFile isf =
                IsolatedStorageFile.GetUserStoreForApplication())
            {
                using (IsolatedStorageFileStream stream =
                    new IsolatedStorageFileStream(filename,
                    FileMode.OpenOrCreate, isf))
                {
                    if (stream.Length > 0)
                    {
                        DataContractSerializer dcs =
                          new DataContractSerializer(typeof(T));
                        result = dcs.ReadObject(stream) as T;
                    }
                }
            }
            return result;
        }
```

```
        public static T ReadGraphFromFile<T>(string filename,
          Func<T> seedFunc) where T : class
        {
            if (IsolatedStorageFile.GetUserStoreForApplication().
                FileExists(filename))
                return ReadGraphFromFile<T>(filename);
            else
                return seedFunc();
        }
    }
}
```

With this class in hand, we can now very easily store and retrieve our data model. For our sample application, we're going to create a class called `AppData` to serve as the root of the data model and a class called `Customer` to reside within `AppData` (Listing 14.3).

At this point you might be thinking we're almost done and all we have left to do is bind the UI directly to the classes shown in Listing 14.3. This is actually a very, very (did I mention very?) bad idea. Data on disk has different requirements than data bound to a Silverlight UI. Data bound to a Silverlight UI needs to let Silverlight know when properties have changed (via the `INotifyPropertyChanged` interface) and when collections change (via the `ObservableCollection` class). In addition, data optimized for disk storage or serialization isn't always the same shape as data optimized for user interfaces. In many cases, your view models will have calculated properties and things like converters that allow the UI to be bound to things that appear as colors or images, or even charts and graphs. There are also times when the UI needs to store state, such as whether a record is selected or in some other state that has meaning only to the UI. In these cases, you definitely do not want to be storing that information on disk.

In short, try to avoid tightly coupling your UI to your persistence format wherever possible.

Listing 14.3 **The `AppData` and `Customer` Data Model Classes**

```
using System.Runtime.Serialization;

namespace IsolatedStorageDemo.Models
{
    [DataContract]
    public class AppData
    {
        [DataMember]
        public Customer[] Customers { get; set; }
    }
}
```

```
using System.Runtime.Serialization;

namespace IsolatedStorageDemo.Models
{
    [DataContract]
    public class Customer
    {
        [DataMember]
        public string Name { get; set; }

        [DataMember]
        public string Description { get; set; }
    }
}
```

The `AppData` and `Customer` classes are used only as a means of storing and retrieving data. What the user interacts with is a view model, shown in Listing 14.4. The view model may contain data that looks like our data contract classes, but it also contains very UI-specific features, such as a property called `IsSelected` that we'll use to change the background color of items in a list box. This view model is actually borrowed (okay, borderline hacked) from the view model that comes with the Databound Windows Phone Application Visual Studio template.

Listing 14.4   **MainViewModel.cs and ItemViewModel.cs**

```
using System;
using System.ComponentModel;
using System.Collections.Generic;
using System.Collections.ObjectModel;
using IsolatedStorageDemo.Models;


namespace IsolatedStorageDemo
{
    public class MainViewModel
    {
        public MainViewModel()
        {
            this.Items = new ObservableCollection<ItemViewModel>();
        }

        public ObservableCollection<ItemViewModel> Items
          { get; private set; }

        public bool IsDataLoaded
        {
```

```
        get;
        private set;
    }

    public void LoadData()
    {
        LoadFromIso();
        this.IsDataLoaded = true;
    }

    public void LoadFromIso()
    {
        AppData appData =
            IsoStoreHelper.ReadGraphFromFile<AppData>(
            "appdata.dat", () =>
        {
            AppData seed = new AppData()
            {
                Customers = new Customer[] {
                    new Customer { Name = "First Customer",
                        Description = "This is the first customer" } }
            };
            return seed;
        });

        this.Items.Clear();
        foreach (Customer cust in appData.Customers)
        {
            this.Items.Add(new ItemViewModel { Name = cust.Name,
                Description = cust.Description });
        }
    }

    public void SaveToIso()
    {
        AppData data = new AppData();
        List<Customer> customerList = new List<Customer>();
        foreach (ItemViewModel itemView in this.Items)
        {
            customerList.Add(new Customer { Name = itemView.Name,
                Description = itemView.Description });
        }
        data.Customers = customerList.ToArray();
        IsoStoreHelper.WriteGraphToFile("appdata.dat", data);
    }
}
```

```
}

using System;
using System.ComponentModel;

namespace IsolatedStorageDemo
{
    public class ItemViewModel : INotifyPropertyChanged
    {
        private string _name;
        public string Name
        {
            get
            {
                return _name;
            }
            set
            {
                if (value != _name)
                {
                    _name = value;
                    NotifyPropertyChanged("Name");
                }
            }
        }

        private string _description;
        public string Description
        {
            get
            {
                return _description;
            }
            set
            {
                if (value != _description)
                {
                    _description = value;
                    NotifyPropertyChanged("Description");
                }
            }
        }

        private bool _isSelected;
        public bool IsSelected
        {
```

```
            get
            {
                return _isSelected;
            }
            set
            {
                _isSelected = value;
                NotifyPropertyChanged("IsSelected");
            }
        }

        public event PropertyChangedEventHandler PropertyChanged;
        private void NotifyPropertyChanged(String propertyName)
        {
            PropertyChangedEventHandler handler = PropertyChanged;
            if (null != handler)
            {
                handler(this, new PropertyChangedEventArgs(propertyName));
            }
        }
    }
}
```

Now that we've got a data model that we can load from and write to isolated storage, and we have a view model that is tailored for Silverlight data binding, the only thing we're missing is a UI to put it all together. Listing 14.5 contains the XAML for rigging up the list box to display the customers in our view model. In addition, it contains an application bar with buttons we can use to add and remove customers. Each time a customer is added or removed, we convert the view model into a data model and save it to isolated storage. When the application starts up, the view model tries to reconstitute itself from saved data in isolated storage.

Listing 14.5   MainPage.xaml

```
<phone:PhoneApplicationPage
    x:Class="IsolatedStorageDemo.MainPage"

    ...namespace stuff removed for clarity ...
    d:DataContext="{d:DesignData SampleData/MainViewModelSampleData.xaml}"
    FontFamily="{StaticResource PhoneFontFamilyNormal}"
    FontSize="{StaticResource PhoneFontSizeNormal}"
    Foreground="{StaticResource PhoneForegroundBrush}"
    SupportedOrientations="Portrait"  Orientation="Portrait"
    xmlns:my="clr-namespace:IsolatedStorageDemo.Converters"
    shell:SystemTray.IsVisible="True">
    <phone:PhoneApplicationPage.Resources>
```

```xml
            <my:SelectedColorConverter x:Key="colorConverter"/>
    </phone:PhoneApplicationPage.Resources>

    <Grid x:Name="LayoutRoot" Background="Transparent">
        <Grid.RowDefinitions>
            <RowDefinition Height="Auto"/>
            <RowDefinition Height="*"/>
        </Grid.RowDefinitions>

        <StackPanel x:Name="TitlePanel" Grid.Row="0" Margin="12,17,0,28">
            <TextBlock x:Name="ApplicationTitle"
             Text="Iso Store App"
             Style="{StaticResource PhoneTextNormalStyle}"/>
            <TextBlock x:Name="PageTitle"
             Text="Customers" Margin="9,-7,0,0"
             Style="{StaticResource PhoneTextTitle1Style}"/>
        </StackPanel>

        <Grid x:Name="ContentPanel" Grid.Row="1" Margin="12,0,12,0">
            <ListBox x:Name="MainListBox" Margin="0,0,-12,0"
                     ItemsSource="{Binding Items}"
                     SelectionChanged="MainListBox_SelectionChanged">
                <ListBox.ItemTemplate>
                  <DataTemplate>
                  <StackPanel Margin="0,0,0,17" Width="432"
      Background="{Binding Path=IsSelected,
Converter={StaticResource colorConverter}}">
                        <TextBlock Text="{Binding Name}"
                         TextWrapping="Wrap"
                        Style="{StaticResource PhoneTextExtraLargeStyle}"/>
                        <TextBlock Text="{Binding Description}"
                        TextWrapping="Wrap" Margin="12,-6,12,0"
                        Style="{StaticResource PhoneTextSubtleStyle}"/>
                    </StackPanel>
                    </DataTemplate>
                </ListBox.ItemTemplate>
            </ListBox>
        </Grid>
    </Grid>


    <phone:PhoneApplicationPage.ApplicationBar>
        <shell:ApplicationBar IsVisible="True" IsMenuEnabled="false">
            <shell:ApplicationBarIconButton x:Name="appBarAddButton"
             IconUri="/Images/appbar.add.rest.png"
             Text="Add" Click="appBarAddButton_Click"/>
```

```
        <shell:ApplicationBarIconButton x:Name="appBarDelButton"
          IconUri="/Images/appbar.delete.rest.png"
          Text="Delete" Click="appBarDelButton_Click"/>
      </shell:ApplicationBar>
    </phone:PhoneApplicationPage.ApplicationBar>
</phone:PhoneApplicationPage>
```

And finally, here is the code-behind to the main page shown in Listing 14.6.

Listing 14.6   **MainPage.xaml.cs**

```csharp
using System;
using System.Windows;
using System.Windows.Controls;
using Microsoft.Phone.Controls;

namespace IsolatedStorageDemo
{
    public partial class MainPage : PhoneApplicationPage
    {
        // Constructor
        public MainPage()
        {
            InitializeComponent();

            DataContext = App.ViewModel;
            this.Loaded += new RoutedEventHandler(MainPage_Loaded);
        }

        private void MainListBox_SelectionChanged(object sender,
          SelectionChangedEventArgs e)
        {
            // If selected index is -1 (no selection) do nothing
            if (MainListBox.SelectedIndex == -1)
                return;

            (e.AddedItems[0] as ItemViewModel).IsSelected = true;
            if ((e.RemovedItems != null) && (e.RemovedItems.Count > 0))
            {
                (e.RemovedItems[0] as ItemViewModel).IsSelected = false;
            }
        }

        private void MainPage_Loaded(object sender, RoutedEventArgs e)
        {
            if (!App.ViewModel.IsDataLoaded)
```

```
        {
            App.ViewModel.LoadData();
        }
    }

    private void appBarAddButton_Click(object sender, EventArgs e)
    {
        Random r = new Random();
        ItemViewModel newItem =
            new ItemViewModel { Name = "Customer " +
            r.Next(5, 100).ToString(),
                Description = "Newly Created Customer" };
        App.ViewModel.Items.Add(newItem);

        App.ViewModel.SaveToIso();
    }

    private void appBarDelButton_Click(object sender, EventArgs e)
    {
        MessageBoxResult result = MessageBox.Show("Delete " +
            App.ViewModel.Items[MainListBox.SelectedIndex].Name + "?",
            "Confirm", MessageBoxButton.OKCancel);
        if (result == MessageBoxResult.OK)
        {
            App.ViewModel.Items.RemoveAt(MainListBox.SelectedIndex);
        }

        App.ViewModel.SaveToIso();
    }
  }
}
```

When you run this sample (there are a few files necessary for compilation not included in the source listings in this chapter that you can get from the code downloads for the book), you get something that looks similar to Figure 14.3.

Figure 14.3   Running the isolated storage
sample.

Summary

This chapter started with a discussion about some of the capabilities of Core Data on the iPhone. Because no direct correlation exists between Core Data and WP7, this chapter focused on the capability to store and retrieve entire object hierarchies to and from disk using isolated storage.

With the combination of isolated storage, the WCF Data Contract Serializer, and LINQ for runtime queries of in-memory data, your application can manage virtually any kind of data with relative ease. This chapter showed you how to accomplish that using isolated storage. In the next chapter, you'll see how to deal with remote data by building smart clients.

Building Smart Clients

If Facebook were a country, it would now be the 6th most populous in the world.

InsideFacebook.com

This chapter provides an overview of one of the most powerful application types for mobile devices—the smart client. The days of the massive, monolithic desktop application are numbered. Even applications that sit on modern desktops often communicate with services on the Internet for supplemental information, research, lookups, or even complex calculations.

A smart client is an application that takes advantage of the hardware of the host environment. It is capable of using the GPS, the accelerometer, high-resolution video, audio, and of course, network devices. These applications can be anything from casual games to weather applications to applications such as Netflix, Flixster, Facebook, Twitter, and so on. Although all these applications are fully installed WP7 applications, the real work is done elsewhere, and the real data resides in the cloud. Aside from a few niches, today's mobile phone users often won't even bother installing applications that aren't connected in some way to the world (via the Internet, GPS, Wi-Fi, and so on) around them.

This is the model that this chapter discusses, showing you how to harness the networking and storage capabilities of WP7 to build applications that talk to platform-neutral RESTful services as well as applications that talk to Windows Communication Foundation (WCF) services on .NET-based application servers.

Consuming RESTful Services

REST is an acronym that stands for *REpresentational State Transfer*. To summarize quickly so we can get to the code demos as fast as possible, this boils down to treating the Web like a collection of resources. Every resource has a Unique Resource Identifier

(URI). By using verbs that are part of the standard HTTP vocabulary, such as GET, PUT, DELETE, and POST, and using the URIs as if they were nouns, we can construct a vocabulary that allows us to manipulate and query resources regardless of the underlying platform on which these resources are hosted.

Suppose you have a resource collection called `Users` exposed at a URI like http://my.server.com/Users. Using typical REST assumptions, issuing an HTTP GET request to this URI should give you some representation (almost always XML, often in "feed" form, although lately JSON has become a popular alternative) of that collection. Sending an HTTP GET to http://my.server.com/Users/bob should, according to convention, give you a representation of the resource known as "bob" belonging to the resource collection "Users". Using an HTTP PUT to that same URI will replace the representation of "bob" on the server with the one you sent. Sending an HTTP DELETE to that URI should, assuming you have access, delete the resource known as "bob."

For a full discussion of RESTful architecture, check out the extensive Wikipedia entry on it at http://en.wikipedia.org/wiki/Representational_State_Transfer. Many books talk about the various ways to implement RESTful services in different languages. One such book is *RESTful .NET* (ISBN: 0596519206) by Jon Flanders. If you're into Ruby, the *Practical REST on Rails 2 Projects* book by Ben Scofield is another excellent guide.

It doesn't take very much or deep thought to start to realize some of the benefits of this type of exposure of services. Rather than utilizing someone's fixed remote procedure call (RPC) style interface, where you are invoking proprietary methods, you're just using the basic vocabulary of the Internet itself. RESTful services have rapidly become popular, especially among social networking sites that want to make their information and APIs as easy to use and widely available as possible.

Why LINQ to XML Is Your New Best Friend

There are two parts to communicating with RESTful services. The first is the HTTP communication where your code needs to be able to send payloads utilizing standard HTTP methods such as GET and POST. (PUT and DELETE are often left out to allow for a wider variety of client consumption, but that's a topic better discussed in one of the aforementioned books on RESTful services.)

The second part of communicating with RESTful services is being able to read and write the payload, or resource. In most cases this payload is represented as XML— either as XML that conforms to some custom schema or as a *feed* type of XML, such as Atom or RSS.

This is why LINQ to XML is your new best friend. LINQ to XML will allow your C# code to rip through any XML document (obtained either locally or from the Web), process it, query it, and turn it into usable view model data quickly, efficiently, and in a way that is easy to read and understand by other developers.

The first class you need to talk to RESTful services is the `WebClient` class. Although more robust alternatives are available in the full version of the .NET Framework, `WebClient` is the go-to class that is available to Silverlight developers for making web requests. (Other classes are capable of network access, but `WebClient` is probably the easiest and simplest to use for web service calls.)

Pulling data from a website using a simple HTTP GET couldn't possibly be easier. The `DownloadStringAsync` method does just what its name implies—it downloads the contents of a particular URI as a single string asynchronously in the background and, when the download is complete, raises an event and trigger your code to deal with the response, as shown in the following code:

```
public void LoadStuff()
{
    WebClient wc = new WebClient();
    wc.DownloadStringAsync(
     new Uri("http://my.server.com/stuff"));
    wc.DownloadStringCompleted +=
      new DownloadStringCompletedEventHandler(wc_DownloadStringCompleted);
    }
void wc_DownloadStringCompleted(object sender,
   DownloadStringCompletedEventArgs e)
{
    StringReader sr = new StringReader(e.Result);
    var reader = XmlReader.Create(sr);
    var document = XDocument.Load(reader);
    // Process the XML document
}
```

One of the most commonly performed web activities is a simple HTTP GET to retrieve data. However, smart clients also send data to RESTful services. Suppose our WP7 application submits a new `Customer` to a RESTful service via HTTP POST. To do this, we're going to need a little bit finer-grained control over our web request. We need to set the content type (in this case it will be "text/xml"), we need to change the HTTP method to `POST`, and we need to convert the XML payload into a stream of bytes that we can place into the body of the HTTP POST. It might sound complicated but, comparing the following code to what needs to be done in iOS to perform similar activities, you should be thankful that it is as simple as it is on WP7.

To get started, we're going to use the `HttpWebRequest` class, which gives us fine-grained control over the request as we build it:

```
private void foo_Click(object sender, RoutedEventArgs e)
{
    HttpWebRequest request = (HttpWebRequest)
        WebRequest.Create(
        "http://localhost/Chapter15ServiceHost/RESTfulService.svc/
UploadedCustomers");
    request.ContentType = "text/xml";
    request.Method = "POST";
    request.BeginGetRequestStream(
      new AsyncCallback(GetRequestStreamCallback), request);
}
```

This is the first step in a three-step sequence of asynchronous actions. When the call to BeginRequestStream finishes, it's going to invoke our callback (other languages refer to this as a *completion* or a *monad*, if you're into that sort of thing). This callback is shown next, which builds the body of the request by converting an XML document into a byte array and then performing the request asynchronously:

```
void GetRequestStreamCallback(IAsyncResult result)
{
    HttpWebRequest request = (HttpWebRequest)result.AsyncState;
    Stream postStream = request.EndGetRequestStream(result);

    string xmlPayload =
        "<?xml version=\"1.0\" encoding=\"utf-8\"?>" +
            "<Customer xmlns:xsd=\http://www.w3.org/2001/XMLSchema\
xmlns:xsi=\"http://www.w3.org/2001/XMLSchema-instance\">" +
            "<FirstName>Foo</FirstName>" +
            "<LastName>Johnson</LastName>" +
            "<Address>" +
                "<Line1>1 Fake St</Line1>" +
                "<City>FakeVille</City>" +
                "<State>FA</State>" +
                "<Zip>90210</Zip>" +
            "</Address>" +
            "</Customer>";
    byte[] payloadBytes = Encoding.UTF8.GetBytes(xmlPayload);
    postStream.Write(payloadBytes, 0, payloadBytes.Length);
    postStream.Close();
    request.BeginGetResponse(
      new AsyncCallback(GetResponseCallback), request);
}
```

The next step in the chain is the asynchronous callback triggered by the completion of a response. This response could be an error or it could be success. The only way to find out is in the following callback code:

```
void GetResponseCallback(IAsyncResult result)
{
    HttpWebRequest request = (HttpWebRequest)result.AsyncState;
    HttpWebResponse response =
      (HttpWebResponse)request.EndGetResponse(result);
    Stream responseStream = response.GetResponseStream();
    StreamReader streamReader = new StreamReader(responseStream);
    string responseString = streamReader.ReadToEnd();
    Debug.WriteLine(responseString);
    responseStream.Close();
    streamReader.Close();
    response.Close();
}
```

If you're used to making simple 10-line web service requests in your favorite desktop programming language, don't be so quick to judge. Just because this way might look different doesn't mean it's bad. In fact, after having consumed web services this way (what I call "very asynchronous," although some refer to it as "ridiculously async") on WP7 for a while, I've actually grown rather fond of it.

During each of these steps, there is a chance for a progress bar or some other visual indication of network activity. If you've been using a WP7 device for a while, you are no doubt familiar with the "sliding dots" that appear during most network activity. They are a subtle indicator that some network activity is taking place in the background, but the UI doesn't get cluttered up with giant wheels or other obtrusive "please wait" or progress indicators.

In addition to being able to provide the user with visual feedback, each of these steps is also a very logical place to trap errors. By taking the little bit of extra time and caution required to implement RESTful web service clients in this fashion, you give your users that feeling of quick, unobtrusive network access that permeates the user experience of all Microsoft's stock WP7 applications.

Now that you've seen how to make simple HTTP GET requests, and you've seen how to send XML payloads via HTTP POST, let's take a look at how incredibly easy it is to parse some data from some of the most popular formats: Twitter, YouTube, and RSS feeds.

First, let's look at how easy it is to crack open the 10 most recent tweets from a given user (this API access doesn't require authentication; for more involved Twitter activity you'll need a developer key):

```
public void LoadTweets()
{
    WebClient wcTweets = new WebClient();
    wcTweets.DownloadStringAsync(new
Uri("http://api.twitter.com/1/statuses/user_timeline.xml?screen_name=
ckindel"));
    wcTweets.DownloadStringCompleted +=
        new DownloadStringCompletedEventHandler(
        wcTweets_DownloadStringCompleted);
}
void wcTweets_DownloadStringCompleted(object sender,
    DownloadStringCompletedEventArgs e)
{
    StringReader sr = new StringReader(e.Result);
    var reader = XmlReader.Create(sr);
    var document = XDocument.Load(reader);

    var tweets =
        from tweet in document.Descendants("status")
        select tweet;
```

```
App.ViewModel.Tweets.Clear();
foreach (var tweet in tweets)
{
    Tweet newTweet = new Tweet
    {
        Text = (string)tweet.Element("text"),
        CreatedAt = DateTime.ParseExact(
          (string)tweet.Element("created_at"),
          "ddd MMM dd HH:mm:ss zz00 yyyy", null)
    };
    App.ViewModel.Tweets.Add(newTweet);
}
TweetsLoaded = true;
}
```

This code rips through the list of status updates for the user ckindel (Charlie Kindel is a General Manager for the Developer Ecosystem for Windows Phone 7 with Microsoft) and converts them into a view model form to which we can bind a UI. The UI from the sample application for this chapter is shown in Figure 15.1.

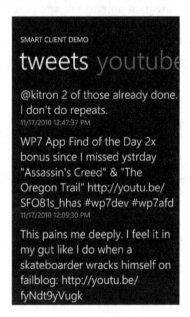

Figure 15.1   Screenshot of smart client application.

And now to sift through the Google Data feed for a particular user's YouTube uploads:

```
public void LoadVideos()
{
    WebClient wc = new WebClient();
    wc.DownloadStringAsync(new
Uri("http://gdata.youtube.com/feeds/api/users/thecrochetdude/uploads"));
    wc.DownloadStringCompleted +=
      new DownloadStringCompletedEventHandler(wc_DownloadStringCompleted);
    this.VideosLoaded = true;
}
void wc_DownloadStringCompleted(object sender,
  DownloadStringCompletedEventArgs e)
{
    StringReader sr = new StringReader(e.Result);
    var reader = XmlReader.Create(sr);
    var document = XDocument.Load(reader);

    XNamespace atom = "http://www.w3.org/2005/Atom";
    var entries =
        from entry in document.Descendants(atom + "entry")
        select entry;

    App.ViewModel.Videos.Clear();
    foreach (var entry in entries)
    {
        App.ViewModel.Videos.Add(new VideoViewModel
        { Title = (string)entry.Element(atom + "title"),
          Description = (string)entry.Element(atom+"content") });
        //Debug.WriteLine(entry.ToString());
        //Debug.WriteLine("Author:" + (string)entry.Element
(atom + "author").Element(atom + "name"));
    }
    VideosLoaded = true;
}
```

Here's very similar code (I've skipped the WebClient bit; by now you should be pretty familiar with that part of the code) to convert an RSS feed into instances of view model objects:

```
void wcBlog_DownloadStringCompleted(object sender,
  DownloadStringCompletedEventArgs e)
{
    StringReader sr = new StringReader(e.Result);
    var reader = XmlReader.Create(sr);
    var document = XDocument.Load(reader);

    var posts =
```

```
            from item in document.Descendants("item")
            select item;

    App.ViewModel.BlogPosts.Clear();
    foreach (var post in posts)
    {
        BlogViewModel blogpost = new BlogViewModel
        {
            Title = (string)post.Element("title"),
            Description = (string)post.Element("description"),
            PublishDate = DateTime.Parse((string)post.Element("pubDate"))
        };
        App.ViewModel.BlogPosts.Add(blogpost);
    }
    BlogLoaded = true;
}
```

As you can see, the amount of code required to consume RESTful web services—whether they belong to Twitter, YouTube, RSS, or your own custom service—is very small. Windows Phone 7 gives your application the capability to talk to web services quickly, easily, efficiently, and asynchronously so that you can perform that communication without negatively affecting the user experience.

As a reader exercise, take the code from the sample application that comes with the code for this chapter and extend the pivot item for the tweets so that it fetches the source user's Twitter icon from the Web and displays it at the top of the page. As a hint, a few chapters back I showed you how to dynamically set the contents of an Image control to a byte array. Learning new technologies isn't about remembering syntax; it's about putting different techniques together to create amazing applications. The code I've given you in this chapter can serve as a catalyst for some pretty cool applications; all you need is a little imagination and patience.

Consuming WCF Services

If you happen to be fortunate enough to be writing both the client- and the server-side of your smart client application, you might actually want to pass on using traditional RESTful services. Although the RESTful architecture is an elegant one and it is great for providing cross-platform functionality without incurring any language or platform-specific dependencies, sometimes there are more practical options.

In the case of building both the server and the Windows Phone 7 application, if you are building the server using .NET and WCF, you might want to consume the WCF services using a service reference rather than using raw HTTP messaging. All the functionality I am about to discuss is completely unavailable on the iPhone and iOS. This is a huge productivity booster and timesaver for those with Microsoft back-ends being exposed to mobile devices.

To add a service reference, you need to tell Visual Studio 2010 the location of the service. You do this by entering in the URL of the WCF service, the URL of a non-Microsoft web service (so long as it exposes standards-compliant WSDL), or you can press the Discover button and it will locate web services exposed by projects in the same solution. Figure 15.2 shows an example of the dialog that appears when you right-click a Windows Phone 7 application and choose Add Service Reference.

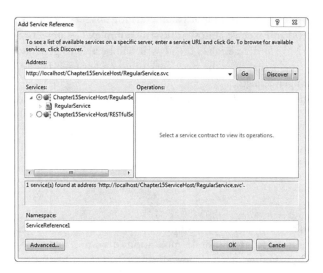

Figure 15.2   The Add Service Reference dialog.

Even though the Add Service Reference dialog can discover RESTful services that are implemented in WCF, you do not want to add a WCF reference to them, because the client-side proxy generation will fail. In our case, I located the WCF service that I built (this is all available in the code sample for this chapter) and added a service reference.

After it is added, you can utilize the service reference's generated client proxy to asynchronously communicate with your WCF service:

```
RegularServiceReference.RegularServiceClient client =
  new RegularServiceReference.RegularServiceClient();
client.GetSomeStringCompleted +=
  new EventHandler<
    RegularServiceReference.GetSomeStringCompletedEventArgs>(
    client_GetSomeStringCompleted);
client.GetSomeStringAsync("foo");
```

The code to respond to the asynchronous completion of a WCF service call looks like this:

```
void client_GetSomeStringCompleted(object sender,
  RegularServiceReference.GetSomeStringCompletedEventArgs e)
{
    Debug.WriteLine("Received reply from service:\n" + e.Result);
}
```

Although the return value and input parameters for this service call were simple strings, you can send and receive almost arbitrarily complex C# objects. So long as WCF knows how to serialize and deserialize the class, it will be able to generate a client-side proxy or client wrapper that does the busywork of going between raw HTTP payload and the client wrapper objects.

You can also invoke methods on a remote WCF service without adding a service reference and without using a generated proxy. This is done using a WCF class called a `ChannelFactory`, but that class and topics related to it are better handled by books written specifically about WCF. For more information about WCF, check out the book *Programming WCF Services* by Juval Lowy.

Summary

Mobile applications rarely exist in a vacuum. Although there are some very popular and notable exceptions, in most cases mobile applications need to make use of network resources somehow. Whether this is to download the latest weather information, stock quotes, or to communicate with a proprietary hosted database, mobile applications are often nothing without their network resources.

This chapter provided you with an overview of how to build network-connected Windows Phone 7 applications. Whether you are using the `WebClient` or `HttpWebRequest` classes to communicate with RESTful services, or using generated WCF client proxies, exchanging data with network resources is simple, easy, and efficient. With networking capabilities now in your WP7 toolbox, you are ready to create amazing applications that users will enjoy and continue to use again and again.

16

Separating Your Concerns

The mother art is architecture.
Without an architecture of our own we have no soul of our own civilization.

Frank Lloyd Wright

This chapter is the culmination of something this book has been building toward for several chapters. As you have been going through the book reading the text, looking at the source code, and running the samples, hopefully a few things have been crossing your mind.

First, hopefully you have been enjoying the code samples and learning something along the way. Second, your keen developer mind might be thinking something like this:

This is great and all for simple "hello world" apps, but how does all this work in real production apps? How can I create elegant, testable, simple, easy-to-maintain code that solves real-world problems? How do I avoid the inevitable spaghetti that plagues most apps of any real size?

If you've been thinking anything like that, this chapter should make you very happy. There is a method to my madness. At the beginning of the book I illustrated simple concepts to get you started using crude, brute-force code samples. As the book progressed, the samples have been getting more involved, and you might have even noticed that in the previous chapter I deliberately separated the data model from the view model. In the next chapter, you'll learn about unit testing and test-driven development (TDD).

This chapter combines a high-level discussion of architectural and design patterns with a walkthrough of an open-source implementation of one of those patterns. We'll look at how the MVC pattern is applied to iOS application development, and we'll see how an adaptation of that pattern can be used to help you in your quest to build amazing WP7 applications and do so in a scalable, testable, maintainable fashion.

A Brief History of MVC

In today's world of software development, techniques and technology that were brand new last year are often considered "old school," and all the cool kids on the playground stop using the old stuff in favor of the hottest new SDK, language, or framework.

Believe it or not, the Model View Controller (MVC) architectural pattern has been around since 1979. That's right, some of you reading this book might actually be younger than this pattern (which makes me feel even older, and I reserve the right to refer to you all as whippersnappers in subsequent chapters).

MVC was first described in 1979 by a member of the Smalltalk team at Xerox PARC. Given this foundational fact, it should come as no surprise to any Objective-C (a language inspired by Smalltalk) programmer that Apple makes extensive use of—and often requires—the MVC pattern in its frameworks, such as in Cocoa and iOS.

At the core of the MVC pattern is a desire to separate concerns. Most developers have experienced the nightmare of attempting to untangle code that has become too tightly coupled. This often happens after an application has been released to production and is working fine. Then someone wants the application to do something no one planned for during the initial release.

When the developers lift the hood and stare down into the engine of the application, what they find scares them. Everything has a tight dependency on everything else. They can't change one piece of code without rewriting another. A somewhat simple change becomes hellish in its complexity and potential time and resource consumption. Worse yet, the code hasn't been written with unit testing in mind, so there's no automated, reliable way of knowing whether the new features haven't broken the previously working features. Because of the interdependent, tightly coupled modules, developers can't even test their code in isolation.

MVC isn't a sprinkle-on magic fairy dust solution that will fix all these problems. It is nothing more than one pattern among many that has as its primary goal the separation of concerns to provide for a more agile, flexible, loosely coupled and yet still highly cohesive application. Again, using MVC doesn't guarantee success, just like using a hammer doesn't guarantee you won't smash your own thumb with it.

I will provide a detailed description of MVC both because it is the primary development pattern on the iPhone and because understanding how MVC works will make understanding how the variant we will be using, MVVM, works.

The way MVC is designed to work is through clear assignment of roles and responsibilities within an application, lumping those responsibilities into three distinct bins:

- Model—The model is responsible for the domain data. This includes more than just storing information. It includes the maintenance of state and the notification of observers of changes in state. The view and controller can both be observers or subscribers to state change information.

- View—The view is responsible for rendering the model in an interactive form. The view is responsible for facilitating the handling of user interaction, but it does not directly react to user interaction.

- Controller—The controller is responsible for responding to user input and manipulating the model in response to this input. You might think that the view is responsible for this, but the distinction is important. If the view renders a button whose state is bound to the model, the view facilitates the act of a user tapping the screen, but the controller executes code in response to this tap.

An illustration of the interaction of these three roles is shown in Figure 16.1.

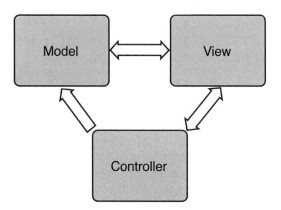

Figure 16.1   An illustration of the Model View
Controller pattern.

What you often see are user interfaces built around these symbiotic MVC trios. A single piece of fully functional user interface will often be the result of a small model, a singular purpose view, and a controller to manage the whole thing.

If you look at the diagram in Figure 16.1, you might notice that there is a bidirectional relationship between the model and the view. This relationship is often facilitated through data binding.

If you have been doing any iOS programming, you probably know that data binding, at least in the sense Mac OS X desktop programmers might be used to, is not available. Instead, the controller takes on a more aggressive role and is often used to force-feed data to the model and also force information into the view. This type of implementation—where the controller directly manipulates the view and the model, and there is little, if any, communication directly between the model and the view—is often referred to as the Passive View pattern (shown in Figure 16.2). This is really the MVC pattern with the controller acting as a middleman for model-to-view communication.

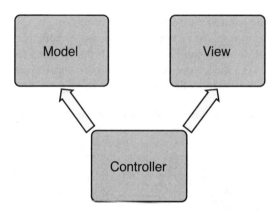

Figure 16.2   The Passive View alternate form of
MVC.

Think of how this might apply to a typical iOS development scenario. One of the most commonly used controllers is the UITableViewController. This controller contains within it a reference to a view hierarchy that, for all intents and purposes, takes the role of the View in the preceding diagram. iOS and Cocoa both make extensive use of the Delegate pattern. Rather than having a reference to a model object with a bunch of properties that the controller can read to manipulate the view, the controller instead maintains a single reference, called delegate, to an object that must expose certain methods.

When a particular user interaction with the view requires some data that the view doesn't have, the controller handles this input (remember the view just facilitates input; it doesn't *handle* it). If the controller needs something that it doesn't already have (such as a UITableViewCell instance for a particular row/group), it can send messages to (call methods on) the delegate object. In this case, the delegate object is serving in the role of the model.

MVC purists often sneer at this particular example because the UITableViewController has the capability to be its own delegate. This means that the controller is providing its own model, and to many this act is borderline offensive.

So far in this book you have seen me create a folder called ViewModels or Models in many of the sample applications. I've done that because even for the simplest of applications, a little separation of concerns goes a long way. I have been informally leading up to this chapter by trying to keep controllers, views, and their corresponding models as separate as possible.

In the next section of this chapter, you'll learn about a variant of MVC called MVVM. We will be using an open-source implementation of this pattern to build an application with clean lines, sexy curves, and separated concerns.

Introduction to MVVM

To explain the progression from MVC to MVVM, I will share an anecdote with you. I was working on one of the most complicated and in-depth applications I've ever developed. It had a high-speed, real-time, streaming back-end that continually fed information to the UI and occasionally took input from the user. I was working on this with Pavan Podila (some of you might know him by his tribal name, Dances with Xaml). We were avid fans of the MVC pattern and were jointly developing a model as he built an amazing UI and I built an equally amazing back-end. It was truly a thing of beauty.

Until we tried a real-world scenario.

This is when the happy synergy started to break down. As I needed more and more functionality on the back-end, I started adding more properties to the model. Because I was adhering as much as possible to the MVC pattern I'd used for so long, I kept as much of the "controlleryness" (this is a technical term, seriously) in the controller. I didn't put any methods on the model that weren't related to state maintenance, manipulation, or notification. Pavan was rapidly adding properties to the model that he needed to facilitate the WPF magic he was creating. We quickly realized that my back-end was getting corrupted by his UI-specific modeling and his UI was being corrupted by implementation-specific details related to my back-end implementation. Worse yet, both of us were utterly abusing the controller and making it do all kinds of things nature never intended a controller to do. Even though we were separating some concerns with MVC, it just wasn't good enough.

The problem we had was that we didn't come to the realization soon enough that a single model that provides both "bindability" (another technical term referring to the fact that an object is designed specifically to be bound to a Silverlight GUI) and persistence. We needed to split those roles. Instead of keeping with MVC, we bled functionality out of the controller and created a back-end Model and a front-end ViewModel.

The ViewModel had properties on it that represented things like the status of toggle switches, bound view states, transition information, and custom aggregations of data that took three or four properties to represent on the back-end. The Model object was pure persistence, data "as it looks on the wire."

This new separation of concerns was an implementation of the Model-View-View-Model (MVVM) pattern. In this pattern, the view communicates with a view model through commands and two-way data binding. The View model alerts the view of important state changes through messages. The view model can talk to the model (as ours did) and the view can, if need be, interact directly with the underlying model.

This interaction pattern is shown in Figure 16.3, which is an illustration of MVVM with a specific slant toward Laurent Bugnion's open-source implementation.

Throughout the rest of this chapter, I'll be walking through the implementation of an application that utilizes an open-source MVVM framework. MVVM is nothing more than a pattern, but the framework provides some very helpful classes that make it easier to keep our concerns separate while building WP7 applications.

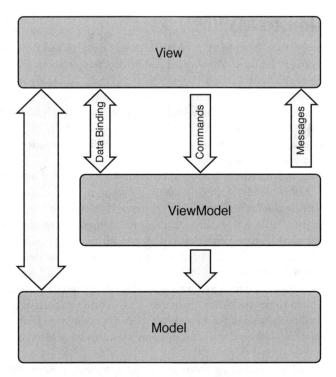

Figure 16.3   Interaction of roles within a typical MVVM
implementation.

Working with MVVM Light for WP7

Before continuing on with this section of the chapter, I must give credit where credit is
due. I learned about MVVM less because I was interested in the pattern and more
because of Laurent Bugnion's implementation of this pattern, MVVM Light, an open-
source product available for WPF, Silverlight, and Windows Phone 7. If you want to learn
something about Silverlight, follow this man on Twitter (@LBugnion) or his blog at
http://blog.galasoft.ch. Better yet, go buy his book, *Silverlight 4 Unleashed*.

In this next section of the chapter, you're going to need a few things to follow along.
Because of the length and complexity of the sample code, I recommend that you read
through this section without trying to type anything in. When you're done with this section, open up the sample code and play with it; run the sample application, and see how
everything works as a cohesive application.

The first thing you'll need to work with MVVM Light is the toolkit itself. The installation instructions might vary between the time of this book's writing and when you're

reading it, so you'll need to follow the installation instructions on the MVVM Light web-site. You can download the library and find documentation and installation instructions at http://www.galasoft.ch/mvvm/getstarted. At this URL you'll find links to the installation instructions, videos, documentation, and a link to download the library.

Before proceeding with the rest of this chapter, make sure that you can create a new MVVM Light (WP7) application and that it compiles and runs. As I sit here writing this book, there is no automated installation utility for MVVM Light. You need to unzip the templates and binaries and put them in the appropriate directories.

To show off the power of MVVM Light, I'm going to walk you through building a sample application. This will be a little different from the samples in previous chapters because MVVM Light is a library that provides code that supports an architectural princi-pal. To see this in action, we need to build a full application. It doesn't make sense to show you tiny isolated snippets without showing you how they actually improve the quality of your application.

This sample application is called Mnemuse, a tool for writers of fiction. This tool allows writers to store and browse characters, places, scenes, inspirations, plotlines, chapter organizations, and more all from their Windows Phone 7 device. This lets them be sure that they'll never lose an important idea or forget what color of hair a particular character had ever again. Note that, at the time of the writing of this book, this app is purely a demonstration and isn't in either application marketplace.

We could build this application in a non-MVVM fashion. I could create a bunch of XAML pages and load up the code-behind with direct data manipulation code. I could put the isolated storage (or web service) I/O in a place that is activated directly by UI controls. I could even have one page instantiate other pages and have master pages manu-ally instantiate and feed data to detail pages. The end user might never know that I've cut these corners or how tightly coupled or impossible to test my application is. To be honest, I could do this and the application might perform just fine as far as my users are con-cerned, and I might even make a lot of money from the app.

But would I respect myself in the morning? No.

And so we're going to do it the MVVM way.

To start with, I'm going to create a new MVVM Light (WP7) project. When you do this you get a MainPage.xaml just like any other WP7 application. But you also get a ViewModel folder, and in that folder is a class called `MainViewModel`. There is usually a 1:1 correspondence between the view (which can be a page or a user control, in my opinion) and the view model. The view model is the first aspect of this application we're going to look at.

Building a View Model

Providing code in support of view models is one of the primary tasks of the MVVM Light library. As developers progress through the learning process, they tire of building applications that produce spaghetti code and want something cleaner and more elegant. Developers often drift naturally in the direction of MVVM.

One speed bump in the MVVM adoption process is often figuring out how to manage the lifetime of view models. Sometimes developers will create a static class that stores references to all the view models so that these models will be around when needed. What happens next is often where developers decide that MVVM isn't a good idea: They try to get binding working between their XAML view and the static view model, and it gets ugly. The act of making this work often produces more spaghetti code than what the developer was originally trying to avoid.

Enter the `ViewModelLocator`. This is a class that is provided for us by the MVVM Light project template. For each of the view models in our application, this class maintains a static property that holds a reference to a singleton instance of that view model. In addition, there are nonstatic properties designed specifically to allow for XAML binding. This fixes one of the most painful aspects of trying to keep the view code "pure" by having a central utility class (which could be considered a Factory if you're into pattern labeling) be responsible for the instantiation, binding exposition, and lifetime management of view models.

In our sample application, the main page displays a list of books because it is a true rarity to find a fiction author who only ever thinks about one book at a time. So not only are we going to need our main view model to maintain a list of books, but we want this view model to be bindable and locatable using the `ViewModelLocator` class.

To rig up a new view model in the `ViewModelLocator` class, I first add a method call such as `CreateMain()` to the instance constructor. You'll put one of these method calls in here for each of your view models.

First you'll see the `MainStatic` property, which provides for the singleton instance of the view model:

```
public static MainViewModel MainStatic
{
    get
    {
        if (_main == null)
        {
            CreateMain();
        }

        return _main;
    }
}
```

Here the _main variable is a private static member. Next we have the nonstatic member that refers to the static member that is used to support data binding.

```
[System.Diagnostics.CodeAnalysis.SuppressMessage("Microsoft.Performance",
    "CA1822:MarkMembersAsStatic",
    Justification =
"This non-static member is needed for data binding purposes.")]
public MainViewModel Main
```

```
{
    get
    {
        return MainStatic;
    }
}
```

Next, by convention we have a method called `ClearMain()` that cleans up our main view model. Use this method to get rid of any resources that your view model might be consuming. In my case, I call the `Cleanup()` method on _main, which is a method that belongs to all view models, and then I set _main to null. The `CreateMain()` method just instantiates a new instance of the main view model. Keep in mind that you must never manipulate the view model directly in the locator class. The locator class is purely a life-time manager and data-binding facilitator. All real initialization code takes place within the view model itself. This brings me to Listing 16.1, the `MainViewModel` class for my books page.

Listing 16.1   **MainViewModel.cs**

```
using GalaSoft.MvvmLight;
using System.Collections.ObjectModel;
using GalaSoft.MvvmLight.Command;
using System.Windows;
using GalaSoft.MvvmLight.Messaging;
using Mnemuse.Messages;
using System.Threading;
using GalaSoft.MvvmLight.Threading;
using Microsoft.Phone.Controls;
using System;

namespace Mnemuse.ViewModel
{
    public class MainViewModel : ViewModelBase
    {
        private ObservableCollection<Book> books;
        private Book selectedBook;

        #region Singular Properties
        public string ApplicationTitle
        {
            get
            {
                return "Mnemuse";
            }
        }

        public string PageName
```

```csharp
    {
        get
        {
            return "Books";
        }
    }

    public string Welcome
    {
        get
        {
            return "Welcome to MVVM Light";
        }
    }

    #endregion

    public ObservableCollection<Book> Books
    {
        get
        {
            return books;
        }
        set
        {
            books = value;
            RaisePropertyChanged("Books");
        }
    }

    /// <summary>
    /// Initializes a new instance of the MainViewModel class.
    /// </summary>
    public MainViewModel()
    {
        Books = new ObservableCollection<Book>();

        if (IsInDesignMode)
        {
            // Code runs in Blend -> create design time data.
            for (int x = 1; x < 6; x++)
            {
                Book b = new Book
                    { Title = "Book " + x.ToString(),
                        Description = "This is book " + x.ToString() };
                Books.Add(b);
```

```
                    }

                }
                else
                {
                    // Code runs "for real"
                }
            }
            ////public override void Cleanup()
            ////{
            ////      // Clean up if needed

            ////      base.Cleanup();
            ////}
        }
}
```

Now that we've got our view model, we need to bind our view to it. In the past (you know, back in the good old days around Chapter 8 or so), I've set the DataContext of a view programmatically in the code-behind. Although this practice will certainly get the job done and a lot of people like doing it this way, I prefer to do everything declaratively and use code only as a last resort. As a result, take a look at the top of my MainPage.xaml markup:

```
<phone:PhoneApplicationPage x:Class="Mnemuse.MainPage"
        xmlns="http://schemas.microsoft.com/winfx/2006/xaml/presentation"
        xmlns:x="http://schemas.microsoft.com/winfx/2006/xaml"
        xmlns:phone="clr
namespace:Microsoft.Phone.Controls;assembly=Microsoft.Phone"
        xmlns:shell=
"clr-namespace:Microsoft.Phone.Shell;assembly=Microsoft.Phone"
        xmlns:d="http://schemas.microsoft.com/expression/blend/2008"
        xmlns:mc=
"http://schemas.openxmlformats.org/markup-compatibility/2006"
        FontFamily="{StaticResource PhoneFontFamilyNormal}"
        FontSize="{StaticResource PhoneFontSizeNormal}"
        Foreground="{StaticResource PhoneForegroundBrush}"
        SupportedOrientations="Portrait"
        Orientation="Portrait"
        mc:Ignorable="d"
        d:DesignWidth="480"
        d:DesignHeight="696"
        shell:SystemTray.IsVisible="True"
        DataContext="{Binding Main, Source={StaticResource Locator}}">
```

The key line here is the binding expression `{Binding Main, Source={StaticRe-source Locator}}`. This line is declaring that I want the data context of my entire view to be set to the `Main` property on the Locator object, which is a global resource. The MVVM Light project template put some code in our App.xaml file that declares an instance of the `ViewModelLocator` class as a global resource:

```
<Application.Resources>
    <vm:ViewModelLocator x:Key="Locator"
                            d:IsDataSource="True" />
</Application.Resources>
```

Now that we have a view model locator, and our view's data context has been set to an instance of a view model (remember, even though it's an instance property it's still pointing to a static singleton), we can bind some of our UI to the view model, as shown next:

```
<TextBlock x:Name="ApplicationTitle"
                    Text="{Binding ApplicationTitle}"
                    Style="{StaticResource PhoneTextNormalStyle}" />
<TextBlock x:Name="PageTitle"
                    Text="{Binding PageName}"
                    Margin="-3,-8,0,0"
                    Style="{StaticResource PhoneTextTitle1Style}" />
```

The first phase of our adoption of MVVM is complete: the use of a view model. At this point a lot of developers and many architects sit back and think: *Was this trip really necessary?*

The answer is no. And yes. As I mentioned before, you can rig all this up spaghetti-style or you can do everything in code-behind. All we've done so far is provide a means for our application to make use of view models. So far you haven't seen any of the real benefits because you've seen data binding before and it shouldn't be that new to you. What comes next are the features of the MVVM Light toolkit and the benefits of MVVM adoption that could (and I'm not joking) change the way you write applications forever.

Yes, But Will It Blend?

Developers familiar with building applications for the iPhone and iPad are intimately familiar with this problem: The design surface almost never reflects an accurate representation of the live, running application. It depends on the individual developer, but often the design surface experience of Interface Builder is so completely different from the runtime experience (especially when dealing with custom views with custom rendering) that developers simply skip IB entirely and do everything in code.

This is also true, to an extent, with Silverlight, WPF, and Windows Phone 7 applications. It is very easy to build an application that is so unfriendly to design tools that developers ignore the fact that design tools exist, and they do all their UI building the "notepad way"—by hand-entering XAML into Visual Studio.

There is a cure for design tool exclusion, and its name is MVVM. The biggest problem with being able to use design tools to build UIs is their lack of cooperation and integration with the underlying data model. Typically, designers don't care about (nor do they have access to) data models generated by C# classes that come from web service proxies, and so on. However, if your UI is tightly coupled to service proxy classes, it can be very difficult to work with your UI in a tool like Blend.

In Listing 16.1, you might have noticed a line of code in the constructor of the `MainViewModel` class that looks like this:

```
if (IsInDesignMode)
```

This property (handily provided for us by MVVM Light) gives the constructor of our view model the capability to create some dummy data. Blend follows the chain of data binding and executes constructors in our view models *at design time*. By playing nicely with MVVM, our view models can provide design tools such as the built-in Visual Studio designer and Blend with sample data that we (or better yet, professional designers) can use to build incredible user interfaces. I'll cover another technique later in this chapter with service providers that will even hide the if statement from the view model's constructor, making our code even more clean—and who doesn't love clean code? Figure 16.4 shows a screenshot of what our main page looks like in Blend. Note how programmatically generated data is showing up on a design surface.

Figure 16.4   A view bound to a view model
rendered in Blend.

Working with Commands

Now that we've got a view, a view model, and we even have data binding between the view and view model, we want to add some interactivity. At some point users are going to have to interact with our application. When they do, we're going to want to execute some code in response to that interaction.

In a non-MVVM application, we might put all the code that responds to user interaction in the code-behind of the view page (for example, MainPage.xaml.cs). Although there is nothing inherently wrong with this, this practice makes for code that is hard to test (as you'll see in the next chapter), hard to maintain, and is generally inflexible and not as clean as it could be. Certainly, there are times when code-behind code is required, but as I mentioned, I like to do everything declaratively until the last possible moment.

The piece of interactivity that I want to show you is the capability to delete a book from the list. To do this, we'll use a control available within the Silverlight/WP7 Toolkit that you can find on Codeplex at http://silverlight.codeplex.com. This control is the ContextMenu control.

Let's take a look at the data template that I'm using for books when they appear in my main page's list box. This data template is defined in the resource dictionary for the page rather than directly on the list box. I like this approach rather than the one I've used previously in the book because it makes that data template more reusable, and it makes the markup for my list box much easier to read.

```
<DataTemplate x:Key="bookItemTemplate">
    <StackPanel Width="480">
        <toolkit:ContextMenuService.ContextMenu>
            <toolkit:ContextMenu>
                <toolkit:MenuItem Header="delete book"
                                  Command="{Binding RemoveBookCommand}" />
            </toolkit:ContextMenu>
        </toolkit:ContextMenuService.ContextMenu>
        <TextBlock Text="{Binding Title}"
            Style="{StaticResource PhoneTextLargeStyle}"/>
        <TextBlock Text="{Binding Description}"
            Style="{StaticResource PhoneTextNormalStyle}"/>
    </StackPanel>
</DataTemplate>
```

Each book is going to be represented by a stack panel with a couple items in it, including text blocks for the title and description. This is pretty straightforward. The new control here is the context menu. Within the menu is a menu item. This is where the fun starts.

Rather than seeing what you've seen so far in this book, a typical "click" event handler, there is now a command. Even better, this command is a property on the view model. Commands are really nothing more than instances of objects which contain references to executable code. They provide for a way to bind user interface elements to code that executes without having to tightly couple that code to a code-behind. In other words, with the command as part of the view model, that code is now shared and stored on the view model itself. This makes the code easier to find, easier to maintain, provides a single point of execution (rather than potential multiple entry points like you typically see in code-behind implementations), and can even be reused by different views that reuse the same view model.

Let's take a look at the command property on the view model that we add to support deleting books. If your brain has already calibrated itself to the MVVM way of thinking, you might already be asking yourself: Is this command on the Main View model or the Book view model? The answer is on the Book view model. This is because this data template is bound to a list of books, and each of those books is an instance of the Book view model.

Listing 16.2 shows our Book view model in its entirety.

Listing 16.2   **Book.cs**

```
using System;
using System.Net;
using System.Windows;
using System.Windows.Controls;
using System.Windows.Documents;
using System.Windows.Ink;
using System.Windows.Input;
using System.Windows.Media;
using System.Windows.Media.Animation;
using System.Windows.Shapes;
using GalaSoft.MvvmLight;
using GalaSoft.MvvmLight.Command;
using GalaSoft.MvvmLight.Messaging;
using Mnemuse.Messages;

namespace Mnemuse.ViewModel
{
public class Book : ViewModelBase
{
    private string title;
    private string description;

    public Book()
        : base()
    {
        InitializeCommands();
    }

    public RelayCommand RemoveBookCommand { get; private set; }
```

```
public string Title
{
    get
    {
        return title;
    }
    set
    {
        title = value;
        RaisePropertyChanged("Title");
    }
}

public string Description
{
    get
    {
        return description;
    }
    set
    {
        description = value;
        RaisePropertyChanged("Description");
    }
}

private void InitializeCommands()
{
    // when someone uses a context menu to delete THIS book,
    // broadcast a message so any affected viewmodels
    // can handle it (e.g the global book list)
    RemoveBookCommand = new RelayCommand(
        () =>
          Messenger.Default.Send<RemoveBookMessage>(
          new RemoveBookMessage(this)));
}
}
}
```

RelayCommand is a class that comes with the MVVM Light framework. This class provides a wrapper for code that will be executed when the command is executed. In addition, it also provides a wrapper for code that will be executed to determine whether a
command is executable. When you bind regular buttons to commands, they will run the
custom code in the RelayCommand that returns a true or false. When the code returns
false, the button will be disabled.

To summarize, commands provide a way to bind UI elements declaratively to a reusable wrapper around a block of code. These commands can be bound using Blend or Visual Studio 2010's designer or by typing the XAML in by hand. Again, I like to keep things declarative as long as possible, so I'm a huge fan of using commands to react to UI events whenever possible.

There is one spot in WP7 that isn't compatible with commands: the application bar. The application bar controls aren't real Silverlight controls and, despite efforts to make them look like real controls, they don't behave the same way Silverlight controls behave. This is because the application bar exists outside the application's main frame and can shrink or grow the application based on the opacity setting of the app bar. With the application bar menu items, you're still going to have to respond to the click event. However, that doesn't mean you have to embed code directly in the code-behind; you can forward that click to a command. In the following code, I forward the click from the Add button on the app bar to a command that adds books to the main view model:

```
private void addBookButton_Click(object sender, System.EventArgs e)
{
    var vm = DataContext as MainViewModel;
    if (vm != null)
    {
        vm.AddBookCommand.Execute(null);
    }
}
```

Finally, at the bottom of Listing 16.2 you might have noticed the `Messenger.Default.Send` code. By sheer coincidence, this leads me to my next topic: messaging.

Sending Messages with MVVM Light

When trying to maintain a clear separation of concerns, one of the hardest things to do is avoid making direct method calls on dependent objects. The reason this is a problem is that every time you do this, you string another piece of spaghetti between two layers of your application and eventually, that spaghetti becomes so hard to untangle (without breaking) that the only way to maintain your application is to just keep heaping more meatballs on top.

Messaging is another way of maintaining a clear separation of concerns as well as ensuring that all the actors in your MVVM application stick to the script. Messaging (also referred to as "pub/sub" or just "pub sub" by many) allows components of your application to advertise when important things happen without actually knowing ahead of time what needs to take place in response. This decouples the pieces of your application that are performing notable events from the pieces that respond to them.

In Listing 16.2, you saw the following code that creates an instance of the Remove-BookCommand object:

```
RemoveBookCommand = new RelayCommand(
    () => Messenger.Default.Send<RemoveBookMessage>(
    new RemoveBookMessage(this)));
```

In this code I'm saying that every time the `RemoveBookCommand` is executed (regardless of how or why it is executed) that the current view model (`Book`) will send a message to all subscribers indicating that a book has been marked for removal.

Why not just make sure that each instance of the Book view model has a reference to the Main View model? This way the book could just remove itself directly from the list. The problem with this pattern is that it violates the "don't look up" principal of MVVM development, and it means that anytime we want any other view model to respond to the deletion of a book, we have to put that code in the Book view model rather than in the appropriate view models.

Don't Look Up

Jesse Liberty has a very popular quote about MVVM development that says, quite simply, "don't look up." Keep this in mind when building your view models and it will help guide you to a better MVVM architecture. In short, never reference anything from a view model that is "higher" than the view model. That means your view model shouldn't be able to reference parent view models directly, nor should it ever have a direct reference to the view page (XAML) associated with that view. In our case, the Book view model should never have a reference to the `MainViewModel`.

Instead of maintaining a direct reference to the main view model and directly manipulating the book list, we instead publish a message (`RemoveBookMessage`). Any view model that is subscribing to that message, regardless of where it resides in the application, will be informed about this message when it is sent.

The following code from the constructor inside `MainViewModel` shows how we subscribe to the book removal message and perform the final book deletion without violating the separation between the two view models:

```
Messenger.Default.Register<RemoveBookMessage>(this, RemoveBook);
```

And then the implementation of the `RemoveBook` method performs the actual view model manipulation:

```
public void RemoveBook(RemoveBookMessage removeMessage)
{
    DeleteBookFromList(removeMessage.Book);
}
```

Worth pointing out here is that the only thing we have been manipulating up to this point has been the view model. When we get to the service provider topic, you'll see how we can cleanly and elegantly wire this view model up to a backing or persistence store.

Look Ma, No Code-Behind!

Another thing that you can do with messaging is combine it with the notification of property changes. This allows you to notify other view models automatically when properties change, essentially extending the reach of the standard property change notification system to MVVM Light's message "bus."

To show you how to do that, I will walk you through a solution to a classic problem in applications that need to maintain clear separation of concerns: transitioning between pages. For our sample application, when users tap on a book, they will be taken to another page. This page contains a pivot view that lets the user flip through the characters, places, plots, inspirations, and scenes for that book.

How do you transition from one page to another when tapping on an item should be handled by the view model and not the code-behind? Isn't it a violation of concern separation to directly instantiate the details page from the master page and navigate to it? This particular debate will probably rage on for hundreds of years, but my personal view is that if I can avoid a direct coupling between the pages, I will.

Take a look at the XAML for the declaration of my list box:

```
<ListBox x:Name="bookListBox"
        ItemsSource="{Binding Books}"
        ItemTemplate="{StaticResource bookItemTemplate}"
        SelectedItem="{Binding Path=SelectedBook, Mode=TwoWay}">
</ListBox>
```

What I've done here is bind the `SelectedItem` property of the list box to a property I have in my view model called `SelectedBook`. This binding is bidirectional so I can affect the UI by changing this value from the code, or the UI can affect my code when the user taps an item. Here's the definition of my `SelectedBook` property:

```
public Book SelectedBook
{
    get
    {
        return selectedBook;
    }
    set
    {
        var oldValue = selectedBook;
        if (oldValue == value) return;

        selectedBook = value;

        // broadcast this to all listening viewmodels, not just bound UI
        RaisePropertyChanged("SelectedBook", oldValue,
          selectedBook, true);

        this.SelectedBook = null;
```

```
        // clear this so user can hit back and re-tap same item
    }
}
```

The "get" accessor is pretty straightforward here. In the setter I trap the condition that the value of the selected item changed, but the new value is the same as the old. This keeps me from republishing events that don't need to be published. Next, I use an overload of the MVVM Light method `RaisePropertyChanged` that causes a message send to take place, notifying any interested view models that this particular property changed. Next I set the `SelectedBook` property (which in turn sets the `SelectedItem` property on the list box because of two-way binding) to null. This allows the user to reselect the same book after tapping the back button to go back to the book details page. Without clearing this, users would have to tap a *different* book every time they tap the back button to go to a details screen.

So which view model should respond to this message? In the case of the sample application, I'm going to subscribe to this message in the `CharactersViewModel` class. This is because the character view is the first view in the book details pivot. I could make the book pivot view model listen for this message, but I don't actually have a view model for the pivot itself. Instead I am using the pivot as an empty shell that provides navigation between multiple views (and their corresponding view models). You'll see how this works if you look at the Mnemuse source code associated with this chapter.

Here is the code in the character view model that listens for a change in the currently selected book. First, we register for the message and call the `LoadCharactersFromBook` method in response to this message:

```
Messenger.Default.Register<PropertyChangedMessage<Book>>(
    this,
    (action) => DispatcherHelper.CheckBeginInvokeOnUI(
        () => { if (action.NewValue != null)
                LoadCharactersFromBook(action.NewValue); }));
```

The following is the implementation of the `LoadCharactersFromBook` method:

```
private void LoadCharactersFromBook(Book b)
{
    if (b == lastBook) return;
    lastBook = b;

    PhoneApplicationFrame frame =
      (PhoneApplicationFrame)App.Current.RootVisual;
    if (!frame.CurrentSource.ToString().Contains("BookPivotView.xaml") )
        frame.Navigate(new Uri("/BookPivotView.xaml", UriKind.Relative));

    Debug.WriteLine("Loading characters from book '" + b.Title + "'");
    Characters.Clear();
    for (int x = 0; x < 5; x++)
    {
```

```
        Character c =
         new Character
          { Name = b.Title + " character " + (x + 1).ToString() };
        Characters.Add(c);
    }
}
```

First there is a check to see whether the book being loaded is the same one the view model loaded last time. If so, the method cancels. This prevents the application from accidentally navigating to a detail view when a book is deleted from the middle of a list (for fun, comment out this guard clause and see how it affects the application's behavior).

Next you see we're getting a reference to the phone's application frame. If the application is not currently sitting on the book pivot view page, this code navigates to it. Finally, there is some code to populate the list of characters with some dummy data that we'll need to replace with real data from a service provider.

This, by pure happenstance, leads me to my next topic: service providers.

Using Service Providers

As the name implies, a service provider does just that: provides a service. From a programming and patterns standpoint, a service provider is an abstraction around a particular logical grouping of functionality. One reason to use service providers in an MVVM application is to take care of data persistence. In this case, I want a service provider based on an interface so that I can swap it out easily in the future with something else. For example, my first implementation of a service provider is going to be one that takes model data and communicates with isolated storage. In the future I might want to swap this out with a service provider that communicates with a web service. Even further into the future, I might want to write a service provider that talks to a web service and keeps local caches of web service queries in persistent isolated storage for those occasional periods of time that the application cannot establish a network connection.

The first thing I want to do is define an interface for my service provider:

```
using System;
using System.Collections.Generic;
using System.Linq;
using System.Text;

namespace Mnemuse.Model
{
    public interface IMnemuseServiceProvider
    {
        void SaveCharacters(Guid bookId,
        IEnumerable<Character> characters);
        IEnumerable<Character> LoadCharacters(Guid bookId);

        void SaveBooks(IEnumerable<Book> books);
```

```
    IEnumerable<Book> LoadBooks();
  }
}
```

It's a fairly simple interface at this point, but will be expanded in the future. It is responsible for saving characters, loading characters, saving books, and loading books. Next comes the concrete implementation of this interface. Note that this service provider operates only on objects in the Model namespace—it doesn't know anything about view models or view model objects, and that is by design.

```
using System;
using System.Net;
using System.Windows;
using System.Windows.Controls;
using System.Windows.Documents;
using System.Windows.Ink;
using System.Windows.Input;
using System.Windows.Media;
using System.Windows.Media.Animation;
using System.Windows.Shapes;
using System.Collections.Generic;

namespace Mnemuse.Model
{
public class MnemuseServiceProvider : IMnemuseServiceProvider
{

    public void SaveCharacters(Guid bookId,
      IEnumerable<Character> characters)
    {
        IsoStoreHelper.WriteGraphToFile(
          bookId.ToString() + "-chars.dat", characters);
    }

    public IEnumerable<Character> LoadCharacters(Guid bookId)
    {
        return IsoStoreHelper.ReadGraphFromFile<Character[]>(
          bookId.ToString() + "-chars.dat");
    }

    public void SaveBooks(IEnumerable<Book> books)
    {
        IsoStoreHelper.WriteGraphToFile("books.dat", books);
    }

    public IEnumerable<Book> LoadBooks()
    {
```

```
        return IsoStoreHelper.ReadGraphFromFile<Book[]>("books.dat");
    }
}
}
```

Remember the `IsoStoreHelper` class we wrote a couple chapters ago? It's going to come in very handy for the implementation of our service provider. Now that we have a service provider, we need to make sure that each of our view models is given a proper reference to this service provider without violating any concerns. This sounds like an ideal job for the `ViewModelLocator` class, which is responsible for creating instances of new view models. I've modified this class so that it hands a reference to a service provider instance in each of the view model constructors (which means I've also modified the view model constructors to expect objects of type `IMnemuseServiceProvider` as a constructor parameter).

To put this service provider to use, let's modify the `AddBookToList()` method in the `MainViewModel` class to include a call to the service provider. This will persist the modified book list to isolated storage every time it changes.

```
private void AddBookToList()
{
    Random r = new Random();
    Book b = new Book {
        Title = "Book " + r.Next(1, 100).ToString(),
        Description = "This is a new Book",
        ID = Guid.NewGuid()
    };
    Books.Add(b);
    serviceProvider.SaveBooks(this.Books.ToModelArray());
}
```

Note the call to the `ToModelArray()` method that appears to be part of the observable collection of books in the property called `Books`. Instead of violating our separation of concerns by adding custom methods to a custom class to translate between model and view model, I've created some static extensions that convert between model and view model domains:

```
public static class BookExtensions
{
public static Book[] ToModelArray(
    this ObservableCollection<ViewModel.Book> sourceBooks)
{
    List<Book> bookList = new List<Book>();
    if (sourceBooks != null)
    {
        foreach (ViewModel.Book book in sourceBooks)
            bookList.Add(new Book
              {
```

```
                    ID = book.ID,
                    Description = book.Description,
                    Title = book.Title
                });
    }
    return bookList.ToArray();
}

public static ViewModel.Book[] ToViewModel(
    this IEnumerable<Book> sourceBooks)
{
    List<ViewModel.Book> bookList = new List<ViewModel.Book>();
    if (sourceBooks != null)
    {
        foreach (Book book in sourceBooks)
            bookList.Add(new ViewModel.Book
            {
              ID = book.ID,
              Title = book.Title,
              Description = book.Description });
    }
    return bookList.ToArray();
}
}
```

Although these extensions aren't part of the types they're extending, when the extensions are in scope it looks like they are methods on those classes. This gives me the capability to translate between model and view model domains without corrupting either the
model or the view model object; I can do the translation in a class separate from either
domain.

The AutoMapper

There is a project available on CodePlex that is an implementation of the "mapper pattern." This class essentially automates the conversion between domain models when the
property names and data types of those classes match. You can also define custom mapping rules that aid in mapping from one object type to another. For example, we could
use this automapper to map from a `ViewModel.Book` to a `Model.Book` instance rather
than using the static extensions I've written previously. At the moment, my models are
simple enough that I don't feel the need to use the automapper. If the complexity rises,
however, I might need to go get this. Fortunately, a WP7 port is available on Jay Kimble's
SkyDrive. You can read his blog post here: http://jaykimble.net/my-library-port-
releasing-continues-automapper-and-castlecore-for-wp7.aspx. I've taken the liberty
of creating a tinyurl for this in case you don't feel like typing the preceding one:
http://tinyurl.com/automapper-wp7.

Now that we've modified the view model to save the list of books to isolated storage, we need to modify it to read from isolated storage when the view model is created by the view model locator. I've added a method called `LoadBooks()` to the `MainViewModel` class which reads books from isolated storage by way of the service provider, uses the static extensions to convert from model to view model domain, and then populates the view model accordingly. Because the view model is data bound, it will see this newly loaded data immediately.

```
private void LoadBooks()
{
    Books.Clear();
    IEnumerable<Book> books = serviceProvider.LoadBooks().ToViewModel();
    foreach (Book b in books)
        Books.Add(b);
}
```

I strongly encourage you to go open up the Mnemuse code sample for this chapter. Play around with navigating between the master view (books) and the details view (the pivot page with a character view model bound). Create books, delete books, exit the application, and return to the application. This will help you get a feel for how all the various parts of MVVM are coming together to help you build a more organized, clean, well-structured application.

As a user exercise, make the calls to service provider asynchronous and turn on an "indefinite" progress bar while calls to the service provider are happening. To do this, you can make use of the callback pattern (much like the delegate pattern or completion blocks for you iPhone developers) to call code when the service provider is finished, which will turn off the "busy" indicator. The busy indicator can be bound to a view model property, so all you really need to do is toggle the Boolean value of an `IsBusy` property to let your users know when data operations are in progress.

Summary

Building "hello world" samples in any language, for any platform, for any device, is relatively easy. Taking the syntactical knowledge you've learned from building dozens of "hello world" applications and applying that to the construction of a well-organized application that will stand up to real-world development life cycles and withstand the rigor of multiperson development teams consisting of designers and developers alike is a daunting task.

This chapter provided you with an overview of the Model-View-View-Model pattern and how it differs from traditional and iOS MVC implementations. Using the MVVM Light toolkit for Windows Phone 7, you can build some pretty complex applications without creating complex, difficult to read and maintain code. By keeping your concerns separate, making sure that each of your application components has clearly defined roles and responsibilities, and by using some lightweight tools and controls, you're well on your way to making applications that you can be confident will stand up to the demands of the WP7 Marketplace users. In the next chapter, we'll look at how to automate testing and create unit tests for applications written using MVVM.

Unit Testing and TDD

The bitterness of poor quality remains long after the sweetness of meeting the schedule has been forgotten.

Anonymous

This chapter provides you with an overview of unit testing and the concepts behind test-driven development (TDD). In the previous chapter we started looking at what it takes to begin moving away from the world of simple demonstration applications and create production-ready, high-quality, complex applications.

In this chapter we'll take the next step. Now that we've started writing code in a way that separates concerns, we're going to take it one step further and write code that is testable. As you'll see throughout this chapter, we'll do this by writing unit tests and exploring TDD concepts. You'll see a couple of tools and frameworks that allow you to write unit tests for Windows Phone 7 applications, and we'll compare that to the unit testing experience for iOS applications.

After finishing this chapter and before you move on to the next, you should be comfortable with the ideas, concepts, and implementation of unit tests for your WP7 applications. Hopefully, you will be excited and inspired enough to want to try a little TDD of your own the next time you start writing an application or module.

What Is Test-Driven Development?

Test-driven development is a software development practice that, as its name implies, embraces the idea of many short development cycles that start with (that is, are driven by) the creation of tests. The concept is to write automated tests that start out by failing. You then write the code to make these tests pass. In practice, however, TDD isn't quite that simple. This is why many books have been written on the subject, including the one most people refer to as the TDD bible, *Test-Driven Development* by Kent Beck.

Generally in TDD a developer will have been given some set of business or functional requirements. From these requirements, a developer and/or the team will come up with a list of things that a specific module of code must do. It's at this point where TDD often goes horribly, terribly wrong.

The wrong way to do TDD: Many developers new to TDD will take the functional requirements and use that to design a class. They often think they're doing "test-driven" development because the class they have designed is just empty stubs; they claim they haven't started coding yet. Next they write automated tests (we'll see some frameworks for doing this throughout the chapter, but one of the most popular in the .NET world is nUnit). These automated tests exercise the stub methods on the predesigned class. At some point developers get frustrated because the tests don't quite fit the class, and so they start rewriting the tests to fit the class. Finally, the developers quit the idea of TDD entirely because they spend so much time writing tests that "don't fit right" that they think the whole thing is a waste of time. Unfortunately, this was my first experience with TDD and I, too, thought it was a waste.

Then I was born again when I met Eric Evans, author of the book *Domain-Driven Design*. He was giving a presentation on domain-driven design at the time, and during a conversation, I managed to get him off on a tangent to talk about TDD. It was a 20-minute conversation that literally changed the way I write code.

The right way to do TDD: *red, green, refactor*.

Red, Green, Refactor

The mantra "red, green, refactor" is one that you will hear at virtually any development shop that has embraced TDD. It is a chant that, at a basic level, reminds you of the order in which you should be writing your code. There is more to it than that, however. Note that *refactor* comes *last*. This is such a wonderful nugget of wisdom stuffed densely into a single, easy-to-remember phrase.

The first thing you need to do, before you get to "red," is to push yourself away from the keyboard. Sit and think about the kind of test that you'll need to write that will get your code moving toward the end of your next sprint (if you aren't using an Agile-type process like Scrum, then replace "sprint" with "release." Then tell your boss you should be doing Scrum). When you've really thought out what kind of test you want to write, that's when you move to *red*.

Red

After you know what your test should prove, write it. This test should be small, and it must fail. The reason it fails is because you're testing a feature that you haven't yet written. There are any number of reasons that it can fail, including the fact that the class you're testing hasn't been written yet. Here, *red* can actually include the scenario where the act of writing your test causes your build to fail. Your mileage may vary, but James Shore's recommendation is that this phase takes around 30 seconds and should only be about 5-ish lines of code.

Green

Now that you've got a failing test, take another 30 seconds to write a very small amount of code. This small amount of code should make the test pass, even if you know it does so in a way that is inefficient, has a bad architecture or "code smell," or in some other way is begging to be enhanced. The bottom line here is to make the test pass, even if you're hardcoding values. This part takes some getting used to, especially for veteran "waterfall" developers who are used to spending weeks upfront figuring out what their code should look like before they write any of it. The *green* here refers to the green indicator from your automated test utility that reports all tests passing.

Refactor

Now that you've got a test that passes, you should have a feeling of confidence. This confidence comes from the fact that you know, for certain, that if you make changes to your code and the light stays green, you haven't screwed anything up. Take your hands off the keyboard and look at the code you've written. If you see room for improvement— hardcoded stuff you can take out, dependencies you can "loosen," or other "code smells" that you can fix, have at it. The trick is to make small, iterative changes while keeping the light green. If you make the light go red during a refactor, and you're really embracing the TDD lifestyle, you should feel your pulse quicken like some Hollywood hacker being forced to penetrate firewalls at gunpoint or risk losing his family. In short, you will become pathologically addicted to keeping the light green at any cost. This can be good but can also be bad—beware the desire to "cheat" just so you can get your tests passing.

For more useful tips on agile development, TDD, and the red/green/refactor cycle, check out James Shore's blog or his book, *The Art of Agile Development*. When you use this pattern often enough in your daily development, it becomes like a biofeedback system that, over time, embeds deep within your soul both a love of TDD and a bitter hatred of the color red.

Mocks and Stubs

Often one of the hardest parts of unit testing to grasp is the word "unit." When people start off testing, they will write tests and sure enough, those tests might often work, and they might even show green from time to time. The problem, though, is that the developers aren't testing code in isolation. They aren't unit testing, they are integration testing.

For example, if you test a class and that class makes a web service, database, or disk I/O call as a result of your test, this isn't a unit test. This is an integration test, and the test itself cannot be considered to be in isolation.

This is typically where developers throw up their arms and get very frustrated. "I can't test my code without calling the database!" they shout. "I can't test this class without it making web service calls!" they plead. "There's no way to test this code in isolation!" they whine. These are all actually very productive responses to the attempt to write unit tests. When you hear yourself saying any of these things, you know you've got some refactoring to do. You need to refactor your code so that it is *mockable*.

A mockable class is one that has loose coupling with its dependencies. In an ideal world, all dependent functions are performed by classes that conform to an interface or contract. In an even more ideal world, the implementation of these dependencies is supplied at runtime to the class through a constructor, through a property, or in many cases, through an Inversion of Control (IoC) framework such as Castle Windsor or Microsoft Unity.

An IoC framework's job is to look at a class, see all the dependencies (properties or constructor parameters that conform to interfaces that are referenced in configuration files), and inject an appropriate implementation of that dependency. These frameworks can often be configured to inject real implementations at runtime and mock implementations at test time.

Because, at the time of this book's writing, I have been unable to get a Dependency Injection or Inversion of Control framework working properly on Windows Phone 7 due to its limitations with Reflection, we have to create our mocks the old fashioned way: code them.

Suppose you want to create unit tests for a class called `TaxHandler`. This class takes a product Stock Keeping Unit (SKU) and a delivery ZIP code and gives back a decimal amount indicating the sales tax to be charged for that item.

As a first knee-jerk reaction, we might create a class called `TaxHandler`. Inside this class, it contains a web service proxy called `InventoryClient` that talks to the inventory service to get full pricing information. In addition, another web service proxy called `TaxClient` talks to the company's internal tax service and gets sales tax rates for particular ZIP codes. The `TaxHandler` class invokes both of these clients in the `ComputeTax` method that takes a product SKU and a ZIP code.

When we write a unit test for this application, we might manually go figure out what the sales tax rate is for ZIP code 90210, figure out the tax on a product that costs $99.99, and then run the `ComputeTax` method. Our assertion would be that the return values match the expected values. Being good little developers, we would then write two more tests: one that verifies that the wrong values won't match the actual output (for example, we deliberately set our expectations wrong and assert failure, which creates a passing test) and one test that takes completely bogus parameters such as an invalid ZIP code. Our assertion here is that an exception gets thrown. When said exception is thrown, our test passes.

We run our tests and, after a small delay, we get a green light. So what's wrong? We got a green light, so we're good under the "red, green, refactor" rule, right? Wrong. Every time we execute this test, we're making two network calls to two different web services. Our purpose in testing the `ComputeTax` method isn't to test the web services, it's only to test that the `ComputeTax` method *calls* those web services with the parameters we indicate. This is a little hard to swallow at first. The purpose of unit testing is to test each small piece of code *in isolation* (for example, as a unit). We must assume that another suite of unit tests has already proved that each of the web services function as expected. As a result, we need to mock those clients so that nothing about our unit test ever leaves a logical area, least of all an entire application tier or layer.

What if we modified the constructor of our `TaxHandler` class so that instead of creating instances of concrete web service client proxies, it accepts instances of objects that implement contracts? These contracts can correspond to the functionality of the web services, but they're just contracts. The implementation now is up to the client consuming the `TaxHandler` class. In our case, that's either the real application or a suite of unit tests.

So, in C#, we might change the constructor to look like this:

```
public TaxHandler(ITaxService taxService, IStockService stockService)
{
    this.TaxService = taxService;
    this.StockService = stockService;
}
```

Now when the client code calls the `ComputeTax` method, the `TaxHandler` class will invoke methods on objects that implement a contract. There won't be any tight coupling between the `TaxHandler` class and the physical implementation of the application tier that supports it.

Whether we use a Dependency Injection framework to automatically supply configuration-controlled instances of these objects or whether our test methods define their own implementations of these contracts, the end result is the same: We can now test just the `ComputeTax` method in isolation and verify that it does as we expect—it makes two web service calls and returns a result that is an aggregate of the results.

I'll show you more test implementations later in this chapter and walk through more examples of refactoring tightly coupled classes so that their dependencies are pulled away, allowing us to test in isolation. This is especially useful when we want to test view model classes like the ones we created in the previous chapter.

Unit Testing iOS Applications

Back in the early days of iPhone development, the unit testing framework that was bundled with Xcode for desktop Mac development, SenTest, didn't work properly on the iPhone. With newer versions of the iOS SDK, however, unit testing capabilities are built right into Xcode for any of your iOS projects. Thankfully, you don't have to install any additional software, nor do you have to do any extra configuration. As you'll see later in the chapter, in the area of unit testing Microsoft suffers from a bit of "v1-itis" in that the first release of its tools are just not mature when it comes to built-in support for TDD and unit testing.

Unit testing support within Xcode is based on the open-source unit testing framework SenTestingKit. This framework has classes and command-line tools that will help you build automated tests and, ideally, embrace TDD within your iOS applications.

You can write two different kinds of unit tests in iOS: logic tests or application tests. In general, you can think of logic tests as what we might think of as traditional unit tests, and application tests might be considered integration tests or UI automation tests.

Logic Testing

To set up logic testing in your iOS application, you'll need to create a new target. I like to put the suffix "Test" (or better yet, "LogicTest") on the end of my target name so I can quickly and easily determine the purpose of the target without relying on a cheat sheet. In the past, I have had Xcode applications with so many different targets that I had to keep a piece of paper nearby that explained each target and its purpose. If this ever happens to you as an iOS developer, know that if you continue down this path, you could conceivably rip a hole in the fabric of space-time itself.

After you have a logic testing target bundle created, set it as the active target. Next, create a new file by selecting the File, New File menu option and pick iOS, Cocoa Touch Class, Objective-C test case class from the available templates. Regardless of whether I'm writing tests for iOS or for WP7, I prefer to have a single test class for a single target class. In other words, if I have a class called `Porsche` and I want to test it, I will create a single test class called `PorscheTests` or `PorscheLogicTests`. Empty out the class header file so it contains an empty interface, as shown:

```
#import <SenTestingKit/SenTestingKit.h>
#import <UIKit/UIKit.h>

@interface PorscheLogicTests : SenTestCase {
}
@end
```

Next, empty out the implementation with the exception of a single passing test method, as shown:

```
#import "PorscheLogicTests.h"

@implementation PorscheLogicTests
- (void) testPassesAlways {
    STAssertTrue(TRUE, @"This test always passes.");
}
@end
```

When you compile the active target (your logic test target), the compilation will fail if any of your unit tests fail, and the compilation will succeed if any of your unit tests pass. This is a very important distinction because these tests are executing at build time. Any runtime facility on which your code relies for functionality will not be available during these tests. For that you'll need to write application tests.

The reason I'm showing you this is so that if you're already familiar with logical unit testing on iOS, it won't look at that different to you when we start writing Windows Phone 7 tests. If you've never seen iOS code before, this is a good example of one area where the two environments have common ground based on time-proven standards such as automated testing.

All the information you need for setting up logic tests in iOS can be found on the developer.apple.com website.

Application Testing

Building a suite of application tests is similar to building logic tests. The difference is that instead of creating a new target that executes tests at build time, you create a clone of your application target. Into this cloned application target you insert application tests. These will execute at runtime when your target clone is running either on a tethered device or in the simulator. This gives your tests the capability to run atop dependencies such as hardware, OS facilities, and other runtime facilities not available to logic tests (such as a functioning UI). I won't get into the details of how to create the application test bundle because Apple does an excellent job of documenting the process on its developer website, and this is a WP7 book, after all.

In this sample taken directly from Apple's documentation, you can see that an application test has access to everything that the running copy of your application does:

```
#import "MyAppTests.h"


@implementation LogicTests
- (void) testAppDelegate {
    id app_delegate = [[UIApplication sharedApplication] delegate];
    STAssertNotNil(app_delegate, @"Cannot find the application delegate.");
}
@end
```

Unit Testing Windows Phone 7 Applications

At the time of the writing of this book, native tool support for Windows Phone 7 unit testing within Visual Studio 2010 is completely nonexistent. However, I am writing this book on the first nonbeta release of the development tools, and Silverlight itself doesn't have any native Visual Studio 2010 unit test tooling. You must use an open source toolkit that you have to download from codeplex.

Given the speed with which Apple integrated the unit testing framework directly into its iOS development tools, I have to assume that Microsoft will follow similar suit. The more developers who use Silverlight as their primary development framework on Windows Phone 7, the more demand there will be for better integrated unit testing tools. So the next time you see a Microsoft evangelist or group product manager, make sure you yell at them and complain about the sad state of affairs when it comes to their unit testing capabilities on Windows Phone 7.

However, unit testing is still possible and relatively painless, depending on the approach you take. The following section walks you through the various ways you can get unit testing to work on Windows Phone 7. I also provide my recommended approach (at least the one I recommend given the tools available to me at the time I wrote this book).

Working with nUnit

Several guides available on the Internet at the moment explain various ways to get nUnit working for Windows Phone 7. In general, what you do is this:

- Download a Silverlight 3 port of the nUnit 2.5.5 library.
- Download the Silverlight Unit Test Framework, a part of the full Silverlight (not WP7!) version of the Silverlight Toolkit available from silverlight.codeplex.com.
- Create a new Silverlight Unit Test application and drop the framework target from Silverlight 4 to Silverlight 3.
- Add references to the Silverlight 3 ported versions of the nUnit assemblies.
- Add a reference to the WP7 application from the Silverlight unit test framework.
- This is where it gets fun: Unload the Silverlight project, edit the .csproj file, and manually edit the `ProjectTypeGuids` XML element so that VS2010 will allow references to WP7 projects and class libraries.
- Make some adjustments to the metadata configuration of the Silverlight Unit Test Framework so that it will execute nUnit tests instead of Microsoft Test (MSTest) tests.
- If you've managed to do all this without messing anything up, in theory you can use nUnit to execute tests against your Silverlight application. However, it isn't always that easy, and the presence of references like GalaSoft's MVVM Light framework only serves to complicate things further.

For this last reason, among many others, I don't recommend that you bother with trying to get nUnit tests working on Windows Phone 7. I am a huge fan of the nUnit test framework, and in general I prefer it to that of the MSTest framework. However, the tooling and integration support for Windows Phone 7 are just not available at the moment.

The other thing I don't like about this approach is that the test execution environment is a real Silverlight environment. Despite the hackery done to the Visual Studio projects, it is still possible that the tests you write could attempt to do something that isn't possible in a Windows Phone 7 application and your tests will still pass. I much prefer executing my unit tests in a true WP7 environment, as I'll show in the next section.

If, by the time you have purchased and read this book, the native support for nUnit on WP7 has gotten better, easier to use, and more integrated into Visual Studio, by all means feel free to use that as your testing framework of choice.

Working with the Silverlight Unit Test Framework

As I mentioned in my discussion of unit testing on Windows Phone 7 with nUnit, unit testing integration with the native tools and the IDE is virtually nonexistent at the time of this book's writing. Getting Silverlight unit testing working on Windows Phone 7 feels a little on the "hack" side. However, it is worth it if you are at all interested in TDD or automated unit testing. We can also rest assured that in the future the unit testing experience will only get better.

To get started, you need a Silverlight 3 version of the Silverlight toolkit available at http://silverlight.codeplex.com. If you go there today, you will find the Silverlight 4 toolkit and the Silverlight for Windows Phone 7 toolkit. The Silverlight 4 toolkit is incompatible with Windows Phone 7 (you cannot add a reference to SL4 assemblies from a WP7 project) and the Windows Phone 7 toolkit doesn't contain the Silverlight Unit Testing framework. This is where things start feeling somewhat hackish.

If you don't feel like scouring the Internet for precompiled Silverlight 3 binaries containing the Silverlight Unit Test framework, you can use the ones I've included in the code samples that accompany this chapter. These are prebuilt SL3 assemblies that you *can* reference from a Windows Phone 7 application. With that in mind, let's get testing.

First, you'll need an application that you plan to test. For the rest of this chapter I'll continue to use the Mnemuse application because it's already an MVVM application that should, in theory, make it slightly easier to test than a traditional application. Second, you'll need an application that will contain the tests.

If you've ever done any unit testing in Visual Studio 2010 before, or if you've used the nUnit test runner, this should seem awkward. If you've done unit testing in iOS before, this should feel like creating a new application target for application tests. The reason is that there is no UI in Visual Studio 2010 to display the results of tests, nor is there an integrated test runner. In short, we need a WP7 application that will execute our tests and display the results. Thankfully, 99.9% of that UI comes from the Silverlight Unit Test Framework and is compatible with Windows Phone 7.

Now that you have two applications in your Visual Studio 2010 solution—a WP7 app that is your real app, and a WP7 app that is your test app—you need to add some references to the test app:

- A reference to your real application (in our case. this is the Mnemuse project).

- A reference to Microsoft.Silverlight.Testing (this came from the SL Unit Testing framework, often affectionately referred to as SLUT).

- A reference to Microsoft.VisualStudio.QualityTools.UnitTesting.Silverlight (also from the v3 SLUT binaries).

- A reference to GalaSoft.MvvmLight.Extras.WP7.

- A reference to GalaSoft.MvvmLight.WP7.

With those references in place, you now need the UI that will display the results of test execution. Fortunately, the Silverlight Unit Testing Framework's UI is more robust than just a simple display of test results. It actually allows you to selectively choose which test suites you plan to run (you can tag your tests with keywords, as you'll see shortly). Injecting this UI into your test application is fairly simple: All you need to do is modify your MainPage.xaml.cs file so that it looks like the code in Listing 17.1.

Listing 17.1   **MainPage.xaml.cs—Injecting the SLUT Harness UI**

```
using System.Windows;
using Microsoft.Phone.Controls;
using Microsoft.Phone.Shell;
using Microsoft.Silverlight.Testing;

namespace Mnemuse.Tests
{
public partial class MainPage : PhoneApplicationPage
{
    // Constructor
    public MainPage()
    {
        InitializeComponent();

        this.Loaded += new RoutedEventHandler(MainPage_Loaded);
    }

    void MainPage_Loaded(object sender, RoutedEventArgs e)
    {
        SystemTray.IsVisible = false;

        var testPage = UnitTestSystem.CreateTestPage() as IMobileTestPage;
        BackKeyPress += (x, xe) => xe.Cancel = testPage.NavigateBack();
        (Application.Current.RootVisual as PhoneApplicationFrame).
          Content = testPage;
    }
}
}
```

Now we've got an application that has all the right references; its main UI will now provide an interactive means by which we can execute tests and see the results. What could possibly be left to do?

Oh yeah. We need tests.

Just to see whether the whole testing framework is working, we're going to create a test class with a single test. This single test will always return true. If we run the application and then run all the tests (which happens automatically if we don't tap anything for a few seconds), we should see a single successful test. If we see that, we know that at least the unit testing framework is working properly.

Create a new subfolder in the test project called Tests (we will be needing other folders later, in case you're wondering if this is redundant). In that folder, put a test class called EmptyTest containing the code shown in Listing 17.2.

Listing 17.2   **EmptyTest.cs**

```
using Microsoft.VisualStudio.TestTools.UnitTesting;
using Microsoft.Silverlight.Testing;

namespace Mnemuse.Tests.Tests
{
[TestClass]
public class EmptyTest : SilverlightTest
{
    /// <summary>
    /// This method tests the actual test harness to make sure we
    /// always get a green light when there are no tests in the system.
    /// </summary>
    [TestMethod]
    [Description(
      "This is a dummy test that will always pass. If this fails, test framework
is broken.")]
    [Tag("framework")]
    public void AlwaysTrue()
    {
        Mnemuse.ViewModel.Book b =
          new ViewModel.Book(); // make sure we can see our target app!
        Assert.IsTrue(true);
    }
}
}
```

The first thing you should notice is that the test class inherits from the base class SilverlightTest. This isn't completely necessary for empty tests like this one, but when we start writing tests of any complexity, it becomes more important to use this base class.

Next you'll see the TestMethod attribute. Every method decorated with this attribute will be available to the test execution harness. We also provide a description of the method, and then we provide a tag using the Tag attribute. The test execution harness lets us run all tests that match a particular tag or set of tags. This comes in handy if we only want to run select test suites at a given time rather than running every visible test.

Finally, I created an instance of the view model in the test application just to prove that we have unfettered access to that project. If creating this instance threw an exception, we would know that we have some issues with the plumbing of our test harness and need to fix it before proceeding with any other testing. Last, we just Assert that the value true is true. This should always create a "green" (passing) test, as shown in Figure 17.1.

Figure 17.1   A passing test in the SLUT WP7
test harness UI.

Now that we're confident that the unit testing framework configuration is working properly and that the test execution UI will work, let's write a more complicated unit test. Had we been doing TDD all along, one of the tests we might have written is that whenever the `RemoveBookCommand` command is executed on an individual book, this execution results in the sending of a `RemoveBookMessage`.

This might seem like a trivial test to write, but we need to consider that messages are sent asynchronously. We'll need to be able to assert that a message was sent. But how do we do that if the message is sent in the background? The answer is our unit test needs to subscribe to this message. The problem then becomes one of correlating the asynchronous reception of this message with the execution of the unit test. Thankfully, the Silverlight Unit Test Framework comes with a very handy attribute that we can use to decorate methods specifically for this purpose: `Asynchronous`.

Create a new test class called `BookTest` in the Tests folder and make the code look like that of Listing 17.3.

Listing 17.3   **BookTest.cs—Asynchronous Unit Testing**

```
using Microsoft.Silverlight.Testing;
using Microsoft.VisualStudio.TestTools.UnitTesting;
using GalaSoft.MvvmLight.Messaging;
using Mnemuse.Messages;
using Mnemuse.ViewModel;
```

```
using System.Diagnostics;

namespace Mnemuse.Tests.Tests
{
[TestClass]
public class BookTest : SilverlightTest
{
    [ClassInitialize]
    public void Init()
    {
    }

    [TestMethod]
    [Asynchronous]
    public void RemoveCommandExecuteSendsMessage()
    {
        Messenger.Default.Register<RemoveBookMessage>(this,
            (m) => {
                Debug.WriteLine(
                  "Received book removal message from Book view model.");
                EnqueueTestComplete();
            });
        Book b = new Book();
        b.RemoveBookCommand.Execute(null);
    }

    [ClassCleanup]
    public void Cleanup()
    {
    }
}
}
```

The key here is the `EnqueueTestComplete` method. An asynchronous test method without this call will never finish, and a test that never finishes is a failing test. We call this method as soon as our test code receives the `RemoveBookMessage`. Because our test code is the only code sending messages at the time, we know that the Book model passed our test because we executed the `RemoveBookCommand` and, as a result, asynchronously received a `RemoveBookMessage` instance.

If we wanted to be a bit more thorough in the unit test, we could make sure that the removal message we receive contains the same book that we created for the test:

```
[TestMethod]
[Asynchronous]
public void RemoveCommandExecuteSendsMessage()
{
```

```
      Book b = new Book();
      Messenger.Default.Register<RemoveBookMessage>(this,
          (m) => {
              Debug.WriteLine(
                "Received book removal message from Book view model.");
              Assert.AreEqual(b, m.Book);
              EnqueueTestComplete();
          });
      b.RemoveBookCommand.Execute(null);
}
```

Mocking and Stubbing

We are now happy developers filled with the confidence and joy that can only come from having built a set of tests that produces a 100% passing (green) result. With this newfound confidence, we dive into the next view model: `MainViewModel`.

`MainViewModel` is created by and maintained by the `ViewModelLocator`. I want to make sure that my view model testing mimics as closely as possible the same situations that are present when the application is running, so I want to get my test instance of `MainViewModel` from the `ViewModelLocator` class.

I've been around the testing block a few times, so I know that the service provider is a dependency that will completely mess up my capability to test in isolation. I'm going to need to create a dummy one of those that my view model can use during testing. I'll need this for two main reasons: first, to remove a dependency on the underlying persistence mechanism from the view model (which could be a web service instead of isolated storage) and second, to guarantee predictable values as a result of service provider method calls. These predictable values give me the values against which I can compare during my assertions.

As a result, my service provider is built against an interface. This lets me create a mock service provider, as shown in Listing 17.4.

Listing 17.4   **MockMnemuseServiceProvider.cs**

```
using System;
using Mnemuse.Model;
using System.Collections.Generic;

namespace Mnemuse.Tests.Mocks
{
    public class MockMnemuseServiceProvider : IMnemuseServiceProvider
    {
        private List<Book> bookList;
        private List<Character> characterList;

        public MockMnemuseServiceProvider()
```

```
        {
            bookList = new List<Book>();
            bookList.Add(new Book
{ ID = Guid.NewGuid(), Title = "Mock Book 1",
  Description = "Mock Book Number 1" });
            bookList.Add(new Book
{ ID = Guid.NewGuid(), Title = "Mock Book 2",
  Description = "Mock Book Number 2" });

            characterList = new List<Character>();
            characterList.Add(
              new Character { Name = "Mock Character 1" });
            characterList.Add(
              new Character { Name = "Mock Character 2" });
            characterList.Add(
              new Character { Name = "Mock Character 3" });
        }

        public void SaveCharacters(Guid bookId,
         System.Collections.Generic.IEnumerable<Character> characters)
        {
            characterList.Clear();
            characterList.AddRange(characters);
        }

        public System.Collections.Generic.IEnumerable<Character>
           LoadCharacters(Guid bookId)
        {
            return characterList.ToArray();
        }

        public void SaveBooks(
          System.Collections.Generic.IEnumerable<Book> books)
        {
            bookList.Clear();
            bookList.AddRange(books);
        }

        public System.Collections.Generic.IEnumerable<Book> LoadBooks()
        {
            return bookList.ToArray();
        }
    }
}
```

I could have used a tool like Moq that lets me define expected return results from various method calls, and Moq would then dynamically construct a bogus object in memory and save me the effort of hand-coding the mock class. This is perfectly valid, and I do this all the time for my desktop and web applications. Again, I might have chosen this route had all of the other unit testing integration been cleaner and simpler. In the future I would hope the act of getting nUnit and Moq working on a WP7 application in Visual Studio 2010 will be an utterly brainless effort. Until then, pick and choose your hackish implementations at your discretion.

Arrange, Act, Assert

When writing unit tests, there is a mantra that many people recite to help keep those tests organized: arrange, act, assert.

- Arrange—Set up everything that needs to be set up at the beginning of your unit test. This includes creating instances of objects under test, creating instances of mock objects, initializing dummy data, and so on. Note that some or all of the arrange step can take place in a method marked as `ClassInitialize` that executes once to initialize any state global to that test class.

- Act—After everything is set up as it needs to be to prepare for the test, you act. This means invoking the method or module under test and storing the result.

- Assert—When you have finished acting, you should have a set of variables that indicate the values you expect to see, and you should have a set of variables that contain the results of the act phase that are the actual results. This is now where your test performs assertion that the expected values match the actual values (or that no exception was thrown, an expected exception was thrown, and so on).

So let's see what it looks like when we try to write a unit test for our `MainViewModel` class using the dummy service provider following the "arrange, act, assert" mantra, show in Listing 17.5.

Listing 17.5   **MainViewModelTest.cs—Arrange, Act, Assert**

```
using Microsoft.Silverlight.Testing;
using Microsoft.VisualStudio.TestTools.UnitTesting;
using Mnemuse.ViewModel;
using Mnemuse.Model;
using Mnemuse.Tests.Mocks;

namespace Mnemuse.Tests.Tests
{
[TestClass]
public class MainViewModelTest : SilverlightTest
{
    private MainViewModel main;
    private IMnemuseServiceProvider dummyProvider;
```

```
    [ClassInitialize]
    public void Init()
    {
        dummyProvider = new MockMnemuseServiceProvider();
        ViewModelLocator.CreateMain();
        main = ViewModelLocator.MainStatic;
    }

    [ClassCleanup]
    public void Cleanup()
    {
        main.Cleanup();
        main = null;
    }

    [TestMethod]
    [Description(
"Verifies that executing the AddBookCommand adds a book to book list")]
    public void AddCommandExecuteAddsBook()
    {
        // Arrange
        int oldBookCount = main.Books.Count;

        // Act
        main.AddBookCommand.Execute(null);

        // Assert
        Assert.AreEqual(oldBookCount + 1, main.Books.Count);
    }
}
}
```

This all looks pretty straightforward. Looking at the code for the AddCommandExecuteAddsBook method, we can see the three steps of the mantra. In the arrange step, we take a snapshot of the number of books currently stored in the view model. We then act by executing the AddBookCommand. Finally, we assert that, after our actions are completed, we have one more book in the list than we started with.

This seems okay, but at this point something is making the hair on the back of my neck stand up, and it's not my cat breathing on me. I created the dummy service provider; I created the view model and initialized it; I arranged, acted, and asserted.

Oh no.

I've got no way of telling the view model to use the dummy service provider! I know that whenever a book is added to the view model, the service provider is invoked to save the book's model. This might (accidentally) work for isolated storage, but if I move to a web service, my testing is going to get ugly quickly. This is why the test cycle is called "Red, Green, Refactor" not "Red, Green, You're Done."

Refactor. Again.

Thankfully, we don't have to do much to make this work. We just need to add a public setter to the `ServiceProvider` property on the `ViewModelLocator` class. This will let us supply our own implementation of a service provider so that when the `CreateMain()` method of the `ViewModelLocator` class is called, the `MainViewModel` class will be handed the appropriate service provider instance.

Here's the new `ServiceProvider` property:

```
public static IMnemuseServiceProvider ServiceProvider
{
    get
    {
        if (serviceProvider == null)
            serviceProvider = new MnemuseServiceProvider();
        return serviceProvider;
    }
    set
    {
        serviceProvider = value;
    }
}
```

Then we modify the `Init()` method on our test class to make sure the `ViewModelLocator` class uses the dummy service provider:

```
[ClassInitialize]
public void Init()
{
    dummyProvider = new MockMnemuseServiceProvider();
    ViewModelLocator.ServiceProvider = dummyProvider;
    ViewModelLocator.CreateMain();
    main = ViewModelLocator.MainStatic;
}
```

Now we can run our test application to see whether we end up completely green. As shown in Figure 17.2, we do indeed have a 100% pass rate on our unit tests. We can now proceed with TDD to add new features and functionality to our view models, as well as create additional unit tests to test functionality that might have already been written. This ensures that, going forward, we can be confident that new code additions don't break code that used to work.

Figure 17.2   All tests are green.

Summary

Developer opinion about unit testing varies widely. Some developers think it's a complete waste of time in the face of actual, manual, physical testing of the application. Other developers will do it, but only because their bosses make them do it. Yet other developers are passionate to the extreme about unit testing and won't let QA even see a running version of their application until they've gotten as close to 100% code coverage with unit tests as possible.

I'm not here to preach to you about whether you should be doing unit testing or test-driven development. This chapter provided you with an overview of how TDD and unit testing can be done on Windows Phone 7, and we compared that experience with a little sample of how unit testing works in the iPhone world. Unit testing using Visual Studio 2010 for Windows Phone 7 is still an early experience and has a lot of room for improvement. However, don't let that keep you from doing it. Building unit testable applications doesn't just make them testable. As you saw during the last refactor session in this chapter, in the process of making a class testable, you often find ways to refactor that can make the class better, less loosely coupled, more cohesive, and so on.

Now that you're well armed with the capability to create applications, create view models, and identify areas where you can keep the concerns of your application separate, you're ready to move on to the next few chapters, including security, social networking and gaming, and deploying applications to the Marketplace.

18

Building Connected Social Games

Just play. Have fun. Enjoy the game.

Michael Jordan

This chapter sheds some light on the oft-neglected arena of casual gaming on mobile devices. When developers think of mobile games, they typically think of OpenGL ES games for iOS devices such as the iPhone and iPad, or they think of Direct3D via the XNA developer toolkit on Windows Phone 7. The goal of this chapter is to remind you that there are more gaming options than going with high-production, render-engine type games. There is a lot to be said for favoring gameplay, community, and connectivity over graphics.

Many of today's most popular mobile games are popular more because of their social aspects and pure, simple gameplay and less because of their graphics (although making a game look good certainly doesn't hurt).

This chapter discusses the connected, social gaming features that are available on today's modern mobile gaming platforms such as Windows Phone 7, the iPhone, and the iPad. After discussing these features, I'll talk about the features that are available in Apple's gaming toolkit and how you might go about implementing those features as a Windows Phone 7 developer. By the time you finish reading this chapter, you should have a good handle on the capabilities, benefits, and drawbacks of Windows Phone 7 when it comes to building community-oriented gaming experiences. If you want to know how to build arcade-style, fast-paced 3D or 2D games using Direct3D on Windows Phone 7, you'll want to pick up a book on XNA Game Studio 4.0. XNA Game Studio is beyond the scope of this book.

If you have no interest in creating games for Windows Phone 7 or learning about mobile gaming in general, feel free to skip this chapter. Then, when you realize you really did want to know about mobile gaming, feel free to come back and read it. This chapter is as much about game theory and concept as it is about game development.

Features of Connected Mobile Gaming Platforms

In this next section I want to spend a little bit of time talking about mobile gaming platform features. Before I get to a straight-up comparison between iOS and Windows Phone 7, I want to make sure that you know exactly what I'm comparing and why. To that end, I'll spend a little time talking about the features that I consider essential to a modern, connected, highly social gaming platform. Remember that I'm not comparing features that show up only in high-end graphical mobile gaming platforms such as the Nintendo DS or the Sony PSP, just features that enable multiplayer gaming and social features like cooperation, competition, leaderboards, achievements, and so on.

Lobbies and Matchmakers

Many multiplayer games need some way for players to find each other. This is because not all games allow you to play against or with people standing right next to you. It's not only possible, but it is becoming increasingly common that the other players in your game are in different locations, time zones, or even countries.

These games need some way of figuring out who the players are and what devices they are using. Typically, these games have a limited number of players and the gaming sessions are temporary. In other words, the game world in which these games take place isn't persistent. You might see games like this where players take part in matches of a strategy game, individual sessions of chess, or specific multiplayer missions of a combat or military simulation game.

In multiplayer games where small groups of players meet up and take part in a short-lived gaming session, there is usually a piece of software running on a server somewhere that is responsible for putting these players together and facilitating the multiplayer session startup and teardown. These software agents are usually referred to as *lobbies* or *matchmakers*.

To summarize, these agents are typically responsible for some or all of the following:

- Locating players based on any number of filters, including geographic, game preferences, relative skill level, status of locked or unlocked portions of the game, and so on
- Facilitating communication between players after they are grouped together
- Facilitating the transition of players from a lobby to an instance of a running game
- Handling the transition of players from a terminating game instance back into a lobby

When playing games on consoles like the Xbox 360, these lobbies often contain rich displays of statistics or information about the map or game session that is currently loading. Additionally, if the system allows voice communication in-game (both Xbox 360 and iOS GameCenter games have this capability), players can often communicate while waiting in the lobby to formulate strategies, talk about the impending zombie apocalypse, or discuss the latest changes in the weather.

Whether you write the code for the lobby on your own servers, write lobby code that gets hosted on a third party, or whether your gaming framework provides lobby facilities on your behalf, transient multiplayer gaming sessions are rarely possible without some kind of lobby or matchmaking agent.

Leaderboards and Achievements

When you stop to think about some of the gameplay elements that create the most memorable, most addictive, most highly played games, those elements can often be boiled down to two core features: *progress* and *competition.*

Mobile devices are inherently different from consoles with controllers that are typically hooked up to ridiculously large televisions and absurdly loud surround-sound systems. Typical mobile gamers want to pull out their phone when they're bored or idle for a few minutes and pass that time playing the game. When reality calls, they want to put the phone back in their pocket and go on with their lives. As a result, your game needs to compel people to come back into the game, to keep playing long after they initially purchased the game.

One way game developers get players to continually come back for more is through *progress.* Whether it's by having a hero gain experience points, levels, gold, and loot through adventuring, or whether it's by accumulating stats such as kills or wins, players crave progress. They love that there is something tangible (as tangible as a bunch of bytes in a portable device can be) to show for their effort—that their increasing skill at the game is rewarded in some way.

Another way to show players' progress is through a reward system. Games with these features are becoming increasingly popular. Facebook is positively littered with reward-based games where people have long ago lost track of the original plot of the game and are purely in it to collect as many rewards as possible. Games can give out badges, achievements, or awards for accomplishing something that took a lot of effort, time, exploration, or just plain luck. Players love the sense of accomplishment they feel when they look at the collection of awards they've amassed.

As players gain in experience, points, levels, and amass their horde of achievements, they can compare that progress against friends they know as well as the rest of the world. This is where leaderboards come in. Games that keep track of the top players in a variety of categories give players incentive to keep coming back to play more and more, hoping that eventually they might get their name to show up on one of the global leaderboards. Fame is a big motivator for many gamers, whether that fame involves being better than their co-workers or better than the rest of the world.

As with lobbies and matchmaking agents, some gaming platforms come preloaded with APIs for manipulating achievements and leaderboards, and some require you to maintain your own. Whether you roll your own achievements and leaderboards or whether you use the ones provided by your gaming development platform, don't underestimate the addictive replay value that progress and competition can add to an already great game.

Turn-Based Game Play

When we think about multiplayer games, often our minds drift to scenes of players furiously kicking, punching, shooting, or scoring goals against other players. Although this is certainly a common type of game, on mobile devices it's often not the most popular way of doing multiplayer games.

On mobile devices, the network connection is prone to brief interruptions. If you're on a train that goes under a tunnel, if you step into an elevator, or stand under a steel bridge, you can lose your cellular data connection. If you're playing a high-speed, fast-paced multiplayer action game, this kind of connection interruption can rapidly sour you on the entire gaming experience as you watch your player die a horrible, lag-induced death. There is a kind of multiplayer game that is more suited to mobile devices that experience random periods of poor-to-nonexistent connectivity: turn-based games.

Think about the simple games of chess, checkers, Battleship, Go, or Connect 4. These games are all turn-based games. From an occasionally connected mobile device, these types of games can be lots of fun when tailored to the on-the-go lifestyle of the typical smartphone user.

Instead of sitting down in a room together to play chess, two people can maintain a long-running game of chess that might last for days or weeks. When your opponent makes a move, your smartphone can get a push notification to let you know that your opponent moved. This lets you either make your move right away, or you can put the phone away and make your move later. It's a very loose, casual style of gameplay that fits extremely well as a multiplayer mobile phone game. These types of games are also often very easy to build in UI frameworks like Silverlight or Apple's UIKit, and graphic-intense frameworks such as Direct3D and OpenGL ES are often overkill for this type of gameplay.

I was once having dinner with a friend when his phone vibrated. He pulled it out, tapped a few things, and then put the phone back in his pocket. When I asked him if it was anything important (thinking it might have been his office), he replied, "No, someone just attacked my base. I sent some troops to take care of it. You gettin' the nachos?" That's when I truly fell in love with the idea of the long-running, turn-based game as played out on mobile devices.

These games have a lot of potential from a development standpoint because it is possible to create these turn-based games with very little server infrastructure. After you've managed to find the other players for your match (see the previous section on lobbies and matchmakers), it's possible to manage the rest of the gameplay through clever use of push notifications and peer-to-peer state synchronization techniques. Additionally, the state of a match often takes very little storage space, and so a small amount of infrastructure can typically host an enormous number of long-running, turn-based games.

Real-Time Multiplayer Gaming

With this type of game, "real-time" refers to the fact that there is little to no delay between player actions and when they take place. Additionally, all the players in a real-time game often exist in the same virtual world. For example, in an MMORPG (massively multiplayer online role-playing game), players from around the world might team up to defeat a single dragon.

In another type of game, three or four players might compete on the same map in a real-time strategy game, ordering units to attack, defend, harvest, and build their way to victory. Other players in the game can react to player movements immediately, and changes to the shared game state are reflected in real-time on every player's device.

Games like this are usually very heavy consumers of network resources. Depending on how the game is played, slow or intermittent network connections can mean the difference between death and victory. As a result, players usually choose to play these games over more reliable Wi-Fi networks.

Overview of Apple's Game Center and GameKit API

Now that we've gone over some of the basic terminology and concepts related to casual and social gaming on mobile devices, this section of the chapter provides an overview of what Apple provides for its iOS developers. If you're an iOS developer, some of this should seem familiar. For Windows Phone 7 developers, it might help to know what facilities are available out-of-the-box for iOS developers in terms of enabling social, competitive, collaborative, and casual gameplay.

Game Center is Apple's rough (emphasis on rough, as you'll learn by reading the rest of this chapter) equivalent of Xbox Live. It provides a core set of services to players revolving around their iTunes identity. The use of the iTunes identity makes perfect sense because most iPhone and iPad users have an iTunes account they use for purchasing applications and music.

Through Game Center, players can establish friend lists, see leaderboards, and find friends with whom to play Game Center-enabled games. The process of enabling an application for Game Center, at least from an AppStore point of view, involves checking a box in iTunes Connect indicating that Game Center is enabled for the application.

Achievements

Achievements (or badges, awards, or whatever you want to call them) are unlockable rewards given to players who perform specific tasks in a game. These tasks can be anything from killing a certain number of enemies, dying in a spectacular fashion, or finding a hidden area on the map.

An API that is part of GameKit allows you to query for the list of achievements a player has already unlocked within your game. You can also programmatically grant or revoke achievements. The list of achievements that are possible in your game, including the culture-localized descriptions of those achievements, are all defined by logging into the iTunes Connect portal and modifying the Game Center settings for your application. To unlock an achievement, just pass the unique ID of the achievement to the appropriate method in the GameKit API.

The GameKit API is isolated. This means that you are limited by the API to only reading and writing data that pertains to your application. You cannot query the list of achievements earned from other applications, nor is there a global achievement list. This view differs from the classic Xbox Live view, where you can navigate to a list of every unlocked achievement in every game by viewing the gamer's profile.

Leaderboards

Leaderboards, also configurable through iTunes Connect, allow your application to keep track of statistics of players and make those statistics available globally. Any device running your application can access the global leaderboards. All you need to do is set the numeric value for a particular player's profile, and the leaderboard configuration does the rest.

You can rank players by kill count, experience points, levels, or any other arbitrary value that is representable as some number. Again, the leaderboards are sandboxed to your application so that your code has access only to leaderboards belonging to your application. Your app can access the leaderboards programmatically to provide a custom or themed UI, or it can launch the standard Game Center Leaderboard UI.

Networking API

Just providing unfettered access to leaderboards and achievements makes writing Game Center games with GameKit a compelling proposition. Add the fact that GameKit also comes with a robust set of networking APIs, and Game Center games become a nearly irresistible target for independent and, in many cases, commercial game developers.

The GameKit APIs provide the capability to find friends and other nearby players through a number of means. First, the application can use stock UI dialogs provided by Apple to find players nearby through either Bluetooth or on the local Wi-Fi network. If this isn't enough, the game can use custom services written by the game developer or global services provided by Apple for finding connected friends, regardless of the means by which those friends are connected.

Once in the game, GameKit provides developers with the capability to halt game sessions programmatically. They can also send messages containing arbitrary data to individual players or all connected players, facilitating both direct and broadcast data.

This means that a Game Center game developer can create a multiplayer game that allows friends to play with each other anywhere in the world *without having to write a single piece of server code or pay the expense of standing up a game server in the cloud*. Certainly some larger and more involved games might need their own custom game servers, but the fact that the basics are already provided for Game Center developers *for free* makes it a very appealing platform.

In-Game Voice Chat

Without having to know the first thing about audio recording, transcoding, or Voice Over IP (VoIP), developers can add audio chat channels to the game data communication channels already available to Game Center games.

For example, if you were building a Battleship-style game on Game Center, you could provide the capability for your players to talk to each other live while playing the game, as well as utilize the GameKit API for sending game-data messages to transmit the moves players make during each turn. You could even bring more people into the game as observers that could participate in the chat channel and watch the action but not actually play. All of this is available to Game Center developers as part of the basic development kit, and none of these features require game developers to host their own game server.

Connected Gaming Options for WP7

The following section describes the facilities available to Windows Phone 7 developers for building casual, social, and connected gaming experiences. Remember that at the time of the writing of this book, the Windows Phone 7 SDK is a v1.0 product, whereas Game Center wasn't introduced to the iPhone until after the third major release of that platform. For three releases, developers had to "roll their own" gaming experiences on the iPhone and, in many cases, developers will have to do the same for the initial Windows Phone 7 SDK. Keep in mind that with the next scheduled major release of Windows Phone 7 (code named "Mango") there are more opportunities and facilities for game development.

Lobbies and Matchmakers

From a code perspective, lobbies and matchmakers can be boiled down to two major tasks: state management and player grouping.

The state that needs to be stored on the server is the list of players who are currently connected and running the game. Lobby code doesn't need to concern itself with offline players because they won't be able to jump into a lobby, nor will they be able to join a game. Some lobby systems also show the status of your friends, including those who are offline.

Player grouping can be as simple as randomly picking players and grouping them together, or it can be as complicated as taking into account relative skill level, gaming history within that game, game style preferences, difficulty preferences, geographic location, network speed, and even network quality (a high-speed network isn't always a good one if it regularly corrupts or drops packets). The code and logic that goes into a matchmaking server is well beyond the scope of this book.

However, if you were to write your own matchmaking server, you might want to start with a WCF (Windows Communication Foundation) service that implemented an interface like the one shown in Listing 18.1.

Listing 18.1   **IHypotheticalLobbyService**

```
using System;
using System.Collections.Generic;
using System.Linq;
using System.Text;
using System.ServiceModel;

namespace ConsoleApplication1
{
[ServiceContract]
public interface IHypotheticalLobbyService
{
    [OperationContract]
    void JoinLobby(string playerId);

    [OperationContract]
    void LeaveLobby(string playerId);

    [OperationContract]
    Player[] FindPotentialPlayers(string playerId);

    [OperationContract]
    void AddToTeam(string teamId, string playerId);

    [OperationContract]
    GameProfile TeamStartGame(string teamId);

    [OperationContract]
    void TeamQuitGame(string teamId);
}
}
```

Keep in mind that this is a random sample just to illustrate some basic concepts and should certainly not be used as a model for a real gaming lobby service.

Windows Phone 7 does not come with any lobby or matchmaking capabilities built into the SDK. The XNA Development Studio provides access to abstractions that borrow Xbox Live's lobby and matchmaking facilities; however, you need to be a full Xbox Live partner to utilize any of that code. Being an Xbox Live partner involves having already published a game for an established and recognized platform and having formally requested this partnership from Microsoft. I discuss some of the reasoning behind this mentality in the next section on leaderboards and achievements.

Leaderboards and Achievements

Just about every type of gamer, from the hardest of hardcore to the most squeamish of the casual players, loves achievements. Progress and competition are two huge motivators in gameplay, and achievements supply both of those in large quantities.

Xbox Live is world-renowned for its achievement system and the Xbox Live Gamerscore value, which is a global score that accumulates as players participate in more and more Xbox Live games. As players accomplish milestones in each game, they earn achievements, and each of those achievements is worth a certain number of points that will be added to a player's overall Gamerscore.

This gives players the sense of accomplishment as they unlock newer and even more rare and hard-to-obtain achievements. They can also compete with their friends and with the rest of the worlds through their gamer score and by trying to unlock more achievements than everyone else.

As mentioned previously, you cannot simply open up Visual Studio and start writing code that works against the Xbox Live achievement system, regardless of whether you're writing your code in XNA or Silverlight. To do anything with XBL achievements, you need to be an XBL partner with a relationship to Microsoft. This is the exact opposite of the Game Center approach where all you need to do is check a box for Game Center support, and you use a web portal to create the list of all the unlockable achievements in your game.

There is, however, a method to this madness. Consider that a Gamerscore is global. Every point you earn by unlocking an achievement in any Xbox Live game is immediately added to your global Gamerscore. Every player on Xbox Live has a Gamerscore that has the same theoretical maximum (the sum total of all points for all achievements on all Xbox Live games). If someone were to create an Xbox Live game where the degree of difficulty to unlock achievements was disproportionately easy or, worse yet, the point value of these achievements was disproportionately large, it would effectively devalue the Gamerscore point.

Think of it this way: Xbox Live is like the Old West gold rush. Everybody is playing games and, over time, they discover gold (Gamerscore points and achievements). The value of gold is relative to the amount of it in circulation. This is why the value of gold has consistently gone up over the years. If I'm holding two bars of gold that took me three years of hard, sweaty labor to obtain and someone suddenly discovers a riverbed that has more gold on it than people can mine, the three years I spent mining that gold become worthless because the same amount of gold can now be obtained with a five-minute trip to this newly discovered riverbed. Faced with this discovery, I would throw up my hands and decide that mining gold is no longer worth my time at all. I might quit the gold mining business and open my own puppet show or become a dentist.

Now think of it this way: You've just spent the last four weeks ignoring your family, friends, and personal hygiene to get all 200 achievements in Kevin Hoffman's Zombie Apocalypse Fitness and Checkers Extravaganza, the newest and most popular Xbox Live title. With unfettered access to the achievement system, someone spends a couple weeks to create a new game, Joe Cheater's Achieve-o-Rama. In this game, achievements only take a few seconds to find, and each one of them is worth a thousand Gamerscore points.

Microsoft recognizes that the relative worth of Gamerscore and achievements within Xbox Live is like an economy within itself. If someone makes a game that is somehow able to reduce the value of achievements and Gamerscore, existing players will get angry and potentially quit. New players will find little to no motivation in playing because it will be so easy to gain points that there will no longer be a satisfying sense of accomplishment that comes from earning new achievements and gaining points.

In short, if Microsoft allowed random game developers access to Xbox Live achievements, they would essentially be allowing anyone to tamper with the Xbox Live economy. In doing that, Microsoft would be ruining the experience for its incredibly large and loyal base. Many people don't realize this, but Xbox Live is currently one of the world's biggest social networks (by some definitions).

If each game could have its own sandboxed achievement and point economy, where the scale and relative difficulty of accomplishment were not relative to some global standard, Microsoft might be able to provide a centralized achievement system like Game Center.

The Future of Xbox Live on WP7

As mentioned, if Microsoft could sandbox the use of Xbox Live resources so that games could have their own local economies of achievements that did not affect global Gamerscores the way "real" Xbox Live games do, theoretically it would be possible for it to provide APIs much like the ones available through Apple's Game Center. The reason Game Center can offer Leaderboard and Achievement APIs the way it does is that the use of those APIs does not devalue in any way the effort required to unlock achievements in other games. I can spend 20 minutes and unlock 20 achievements in one Game Center game, and spend 200 hours in another and unlock only 4. Because these games don't share leaderboards or a common sense of supply and demand for rewards, each game is still enjoyable in its own right, and neither game is affected by the presence of the other on the network. Only time will tell if Microsoft will implement sandboxed Achievements and Leaderboards for mobile devices, but if you want this kind of feature (and you probably do if you're reading this chapter), be vocal: Blog, tweet, and talk to your local Microsoft Developer Evangelists and make your voice heard. Let them know how important this is to you as you consider whether to build your game for the WP7 platform.

Turn-Based Game Play

Aside from the networking facilities available to Xbox Live games written by XBL partners, there are no out-of-the-box facilities for building networked games on Windows Phone 7.

To build a turn-based game server, you basically need to maintain the state (probably in a database) of all running games. Each game usually consists of some shared game state visible to all players, as well as the list of players currently taking part in this game. If the game is a long-running game that can be advanced casually every now and then by players taking a turn here and there whenever they get a chance, you need to make sure that the games are persistent and that you have enough storage to support the shared state of however many concurrent games you think you'll need to support.

A ridiculously simple interface for a central, turn-based gaming service written in WCF might look something like the one shown in Listing 18.2. This contract assumes that games are started up and torn down by a separate lobby service, so all operations take a GUID that indicates the unique ID of the running (and persistent) game. Also remember that this is a completely far-fetched example. The theory and practices behind the design of good mobile, multiplayer games are beyond the scope of this book.

Listing 18.2   **ITurnBasedGameService**

```
using System;
using System.Collections.Generic;
using System.Linq;
using System.Text;
using System.ServiceModel;

namespace ConsoleApplication1
{
[ServiceContract]
public interface ITurnBasedGameService
{
    [OperationContract]
    TurnResult TakeTurn(Guid gameId, string playerId, TurnAction turn);

    [OperationContract]
    GameState GetGameState(Guid gameId);

    [OperationContract]
    Player[] GetPlayers(Guid gameId);

    [OperationContract]
    void SendMessage(Guid gameId, string fromPlayerId,
       string toPlayerId, string text);

    [OperationContract]
```

```
        void Broadcast(Guid gameId, string fromPlayerId, string text);
    }
}
```

The `TurnAction` class in this sample just identifies the intent of the player making the turn. The server is the final arbiter as to whether a move can be done, and it has the final say and can reject a move if there is a problem with it.

```
using System;
using System.Collections.Generic;
using System.Linq;
using System.Text;
using System.Runtime.Serialization;

namespace ConsoleApplication1
{
[DataContract]
public class TurnAction
{
    [DataMember]
    public int DestinationRow { get; set; }

    [DataMember]
    public int DestinationColumn { get; set; }

    [DataMember]
    public int GamePieceId { get; set; }
}
}
```

Again, remember that this is the first release of the WP7 SDK, and it is likely that the out-of-the-box facilities for multiplayer gaming on Xbox Live or some other isolated gaming network will improve over time. If you take some of the advice from my MVVM chapter and perform all your interactions with a gaming back-end using the "service provider" pattern, your WP7 code should be well isolated from any future changes to the gaming platform, even if you end up retiring your home-grown server in favor of running your game on Microsoft's infrastructure in the future.

Real-Time Multiplayer Gaming

The networking requirements of a real-time multiplayer game differ vastly from that of a turn-based game. Through the use of push notifications and a server-heavy back-end architecture, turn-based games can even progress while the application isn't running.

Real-time gaming often requires the use of low-level networking resources, such as sockets (especially those of the UDP variety), to get a barrage of streaming updates from the server that might include things like the ever-changing location of nearby monsters, status updates like a "heartbeat" pulse that periodically updates the client of your character's health and other status. In addition, as your character moves and interacts with the environment, a stream of information needs to flow outward from the client application so that the server can aggregate the information about how you are manipulating and interacting with your environment with the information received from all the other nearby players.

This kind of game is not only hard to implement on the server side (and often carries massive infrastructure requirements), but it's also often very difficult to implement on the client.

Windows Phone 7 does not offer access to any form of TCP or UDP sockets through its Silverlight SDK. This means that the only type of multiplayer gaming you can get at (without resorting to Xbox Live and the previously mentioned partnership with Microsoft) is going to be the consumption of web services. Web services are, in most cases, very high latency and the most efficient way to use those services is to send large payloads less often. This is the exact opposite of the way many real-time multiplayer games operate, which send incredibly frequent updates carrying small amounts of information.

There is nothing I can say here that will make this sting any less. There are a few types of architecture and design that will allow you to use web services, Silverlight, and the Windows Phone 7 networking stack (limited such that it is) to create "near" real-time multiplayer games. The design of this type of game often consists of a single, persistent game world, but it is a game world in which rapid updates are not necessary. In other words, the actions players take against and within this shared world are ones that don't require immediate actions from other players. Games like this might be games where players slowly build empires in a strategy game, but the design of the game is such that players do not need to take immediate (within a few seconds, that is) action to respond to the actions of other players.

Remember that there are optimal game designs for every type of mobile gaming platform. If the game design you're envisioning requires access to UDP sockets to stream blasts of location changes, attacks, heartbeats, and more, perhaps Windows Phone 7 isn't the platform you should be using. Think about the capabilities of the device and especially the most common usage pattern of smartphones (quick in-and-out, casual, and occasionally connected). With this in mind, you should be able to build a casual game that will satisfy plenty of smartphone users and, in the future, be able to utilize even more networking resources as both your game and the WP7 platform advance.

Summary

Windows Phone 7 is, as this book is being written, a v1 product. This means that Microsoft has had to prioritize the list of features available on the platform. Features such as fast, reliable email, web browsing, application market place, rich multimedia, and a decent camera are all features that need to be available in a v1 product.

Some of us might argue that a rich gaming platform SDK like Game Center and GameKit should be available in a v1 product, but it all comes down to building a strong base and implementing the features that smartphone features *demand*, and then progressively implementing those features that WP7 developers *want*.

Windows Phone 7 might not have the same set of out-of-the-box features as Apple's Game Center and the GameKit API that drives it on the mobile device. However, WP7 has incredibly powerful and easy-to-use web service APIs and, as you've seen, rich capabilities to build beautiful, powerful, and smooth UIs that can be used for business or entertainment.

If you take some of the advice learned in the previous chapters around practices for testing applications and using MVVM to build loosely coupled apps, you can use patterns like the service provider pattern to wrap your implementation of gaming services and back-ends in v1 of your product. Then, as Microsoft develops more capabilities for those of us who are not Xbox Live partners into the WP7 SDK, you will be able to quickly and easily adapt to those features, and maybe even retire infrastructure and resources you have running in the cloud that were used to support v1 of your game. In the next major release of Windows Phone 7, Microsoft has stated that it will be allowing Silverlight applications to take advantage of Xbox Live libraries, providing wider potential for casual and indie game developers.

The goal of this chapter has been to inspire you to create a Silverlight-based Windows Phone 7 game. Although some of the social, connected, multiplayer features such as achievements, leaderboards, and peer-to-peer networking APIs might not be available today, nothing is stopping you from building a great casual game now and adding these social features as Microsoft expands the SDK, or rolling your own and replacing your implementation with Microsoft's in the future.

Securing WP7 Applications

Security is mostly a superstition. It does not exist in nature,
nor do the children of men as a whole experience it.
Avoiding danger is no safer in the long run than outright exposure.
Life is either a daring adventure or nothing at all.

Helen Keller

This chapter covers the increasingly important topic of security. Users of smartphone applications, especially those who use their smartphones for work, both expect and demand that the phones and the applications running on them are secure.

Unfortunately consumers and developers often have different definitions of security. To add to the confusion, device manufacturers have certain expectations about what developers will do to secure their applications, and developers have expectations about what device manufacturers will do to maintain the security of the device, the platform, and the operating system.

In this chapter I attempt to clear away some of the ambiguity surrounding the definition of secure applications, devices, and application platforms. In addition, I'll show you some of the built-in security features of the Windows Phone 7 platform and take you through some code samples for encrypting your application's data for secure storage.

What Is a Secure Application?

Security is more about perception than it is about reality. The truth is that given sufficient time, resources, and motivation, in most cases thieves will eventually be able to get what they want from your application.

A secure application is one that makes certain guarantees to the user about the safety of the information contained within that application. In addition, a secure application is also one that, if it were to fall into the wrong hands, would not divulge any trade secrets or sensitive information by virtue of its own source code.

The real trick in building secure applications isn't necessarily making them secure. The trick is making them secure and still providing a good user experience. I have found that an inverse relationship exists between the ease with which a user can interact with your application and the security level of that application. Somewhere right in the middle of that curve is a sweet spot where you have enough security to be practically secure, and you are still providing a compelling, enjoyable, and seamless user experience. Adding more levels of security at this point typically involves herculean coding efforts for little noticeable effect, and removing security from this point can often compromise the entire application's security for barely noticeable improvements in user experience (UX).

An example of where making incremental changes to security can dramatically affect usability is with CAPTCHAs. CAPTCHAs are those prompts we often see on sites that ask us to type in the characters we see in an image. Some of these are fairly easy to read for a human, and I have no trouble satisfying the website's requirement that I am not a robot. However, some sites thought that the CAPTCHAs were too easy for character recognition software to interpret, so they made the characters within the images warped and distorted, and some created hashing effects over the top of the characters to further thwart the attempts of "bots" to read these characters. The problem is that these characters are now so hard to read that I regularly convince sites that I am indeed a robot simply because I can't read the CAPTCHAs. Some let you listen to the CAPTCHAs, but I find the audio recordings even harder to interpret. In my opinion, this is the digital form of the childproof cap for medications. At some point a certain level of security will annoy your legitimate users far more than it deters the illegitimate ones. Many forms of software copy protection, including digital rights management (DRM) for multimedia files, are often more annoying to the people who actually purchased the item than to the ones pirating the items. The last thing you want to do with your application is annoy your users.

The moral of the story is this: If you want to make a secure application, make it secure enough to satisfy your users and not a drop more. Every drop of security you implement above and beyond what is both *practical* and *acceptable* will manifest itself as an annoyance to your users, not a comfort. Different applications in different industries and genres will have different "sweet spots," but taking the time and effort to find the right one for your application is well worth it.

A Fool and His Money

Thomas Tusser, an English farmer and writer, once said, "A fool and his money are soon parted." I have my own version of this saying, "A fool and his money are soon parted because the fool left his safe unlocked."

The world of security, cybercrime, and encryption is full of incredibly complicated topics, concepts, and algorithms. With the massive amount of material available to both enlighten and confuse developers, learning about security can be a daunting task.

To simplify things and to give you a mental image to carry with you when thinking about the security of your own application, consider the following allegory:

You have a very valuable document that contains various account numbers and other pieces of information that, if used by the wrong people, could do a lot of harm. You place this document in the glove compartment of your car and lock the door. Passengers get in and out of your car and, despite their casual attempts to open the glove compartment, none of them see your document. Your friend asks to borrow your car and you're concerned that she could open your glove box and see the private document. Instead of telling your friend she can't borrow your car simply because there's a sensitive document contained within, you give your friend the valet key. This key operates the ignition and the trunk, but will not open the glove box. Your friend returns the car and you check to see that the sensitive document is still safe and secure. Over time you take for granted that your sensitive document is safe, snug inside your car. One day you get out of the car for a minute to grab a coffee. You leave the keys in the ignition and your car is stolen. The thief, who was completely uninterested in your sensitive document, accidentally stumbles on it and eventually sees it for its true value. All your efforts to lock the document in the glove box, giving your friend the valet key, ended up being for nothing because you left your keys in the ignition.

A fool and his data are soon parted because he left the keys in the ignition.

This analogy leads to what is quite possibly the single most important rule of securing sensitive data: *Never, ever leave sensitive data and the mechanism to unlock that data stored on the same physical medium.* If your sensitive data is in the glove box, don't ever leave your keys in the car. If your sensitive data is inside a combination safe, don't ever leave the combination to that safe written on a post-it note in the same house. If you lock your house and expect it to stay that way, don't leave a spare key under a flowerpot by the front door. If you have encrypted data on your windows phone, don't ever store the encryption key on your windows phone. *Ever.*

WP7 Secure by Default

Out-of-the-box, a host of features built in to the Windows Phone 7 platform provide peace of mind for developers and users alike. They include the following:

- Applications are tested, digitally signed, and securely installed on WP7 devices via the Marketplace. This means malicious applications like the ones that plague desktop platforms today can't make their way onto a device.

- SSL is available for communicating securely with back-end services. This gives the developer and user peace of mind knowing that transmitting sensitive information to and from the device cannot be "overheard" by malicious applications anywhere in the middle.

- Applications run inside a secure sandbox with private, inaccessible isolated storage files. Data your application stores in isolated storage can be read only by your application.

- Exchange policies can be used to require phones to enforce a PIN lock code and enable remote wiping of devices. This helps in a corporate environment, ensuring that employees using WP7 devices have passcode-protected phones that can be remotely wiped in case they are lost or stolen.

On most modern desktop operating systems, you will find some mechanism for managing encryption keys. Mac OS X has an application called the Keychain. This application serves as a vault in which encryption keys and certificates (which contain key pairs) can be stored. Much like the glove box holding an important document, the Keychain application is like *another* glove box, which holds a key to the real glove box. Microsoft Windows has a certification store that serves the same purpose. Both of these facilities are accessible programmatically through secure APIs.

Using these APIs, your application can generate a random key and store it in one of these secure repositories and freely use this key to encrypt and decrypt data (the next section of this chapter discusses encryption). These repositories give your applications secure access to the keys without letting anyone (or any application) else see them.

This type of key repository is not available on Windows Phone 7. There is no platform-provided secure means by which you can securely store and use encryption keys. In the next section on protecting data, I'll discuss some of the ways you can still safely protect data on a Windows Phone 7 device without the aid of a key storage facility.

Protecting Data

For many of the most common application scenarios, the security already provided by Windows Phone 7 might be entirely sufficient. Given the relatively small chance that someone might steal a phone owned by one of your users and then find a way to hijack it (decouple it from Zune and the security around the file system in much the same way that iPhones can be "jailbroken"), and then find the isolated storage file for your application, many developers are perfectly fine accepting that level of risk. This might be because the data their application stores isn't sensitive or their users are okay with that level of risk to their personal information.

On the other hand, some developers and users might not be okay with this level of risk. This could be because the users absolutely insist that it be physically impossible for someone to compromise their information or because the type of application has compliance regulations that dictate data protection standards, such as an application that stores patient medical information.

So how do we protect data on a Windows Phone 7 device? We already know that we can't securely store the encryption key on the device using some kind of platform-level key storage service like the ones available on the desktop OS. Also, thinking back to the rules of data security I mentioned earlier in the chapter, we know that we can't store the key in the same physical medium as the data the key protects. In other words, I can't put the encryption key in isolated storage. If both my encryption key and my encrypted data are in isolated storage, I've gone to all that effort of encrypting my data for nothing. This is the equivalent of leaving a spare key under a flowerpot in front of your house. If a thief is standing outside your house looking for a way in, the thief is going to find your spare key. If a hacker has your isolated storage files, the hacker is going to find your encryption key.

One option might be to assign the application a globally unique ID (GUID). Then, when the application needs access to the data, it makes an SSL call to a web service with this GUID and gets in return the encryption key. There are two problems with this scenario. The first is that now you have to figure out how to secure the web service call so that a hacker can't just get the GUID from your app (remember, if they can see your isolated storage, they can see this ID) and make the web service call himself. The second is that this is a type of security that I call "shell game security." You aren't actually adding a level of security, you're just hiding the real security method underneath one of three shells. If a hacker gets into the phone and therefore into your isolated storage file, this level of indirection will probably only slow him down for an few extra minutes. You have to ask yourself if slowing a hacker down for a few minutes is worth days or weeks of development effort. It usually isn't.

The user experience versus security diminishing returns curve also applies to time-to-market. Security features are time-consuming to build and often difficult to implement, and you should always ask yourself whether a given feature is worth the time spent, especially if it might not actually prevent intrusion.. This would be like spending months hand-building a fence around your yard to protect your house—except that the fence is only two feet tall.

The code sample that I'm going to show will ask the user for a password. This password is then going to become the key used to encrypt and decrypt application data in isolated storage. I call this type of key storage mechanism a "meat key," as in a key that is only found in "meatspace" (that area of the universe inhabited by humans as opposed to the Internet). Feel free to reuse that term, I won't charge royalties. Some people call them "passwords," but I prefer "meat key" when these passwords are used specifically for encryption purposes.

There is a definite trade-off here: We've given up a little user experience by forcing the users to type a password every time they launch the application. Remember, we can't store that password for convenience because that's the old "key under the flowerpot" problem. This kind of trade-off should be made only if your application must have this level of security, or if the users of your application are the ones demanding this kind of security. If it was their idea, they're not likely to gripe about having to enter a password. If they choose to store that password on a sticky-note attached to their phone, that's their problem—not yours.

In this next sample application, we'll create a single page with a few controls on it. First, we'll need a text box for entering in the data we want to encrypt, and then two more text boxes—one each for the password and the salt, respectively.

The password and salt are both concepts that apply to the generation of a cryptographic key. A lengthy explanation of what a salt is and how it applies to cryptography is beyond the scope of this book. For now, think of the salt as a way of providing even more uniqueness to the cryptographic key that we're calling a password. As shown in Figure 19.1, the application UI prompts the user for a password, a salt, and some data to encrypt. Chances are that your end users will not know what a salt is. For this reason I often use the UI to label the password as a "username" and the salt as a "password." Usernames and passwords are concepts most users are familiar with, but a staggeringly small portion of the general public is familiar with the concept of a salt as it relates to cryptographic keys.

Figure 19.1   Encryption demo application.

Listing 19.1 shows the code-behind for MainPage.xaml.cs, the code that drives the encryption sample. The first thing you might notice is the use of the `AesManaged` class. This class is one of several cryptographic service providers that are available to Windows Phone 7 applications. This class provides developers with access to symmetric encryption. Symmetric encryption is where the key used to encrypt data is the same as the key used to decrypt it. The opposite of this is asymmetric encryption, also commonly referred to as public/private key encryption. This is because in asymmetric encryption, a private key is used to encrypt data, and the public key is used to decrypt the data. Because our application is using a single meat key generated by the user typing in a password and a salt (or username and password in more user-friendly terminology), we will be using symmetric encryption.

The next thing you might notice is an obscurely named class, `Rfc2898DeriveBytes`. This class is used specifically to derive a cryptographic key from a password and a salt, as you can see by the parameters to this constructor of this class. The `Key` and `IV` (initialization vector) properties of the `AesManaged` class are then set by getting bytes from an instance of `Rfc2898DeriveBytes`. The specific size of the `Key` and `IV` are recommendations from Microsoft. Again, if you're looking for a more in-depth discussion of why these values are the way they are, check out the MSDN documentation on encryption and security or consult your favorite book on encryption algorithms.

Next you'll see that I'm using the `CryptoStream` class. This class takes as constructor arguments a stream (in our case a memory stream), an encryptor or decryptor, and finally an `enum` value indicating whether the stream is being opened for reading or writing. This is an incredibly handy class because after you have a `CryptoStream`, it automatically takes care of encrypting or decrypting for you. Data that is written to a cryptographic stream is automatically processed by the encryption provider. As you can see in Listing 19.1, we use the `CreateEncryptor()` and `CreateDecryptor()` methods of the `AesManaged` class to create streams that either encrypt or decrypt data that is written to the stream.

Last, you might see something that we covered in the chapter on isolated storage. We're using the `IsolatedStorageSettings` class to read and write application settings. In this case, the setting is encrypted so that even if the application and the phone were to be compromised, the data salvaged by a hacker would be useless without the password and the salt, which are not stored anywhere on the device. You don't have to use this class, you can use the `IsolatedStorageFile` class to read and write entire object graph hierarchies in encrypted format, ensuring that every single piece of data in your model is secure.

Listing 19.1   MainPage.xaml.cs Encrypting and Decrypting Data

```
using System;
using System.Windows;
using Microsoft.Phone.Controls;
using System.Security.Cryptography;
using System.IO;
using System.Text;
using System.IO.IsolatedStorage;

namespace EncryptionSample
{
public partial class MainPage : PhoneApplicationPage
{
    // Constructor
    public MainPage()
    {
        InitializeComponent();
    }

    private AesManaged GetAesWithKey(string password, string salt)
    {
        AesManaged aes = new AesManaged();
        Rfc2898DeriveBytes keySource =
          new Rfc2898DeriveBytes(password, Encoding.UTF8.GetBytes(salt));
```

```
        aes.Key = keySource.GetBytes(aes.KeySize / 8);
        aes.IV = keySource.GetBytes(aes.BlockSize / 8);
        return aes;
    }

    private string EncryptString(string secretText,
     string password, string salt)
    {
        AesManaged aes = GetAesWithKey(password, salt);
        MemoryStream ms = new MemoryStream();

        CryptoStream cs = new CryptoStream(ms,
          aes.CreateEncryptor(), CryptoStreamMode.Write);
        byte[] secretBytes = Encoding.UTF8.GetBytes(secretText);
        cs.Write(secretBytes, 0, secretBytes.Length);
        cs.FlushFinalBlock();
        byte[] encryptedBytes = ms.ToArray();
        ms.Close();
        cs.Close();
        return Convert.ToBase64String(encryptedBytes);
    }

    private string DecryptString(string encryptedText,
      string password, string salt)
    {
        AesManaged aes = GetAesWithKey(password, salt);
        MemoryStream ms = new MemoryStream();
        CryptoStream cs = new CryptoStream(ms,
          aes.CreateDecryptor(), CryptoStreamMode.Write);
        byte[] secretBytes = Convert.FromBase64String(encryptedText);
        cs.Write(secretBytes, 0, secretBytes.Length);
        cs.FlushFinalBlock();
        byte[] decryptedBytes = ms.ToArray();
        return Encoding.UTF8.GetString(
          decryptedBytes, 0, decryptedBytes.Length);
    }

    private void decryptButton_Click(object sender, RoutedEventArgs e)
    {
        if (!IsolatedStorageSettings.ApplicationSettings.
             Contains("secret"))
          MessageBox.Show(
"You haven't stored a secret string in isolated storage yet.");
        else
        {
            string encrypted =
```

```
            IsolatedStorageSettings.ApplicationSettings["secret"].
              ToString();
          string decrypted =
            DecryptString(encrypted, passwordBox.Password,
              saltBox.Password);
          MessageBox.Show(
            "Decrypted secret text from Iso Storage:\n" +
            decrypted);
      }
  }

  private void encryptButton_Click(object sender, RoutedEventArgs e)
  {
      string encrypted =
       EncryptString(secretDataTextBox.Text,
         passwordBox.Password, saltBox.Password);

      IsolatedStorageSettings.ApplicationSettings["secret"] = encrypted;

      string decrypted = DecryptString(encrypted,
        passwordBox.Password, saltBox.Password);
      MessageBox.Show("Encrypted text:\n" + encrypted + "\n" +
          "Decrypted again:\n" + decrypted + "\n");
  }
}
}
```

If you're running this application in the simulator, you might notice that every once in a while you'll get a message indicating that you haven't stored an encrypted string yet. This is because the simulator will, depending on certain situations, empty out isolated storage for installed applications.

Protecting Intellectual Property

So far we've covered a few of the ways that you can keep malicious hackers away from your data. You can make sure that you always use SSL to send sensitive data, and if you absolutely need to have completely secure data, you can use the technique from the previous section to encrypt sensitive information using a password- and salt-generated key.

What about your application itself? If you've only ever built applications for the iOS platform before you might not be aware of this, but Java and .NET developers are usually aware that their source code can be reverse engineered from a compiled binary.

If someone were to download your application and somehow manage to copy the Silverlight .XAP (think of this as an iOS "bundle") file to a local hard drive, she could then use any number of freely available tools to decompile the binary assemblies in your application. Even though your application didn't include debugging symbols, some of these disassembling tools are so good that they can generate C# code that looks nearly identical to the code you originally wrote when building the application. Before you panic, keep in mind that the Windows Phone 7 environment is a secure environment, and the likelihood of people being able to do this is slim. It's not impossible, however, so we need to consider the possibility.

If you ignored my advice about never storing the encryption key on the same physical medium as the encrypted data, you might have hardcoded the encryption key as a set of constants in one of your classes. If someone is looking at a disassembled version of your code, even if they haven't reversed it all the way back into C# form, they can easily distinguish the encryption key, and then they will be able to gain access to *anyone's* data on any device running your application. At this point, you've just given away intellectual property because you've been using the same encryption key in *every* instance of your application.

What if your application provides some proprietary algorithm? Hidden deep within your application is some set of instructions that has taken your engineers years to develop, and it is the main reason why people buy your application—because they can't get that algorithm anywhere else. Now let's assume that a single device running your application is tampered with, unlocked, and your application is disassembled. Without much effort, a thief could reverse-engineer your algorithm and either publish it and devalue your application entirely or could release a competing application that does the same thing based on what used to be your proprietary code.

There are tools that can help thwart the tools that reverse-engineer your application binaries back into code, but all they really do is make the job of the thief more difficult. These tools never completely prevent the intrusion. In this case you need to think back to what I said earlier in the chapter—you need to weigh the development cost of implementing a security feature that will merely slow down a thief rather than stop the thief entirely. These tools are referred to as *obfuscators,* and many of them are incredibly simple to use and often take little or no time to work. One such tool that has an established partnership with Microsoft is Dotfuscator Windows Phone Edition. Preemptive Solutions, the maker of the tool, is also offering a monitoring and analytics service to give you insight into the performance of your application in the market. Dotfuscator can do some amazing things, including mask control flow, renaming, encrypt strings, and much more. A suitably complex algorithm hidden underneath a commercial-grade obfuscation tool and deployed securely on Windows Phone 7 should have little chance of discovery.

If, however, you are still paranoid about the discovery of your highly sensitive, proprietary algorithms, you need to consider one of the other rules of security that I live by daily: If you really want to secure what's on the other side of the door, make sure that there's nothing on the other side of the door when someone breaks it down.

If you absolutely cannot live with the remote possibility that someone could take a copy of your application from a device, disassemble it, get around your obfuscation, and reverse-engineer the code in your application, you still have another option: *Defer proprietary algorithm execution to a server.* If, for compliance reasons or out of pure paranoia, you can't put the algorithms in code delivered to a device, you can invoke web services on your servers that will execute the sensitive code. In this fashion you are completely in control of the sensitive code that you cannot let fall into the wrong hands. Again, as with all security decisions, you need to weigh the benefits you get from this architecture with the drawbacks of requiring a device to have connectivity to perform certain functions and the cost of maintaining the server in the cloud, and so on.

Summary

Security is important to everyone, but in varying degrees. What one user wants in terms of security is rarely the same as what another wants. Security can be enforced by regulatory bodies, compliance regulations and committees, or enforced by business people within your organization, or it can come from your own opinion of how secure your small, independent application should be.

When building security into your application, the most important thing to do is weigh the cost of implementation versus the degree of intrusion prevention you get. After you've done that, weigh the negative impact to user experience created by the security feature versus the relative degree of security added to your application. You need to weigh all these factors when building security features because if you don't, you could end up annoying your users with excessive security or losing them through ineffective or nonexistent security.

This chapter showed you how to encrypt and decrypt sensitive information, how you can transmit sensitive information over the wire (the mechanics of which were discussed in previous chapters), and some possibilities for protecting intellectual property from the eyes of unwanted intruders. Hopefully, after having read this chapter, you have a good idea of the degree and manner of security you want to implement in your application and know how you plan to go about it.

Debugging and Troubleshooting

Debugging is twice as hard as writing the code in the first place.
Therefore, if you write the code as cleverly as possible, you are, by definition,
not smart enough to debug it.

Brian W. Kernighan

This chapter discusses debugging, troubleshooting, and analyzing your applications. This is one of the most important steps in application development and is often neglected. Testing an application doesn't stop after all your unit tests pass. You need to make sure that the application runs smoothly and efficiently and, especially on mobile devices, that it isn't abusing resources. Applications that abuse mobile device resources aren't even going to be allowed into the Marketplace.

This chapter shows you how to debug applications to troubleshoot and resolve problems, and it introduces you to some of the other tools available to developers, such as static analysis and code profiling.

Debugging and Tuning iOS Applications

If you've written any iOS applications, this section of the chapter should (ideally) be very familiar to you. Xcode, Apple's development environment, sits atop an open source debugging tool called gdb, which stands for GNU Debugger and is part of the GNU project. For more information on gdb, there is a wealth of information, documentation, and training materials available on the web.

Your mileage may vary, but most developers spend most of their time in the debugger. They run their applications, they poke and prod, they hope nothing breaks, and if the debug session didn't break, the developer is happy.

If something does go wrong, you need to figure out what happened. With iOS applications, this can be particularly tricky. Because of the reference-counted memory management, you can often experience obscure bugs somewhere in your application that are caused by the mismanagement of memory in a completely separate area of the application.

This is why, in addition to the standard capability to debug, set and hit breakpoints, view stack traces and object variables, Apple also provides the capability to record the runtime memory performance of your application. You can watch for all kinds of scenarios, most of which are outside the scope of this book. The biggest, and probably most often used, detection is that of a memory leak. The profiling tool that you can launch directly from Xcode will monitor memory allocation, and it can spot orphaned objects and errors you've made in managing your memory. It takes a while to get used to this tool, but after you get the hang of it, you'll wonder how you ever managed to write applications without it.

If you're clever, you can also write unit tests that ensure that the reference counts of specific objects are identical before and after invoking some library function that you're testing. This doesn't guarantee a flawless, crash-free application, but it will at least give you a little bit of confidence before running the leak-detection tool that a particular method isn't leaking memory allocations.

As with most iOS topics, if you're curious about debugging, troubleshooting, and other low-level refinements that you're definitely going to need to do to publish an application in the App Store, check out *iPhone Programming: The Big Nerd Ranch Guide* by Aaron Hillegass. I personally consider this book the definitive bible for getting started with iPhone programming.

Debugging 101

The mantra I always use when debugging an application is this: *don't just make it break, make it break productively*. Contrary to what many developers might think, the purpose of a debugging session isn't to get from start to finish without breaking. Developers, when testing their own code, will often unconsciously avoid areas of the application about which they are uncertain. When you debug your application, whether it's for the iPhone, Windows Phone 7, or the Commodore 64, you should always be trying to break it. If you're keeping good trace logs and have well-placed breakpoints, breaking the application while under a debugger should give you the information you need to fix that bug. After you fix that one, try to break it again. You're done when you've tried every way you know how to break your application and it won't break. Then, you give it to someone else to break. Another mantra I live by is this: *Never let your customers find your bugs for you*.

Every bug a customer finds that you didn't is a chink in your armor, your reputation with your customer base. In this day of Facebook, email, and social networking across multiple devices, desktop, and mobile platforms, it won't take long for one customer's problem with your application to become everyone's problem with it. Take the extra time to find your bugs before your customers do.

Additionally, you need to make sure that your application properly handles exceptions. The Windows Phone 7 application submission guidelines for the Marketplace explicitly state that if the application ever crashes during the certification process and doesn't present the user with user-friendly, meaningful information about the problem the application just had, the application will be rejected. So not only do you need to find as many of your own bugs as possible, but your application needs to be able to withstand unexpected error conditions and handle all kinds of things that the user, the device, and the cellular network might throw at it.

Debugging Windows Phone 7 Applications

Debugging a Windows Phone 7 application is much like debugging any other application with Visual Studio 2010. If you have been following along throughout this book and running the code samples, you have seen the device emulator that gets launched when you attempt to debug a WP7 application. The application runs inside the emulator while the debugger is attached to the application's process.

This allows you to set and hit breakpoints and to stop, pause, and resume your application at virtually any point during its execution. This lets you see that things are happening the way you expect them to, and it lets you examine the values of variables and other data to help you figure out what went wrong when things do happen unexpectedly.

Using Breakpoints

In the simplest of scenarios, developers can select a line of code on which the debugger should "break" (execution of the application halts and then waits for the developer). At a breakpoint, all the execution context information is available, so you can see the values contained within variables and the call execution stack. You can choose to advance forward one line of code, you can debug "into" a method call, allowing you to follow the execution further down the rabbit hole. You can even drag the pointer indicating the currently executing line of code upward to "rewind" the application back to a particular point. The sheer number of things a developer can do with a basic breakpoint is staggering, but it gets even better.

The following is a list of some of the more advanced things that you can do with breakpoints:

- Location—This is what you normally define when you click into the margin or "tray" on the left side of your code listings in Visual Studio. A red "stop sign" indicator appears in this tray over a location that has a breakpoint set.

- Condition—You can specify a Boolean expression used to determine whether the breakpoint stops execution of the application. This comes in handy for methods that are used over and over throughout your code, but you want to stop execution only when certain conditions are met.

- Hit Count—In addition to a conditional expression, you can also define a hit count. This will allow your breakpoint to be hit "count-1" times. Execution will stop when the breakpoint is hit when the hit count limit has been reached. In other words, if you set the hit count to 10, the application will break on exactly the tenth execution of the line of code where the breakpoint has been set. This can come in handy when you want to test the nth execution within a `for` or `while` loop.

- Process and Thread Filter—You can use a combination of the variables `ProcessId`, `ProcessName`, `MachineName`, `ThreadName` or `ThreadId` to restrict the breakpoint so that it will break only for certain processes or threads. The filter clause accepts Boolean operators such as |, &, and so on to give you very fine-grained control over your breakpoint's configuration.

- Labeling—It might not happen all that often for WP7 applications, but I know that when I build larger, enterprise application suites I can end up with a VS2010 solution that literally has hundreds of breakpoints. Navigating through that mess can be a chore sometimes, and the capability to assign arbitrary labels (you Web2.0 folk can think of these as tags) to breakpoints.

- Execution When Hit—As if all the other breakpoint options weren't enough, you can run a macro or display custom text when the breakpoint does hit. Remember that all these options are cumulative, so you can have a process filter, a condition expression, a hit count, and print custom text when the breakpoint is hit. If you decide to print custom text, you can use several macros to print information about the execution context, such as: $ADDRESS, $CALLSTACK, $PID, $TID, $FUNC-TION, $TNAME, and so on. If you choose to run a macro, the macro will be one of the macros available globally to Visual Studio 2010, and you can pick the macro from a drop-down box.

One thing that I like doing with breakpoints is using the custom print text in a breakpoint "when hit" execution. In addition, I check the Continue Execution box. This allows me to print some information to the debug log (which we'll discuss in the next section in more detail) without having to write code that does that printing. This way, when I want to stop printing that debug information, I can remove the breakpoint rather than commenting out or deleting the code.

Try this out on any random project you have lying around (including any of the samples from this book). Find a spot in your code that you know is executed often and set a breakpoint there. Set it to continue execution "when hit" and print custom text. It's fine to accept the default text that Visual Studio sets for you. If you want to get a little fancier, you can enclose any value you want to display in the custom text in curly braces, as shown in Figure 20.1, which prints the currently selected index in a Pivot control every time the breakpoint is hit.

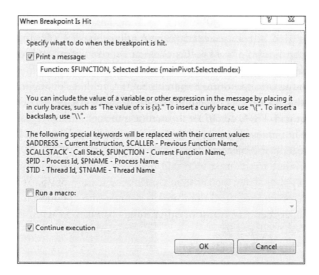

Figure 20.1   Printing custom text upon hitting a
breakpoint.

You might notice that after you make the change indicated in Figure 20.1 to a standard breakpoint and debug your application, the "red ball" shape on the left side changes to a diamond, indicating that there is more to this breakpoint than simply stopping execution on that line. As an added trick, I often label all of my "print debug" breakpoints with the same label so that I can find and deactivate them later. Another useful tip: deactivate your breakpoints instead of deleting them. This way you can turn them back on when you need them. This is especially handy for breakpoints like the one mentioned previously that prints valuable information during a debug session.

When I run the application with this breakpoint active on one of my own apps, I see messages like the following show up in my Debug output window, and execution never stops as I click between active Pivot panels:

```
Function: ApocalypseTrainer.MainPage.mainPivot_SelectionChanged(object,
System.Windows.Controls.SelectionChangedEventArgs), Selected Index: 1
Function: ApocalypseTrainer.MainPage.mainPivot_SelectionChanged(object,
System.Windows.Controls.SelectionChangedEventArgs), Selected Index: 2
Function: ApocalypseTrainer.MainPage.mainPivot_SelectionChanged(object,
System.Windows.Controls.SelectionChangedEventArgs), Selected Index: 3
Function: ApocalypseTrainer.MainPage.mainPivot_SelectionChanged(object,
System.Windows.Controls.SelectionChangedEventArgs), Selected Index: 0
Function: ApocalypseTrainer.MainPage.mainPivot_SelectionChanged(object,
System.Windows.Controls.SelectionChangedEventArgs), Selected Index: 1
```

In Visual Studio 2010, if you click the Debug menu and hover over the Windows option, you should see three additional choices: Breakpoints, Output, and Immediate.

Clicking the Breakpoints option will usually dock the breakpoints window to the bottom of your IDE but, depending on your options, it might show it as a floating window.

This window shows all the breakpoints, their labels, conditions, and hit counts for your solution. Remember when I mentioned that I often use the "labeling" feature to group all my debug-printing breakpoints together. If I use a label like "debugprint," I can then use this window to search for all breakpoints with that label by typing "debugprint" into the search box and pressing Enter. With those results in the window, I can enable or disable all those breakpoints with a single button-click, and I don't have to hunt across hundreds of files in dozens of projects to find all my breakpoints.

Before you continue to the next section, I highly recommend you spend some time playing with breakpoints. They are an often overlooked feature of VS2010. Most developers know how to stop execution all the time on a single line of code, but just as many developers forget that there are a host of other things you can do with breakpoints.

Logging and the Debug Class

You've already seen how to use a special type of breakpoint to print out information to the debug log. In this section, I'll cover a couple of techniques (as well as WP7-specific limitations) for logging other important runtime data as you troubleshoot your app.

If you've written any iOS (or Mac) applications, you're familiar with the `NSLog` function. This function is used extensively by iOS developers to keep track of important information, events, and data as it flows through the application. They use it to make sure that assumptions about data on which their code operates are correct and to print out useful information while developing an application.

The Windows Phone 7 equivalent of the `NSLog` function is the `Debug.WriteLine` method. You use this method in much the same way as you use `NSLog`—to dump whatever information you feel is important to the debug log.

Windows and web developers who have experience with Visual Studio 2010 might be a little disappointed to notice that the number of methods on the `Debug` class are limited and that the `Trace` class is missing entirely. For whatever reason, there is no out-of-the-box method by which you can trace information to a text file in WP7 like there is on desktop or server platforms with VS2010.

It's really a matter of personal preference whether you pepper your code with `Debug.WriteLine` statements or whether you use the breakpoint technique I outlined previously. I personally prefer to use the breakpoint technique because it allows me to toggle different types of output without having to delete or comment out code. Additionally, when I'm ready to submit the application for production certification through the Marketplace, I don't have to worry about tracking down all my `Debug.WriteLine` statements and removing them. On the other hand, if something about a large number of breakpoints bothers you, you might be more comfortable using `Debug.WriteLine` instead.

Using Static Analysis

So, you've been diligent and you've been creating unit tests to make sure your code does what you expect. You've been debugging your code and you've uncovered all kinds of nasty little critters, but you've also managed to squash all those bugs. You're sitting back in your chair thinking that you're ready to upload your masterpiece to the application Marketplace. *But wait, there's more!*

There's another tool in the Windows Phone 7 developer toolbox that can help hone your application code into a finely chiseled blade (a Ginsu, perhaps?). Microsoft has come up with an extensive set of rules, recommendations, and warning signs culled from years of experience and developer feedback. This set of prescriptive guidance has been integrated directly into a static code analysis tool that is built in to Visual Studio 2010. In other words, VS2010 can dig through your code and point out some very common problems and even recommend ways that you might be able to fix them.

For example, the static analysis tool can track the method calls and property accessors in your code and find areas where you might accidentally fall victim to the law of unintended consequences. A very common situation here is when code calls a property accessor and the property accessor then invokes some other function, and that function can be overridden in child classes. This creates a foggy area that allows vast amounts of code to potentially execute as a result of a simple property set that you wrote. A developer unaware of your original intent might be able to come along and override that method and neither of you might immediately notice the consequences of this. Thankfully, the VS2010 static analysis tool is aware of this and thousands of other possible "gotchas."

Figure 20.2 shows what it looks like after code analysis has been run on a Windows Phone 7 application project. To trigger code analysis, all you need to do is right-click a project and choose Run Code Analysis. This will build the application and then perform an analysis of your compiled code.

Figure 20.2   Results of code analysis on a sample project.

In Figure 20.2, you can see that I've got a couple of spots where the static analysis tool is warning me that I should check a call execution chain for unintended consequences. In one of these cases, I really do want those consequences, and I'm stubborn and my boss is yelling at me, and I need to get home to my Xbox, so I want to suppress that warning instead of looking for a way to refactor my code to avoid the warning.

There are a couple of different ways to suppress these warnings. To start, highlight the warning in the list and right-click it. When you choose the Suppress Message(s) option, you can choose to suppress the message "in source" or in a project suppression file.

If you choose to suppress the message in source, this creates an attribute that sits at the scope of the code block that violated whatever static analysis rule triggered the warning. The next time you run code analysis, this warning message will not appear.

Personally, I feel that littering my source code with attributes that only apply at build time and only during code analysis is ugly. Thankfully, I can choose to suppress the static analysis warnings in a project suppression file. If I choose this option, an attribute will be created in a file called GlobalSuppressions.cs.

Listing 20.1 shows a sample of one of the suppressions that I created to avoid doing the real work of refactoring my code.

Listing 20.1   **GlobalSuppressions.cs**

```
// This file is used by Code Analysis to maintain SuppressMessage
// attributes that are applied to this project.
// Project-level suppressions either have no target or are given
// a specific target and scoped to a namespace, type, member, etc.
//
// To add a suppression to this file, right-click the message in the
// Error List, point to "Suppress Message(s)", and click
// "In Project Suppression File".
// You do not need to add suppressions to this file manually.

[assembly: System.Diagnostics.CodeAnalysis.SuppressMessage(
    "Microsoft.Usage",
    "CA2214:DoNotCallOverridableMethodsInConstructors",
    Scope = "member",
    Target = "ApocalypseTrainer.ViewModel.FoodItem.#.ctor()")]
```

I joke about suppressing the static analysis warnings for trivial reasons, but the truth is that you should spend a little bit of time figuring out why the warning appeared and what problems are associated with that warning before you suppress it. Each one of the code analysis warnings has a unique number (such as CA2214 in the preceding sample). If you aren't sure why the static analysis tool is warning you, enter that number into your favorite search engine and see whether anything comes up. I have been pleasantly surprised at how much detail I can find online about some of the CA rules and warnings.

There is another kind of analysis that produces metrics summarizing your code. This type of analysis digs through your compiled code and computes statistics such as a "maintainability index" based on other values such as "cyclomatic complexity," "depth of inheritance," "class coupling," and even the number of lines of code.

Cyclomatic complexity (also called conditional complexity) is a metric used to indicate the complexity of a software program. It measures the number of independent paths through a particular block of source code. A cyclomatic complexity value of 1 indicates that there is only one way to get from the beginning to the end of a block of code. If you introduce an if/else block into code that had a cyclomatic complexity of 1, it will then change to 2, indicating that you can finish that block by either going through the if section or going through the else section. The greater an application's cyclomatic complexity, the harder it is to write unit tests for, and the larger the number of manual tests a developer must do to exercise all the code. This complexity grows naturally as an application grows, but you should keep an eye on it and possibly find ways to reduce this complexity by providing a more linear path through your code. Figure 20.3 shows some sample output from a static analysis run.

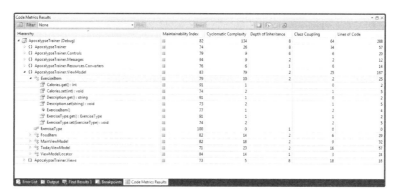

Figure 20.3   Generated code analysis metrics.

Depth of inheritance, as its name implies, refers to the depth of a class within an inheritance hierarchy. The static analysis tool scores the classes in your application with a value indicating the inheritance depth. In general, the deeper a class is within an inheritance hierarchy, the more difficult it is to predict the behavior of that class and the more complex the design. Some of this you need to take with a grain of salt because control hierarchies are often deep before you even start writing your own custom control. However, if you have a view model class with a depth of 8, you might want to consider refactoring to flatten your inheritance tree a little. Figure 20.3 shows the output of the code metrics window, including the depth of inheritance rank, cyclomatic complexity score, and class coupling value.

Class coupling refers to the number of classes on which another class depends. Suppose I've built a class and it has two properties, and each of these properties is a different class. This one class now has a class coupling value of 2 (the static analysis tool ignores built-in .NET types when determining this metric). The general consensus is that the higher the class coupling value for a class, the less stable that class is. In other words, classes with a high class coupling value are far more likely to break after a code change than classes with a low class coupling value. MVVM, as you saw in that chapter, is designed specifically to allow you to build powerful user interfaces with a minimum of class coupling. Another tip to keep in mind is that if you convert a class-typed property into an interface-typed property (allowing for easy mocking or dependency injection via tools such as Unity or Castle Windsor), this will reduce the class coupling metric.

Summary

Before we get into the nuts and bolts of submitting your application to the Marketplace in the next chapter, I wanted to make sure that I introduced you to some of the tools available to Windows Phone 7 developers for debugging, tracing, troubleshooting, and even analyzing code for areas of improvement.

One unfortunate fact of the software development life cycle is that no matter how quickly you manage to complete the main functionality of your application, it is going to take a very long time to hone, refine, tweak, and refactor your application after that point. Knowing how to use static analysis tools, debuggers, breakpoints, and the other techniques presented in this chapter will help take your application from a good app to a rock-solid, stable, reliable application that is more likely to pass the certification process.

Just remember that the purpose of debugging isn't to execute without errors; it's to find errors so that you can fix them. Try to break your application as many ways as you can and use the techniques in this chapter and in previous chapters to find and fix those bugs. Then you'll be ready to submit your application to the Marketplace and hopefully make truckloads of money.

Deploying Applications to the Marketplace

The safe way to double your money is to fold it over once and put it in your pocket.

Frank Hubbard

This chapter is all about deploying your applications to the Marketplace. You've written the code for your application and you're proud of what you've created. You have a good application icon, a tile icon, and you've mastered the techniques of concern separation (possibly with MVVM). You've tested your application with unit testing, and you've debugged it and performed static analysis on the application. You've given the code to your friends or colleagues and gotten them to run the application—and they love it. You're ready to submit your app to the store and start making giant piles of money.

In this chapter you'll see a hands-on walkthrough of taking an application from the point where you're satisfied that it's fast, stable, reliable, and complies with all the certification requirements to the point where it's been uploaded to the Marketplace and you can start collecting your money.

To do this, I'll introduce you to a sample application that I wrote called Zombie Apocalypse Trainer that, interestingly enough, falls into the Health and Fitness category of the Marketplace. I will show you, step-by-step, how I took this application and went through the entire deployment and certification process, including deploying it to a test device to make sure everything worked properly.

Introducing Zombie Apocalypse Trainer

Zombie Apocalypse Trainer is a new twist on the standard calorie-tracker application. Rather than motivating people to lose weight and keep tabs on their calories by shaming them with a log of their eating habits, this application gives people new motivation: avoiding death at the hands of hordes of brain-sucking undead.

The application asks you to set a target weight and a date by which you'd like to reach that weight. This is essentially the Zombie Apocalypse—make-it-or-break-it time. If you don't reach your target weight by the target date, the application assumes that you are simply too overweight to avoid capture and you are going to die a slow, painful death by having your brains eaten by zombies.

Here is the description of the application that I intend to use in the Marketplace:

Are you ready for the Zombie Apocalypse? When the streets are filled with rabid, brain-eating undead, will you be able to outrun them? Use this application to track your calories burned, calories eaten, and weight log. Just tell the app when you think the Zombie Apocalypse will be and start tracking your progress.

From a technical standpoint, Apocalypse Trainer is a standard Silverlight WP7 application that was built with the use of the MVVM Light framework discussed earlier in the book. I tested the application using the unit testing techniques I discussed in earlier chapters. It has three core view models: Main, Today, and History.

The Main view model contains all the information required to supply the home screen with its useful information, such as the number of days remaining until the apocalypse and how long you have gone without being mauled (without exceeding your calorie budget).

The Today view model contains the list of food items you've consumed today and the list of exercises that you've done today. This differs from the underlying persistence medium, which contains a list of *all* food and exercise since you installed the application. Remember that view models are specifically designed to support the UI in its effort to render what the user wants to see, not necessarily what the data looks like on disk (or in a database or on a web service, and so on).

The History view model contains the weight log—the history of weigh-ins since you've installed the application. As you navigate through the application, dialogs appear that allow you to create new data. These are WP7 pages that are bound to individual view models using a view model locator (again, this is all stuff we discussed in the MVVM chapter). When the user taps the Confirm button on a dialog to create a new piece of information, a message is sent using MVVM Light's messaging framework. The view model that holds the collection of items to which the new item will be added has subscribed to this message and, in response to the message, adds the appropriate item to the collection.

Whenever data in the view model changes, the view model asks a subordinate data service to make the changes permanent. In the case of Zombie Apocalypse Trainer, the persistence medium is isolated storage. I use the `IsoStoreHelper` class that was used several times throughout the book to read and write object graphs in and out of isolated storage.

When I do store information in isolated storage, I have three separate files: weight history, exercise history, and food history. The reason I do this is that these three types of view models are never created on the same screen and they are never joined to each other. This minimized the number of isolated storage writes and reads per screen. To convert the data model objects into view model objects, I used C# class extensions to convert one object type to another. Additionally, I used LINQ queries to filter the array of data in the data service to include only the current day's data when I load the view model.

This pattern allows me to do number crunching and analysis (such as determining the length of the current "days without a mauling" streak) on the entire history of information recorded by the application, but the view model displays only a subset of that information to the user. The Today screen never displays more data than what was recorded today, and the Home screen returns only the aggregate information about the days since the last mauling.

Here's some of the code in the Today view model that I used to grab historical information from the data model and convert it to a subset within the view model for rendering:

```
var todayFood =
    from FoodRecord foodRecord in DataService.FoodHistory.FoodRecords
    where foodRecord.RecordDate.Date == DateTime.Now.Date
    orderby foodRecord.RecordDate ascending
    select foodRecord;
this.FoodItems.Clear();
foreach (FoodRecord fr in todayFood)
{
    this.FoodItems.Add(fr.ToViewModel());
}
```

In this case, `DataService` is a property that contains an instance of the helper object I wrote to communicate with the three underlying files in isolated storage. This service is also responsible for computing the number of days since the last mauling. Because the view model can see only today, this naturally becomes the responsibility of the data service, which can see the history of the application since the day it was installed.

The `ToViewModel()` method is an extension method on a separate class. I used this so that neither the `Model` nor the `ViewModel` class has explicit knowledge of how to convert from one to the other, but I'm still able to do it. This is just one option; other options including using the `AutoMapper` class from codeplex, although at the time I wrote this application I couldn't find a reliable port of it for WP7.

If you want to know more about how I built this application, feel free to drop by my blog at http://www.kotancode.com, where I will be sharing stories about WP7 development in general, as well as the experiences I had while building the Apocalypse Trainer application.

Registering and Deploying to Test Devices

Before you can do anything related to the Marketplace, including test your application on a real phone, you need an App Hub developer account. This account is your publisher profile for when you create and publish applications for Windows Phone 7 or for Xbox Live.

The first thing you need to do is go to http://create.msdn.com and sign up for an account. This account will be linked to your Windows Live ID, so if you have multiple Windows Live IDs, make sure you link it to the right one.

Figure 21.1 shows the first step in account creation. In this step you choose your country of origin and whether you are going to be creating an individual account, a company account, or a student (DreamSpark) account.

Figure 21.1   Creating an App Hub account.

After you specify the type of account you want, you will need to specify your personal information and account details, as shown in Figure 21.2. I've left some fields blank to maintain some of my privacy, but you will need to provide a valid email address (you will get an email requesting that you verify this email address, so make sure it's an address that works), at least one phone number, and your home address. Don't worry, this information will not be available to people who buy your application.

Figure 21.2   Supplying additional information for App Hub account.

After you've specified your personal details, you will be asked to pay for your developer account membership. This is currently $99 per year and will allow you to submit an unlimited number of paid applications and five free applications (there is an additional per-application fee for going above the limit of five free apps).

As you go through the process, you will eventually get to step 4, account confirmation. Some time (could be from a few hours to a day) after this, you will receive an email with instructions on how to fill out a survey. This survey will ask you some very detailed questions, including the names of creditors to whom you send money and other information that, in theory, only you could know. This survey is from a company called GeoTrust, which is responsible for verifying the legitimacy of developer accounts. You cannot submit applications to the Marketplace until you have passed the GeoTrust certification process, so make certain that you pay close attention to the instructions and answer all the questions carefully.

For me, the entire GeoTrust process took about 24 hours, although I've heard that it can take a little less time; I've also heard stories where people had problems with the survey and it took several days to sort the mess out.

After your account has been certified and is considered valid, you can register up to five developer devices. To do this, plug the device in and make sure that your Zune synchronization and connection with the device is working properly.

Next, run the developer registration application that came with the WP7 developer tools. This application is installed for you as a shortcut on your start menu. If you can't find it (and you're running Windows 7), open the start menu and type the word "registration" into the search box. The autocomplete list should filter down to an application titled Windows Phone Developer Registration. When you launch the application, you will see a screen that looks like the one shown in Figure 21.3.

Figure 21.3   Registering a device for testing.

After you register a device for testing, go into Visual Studio 2010, and in the debug toolbar, change the active target from Windows Phone 7 Emulator to Windows Phone 7 Device and start a debug session. You will need to make sure that your phone is still plugged in and that if you have a PIN code lock on the device, that you have *unlocked* it before attempting to deploy the application.

Visual Studio 2010 will not deploy applications (debug or release) to WP7 devices when the home screen is currently locked with a PIN code. Always remember to unlock the device before attempting to deploy.

Prepping Your Application for Submission

Before you can deploy your application to the Marketplace, you need to make sure that a few details have been taken care of. First, you need to make sure that your WMAppManifest.xml file has been populated appropriately with your publisher information, the application title, and so on. The following is the WMAppManifest.xml file from my Zombie Apocalypse Trainer application:

```xml
<?xml version="1.0" encoding="utf-8"?>
<Deployment
xmlns="http://schemas.microsoft.com/windowsphone/2009/deployment"
AppPlatformVersion="7.0">
  <App xmlns="" ProductID="{ac5b5d62-573c-4134-b290-0ad4f678ad7f}"
Title="Apocalypse Trainer"
      RuntimeType="Silverlight" Version="1.0.0.0" Genre="apps.normal"
      Author="Kevin Hoffman"
      Description="Track your fitness progress as the Zombie Apocalypse
approaches! Will you survive?"
      Publisher="Kevin Hoffman">
    <IconPath IsRelative="true"
IsResource="false">ApplicationIcon.png</IconPath>
    <Capabilities>
      <Capability Name="ID_CAP_NETWORKING" />
      <Capability Name="ID_CAP_LOCATION" />
      <Capability Name="ID_CAP_SENSORS" />
      <Capability Name="ID_CAP_MICROPHONE" />
      <Capability Name="ID_CAP_MEDIALIB" />
      <Capability Name="ID_CAP_GAMERSERVICES" />
      <Capability Name="ID_CAP_PHONEDIALER" />
      <Capability Name="ID_CAP_PUSH_NOTIFICATION" />
      <Capability Name="ID_CAP_WEBBROWSERCOMPONENT" />
    </Capabilities>
    <Tasks>
      <DefaultTask Name="_default" NavigationPage="MainPage.xaml" />
    </Tasks>
    <Tokens>
      <PrimaryToken TokenID="ApocalypseTrainerToken"
           TaskName="_default">
        <TemplateType5>
          <BackgroundImageURI IsRelative="true"
           IsResource="false">Background.png</BackgroundImageURI>
          <Count>0</Count>
          <Title>Apocalypse Trainer</Title>
        </TemplateType5>
      </PrimaryToken>
    </Tokens>
  </App>
</Deployment>
```

A lot of this information will be rewritten by the certification process, but the essential information here is the application title, the author name, the publisher name, and the links to the artwork like Background.png and ApplicationIcon.png.

You might think that this manifest would control the name of your application as it appears when pinned to your start screen or in the list of installed applications, but this is incorrect. The application title that shows up on the phone itself after installation is controlled by a single attribute in your AssemblyInfo.cs file in the Properties folder. Here's what this attribute looks like in my AssemblyInfo.cs file:

```
[assembly: AssemblyTitle("Apocalypse Trainer")]
```

Also make sure you set the product name and copyright information in this file:

```
[assembly: AssemblyProduct("Apocalypse Trainer")]
[assembly: AssemblyCopyright("Copyright © Kevin Hoffman 2010")]
```

With this in place, build and clean your application and deploy it to a real Windows Phone 7 device. See what your application looks like in the installed applications list as well as when pinned to the start screen. Fiddle with and tweak the various manifest and application settings and properties until your application looks *exactly* the way you want it to. Only when you're done with these tweaks should you consider uploading the application to the Marketplace.

Submitting an App to the Marketplace

So, now you think you're ready to submit your application to the Marketplace. You've tested and debugged the application from every angle you can imagine, including running your application on an actual Windows Phone. If you haven't run your application on a real Windows Phone, you need to go back to the previous section in this chapter. There is no substitution for testing your application on a real device. To make sure that there are no surprises when your application is being tested and certified by Microsoft, you really need to do testing on a real device.

Assuming you've got your application ready to go, you can start the certification process by uploading it to the Marketplace. To start, go to the App Hub at http://create. msdn.com. Log in with the Live ID you associated with your developer account, and click the Submit for Windows Phone 7 button to submit a new application. Make sure you're using Internet Explorer during this process. I know this sounds silly in this modern day and age of HTML5 and high levels of browser compatibility, but I experienced utter failure during step 2 when attempting this process using Chrome. When I switched to Internet Explorer, everything worked properly.

Step 1 of application submission looks like the screen shown in Figure 21.4.

At this step you must supply information about the application, including its name, version number, target platform, and the application package itself. The application package is the XAP file that resides in the Release directory underneath your application's VS2010 project directory. There are some free-form text entry fields here for your own developer notes and notes you can supply that will be read by the certification testers.

Step 2 of the process involves the application description and categorization. Here you supply the detailed description of the application (shown in Figure 21.5), the category, subcategory, and some other information.

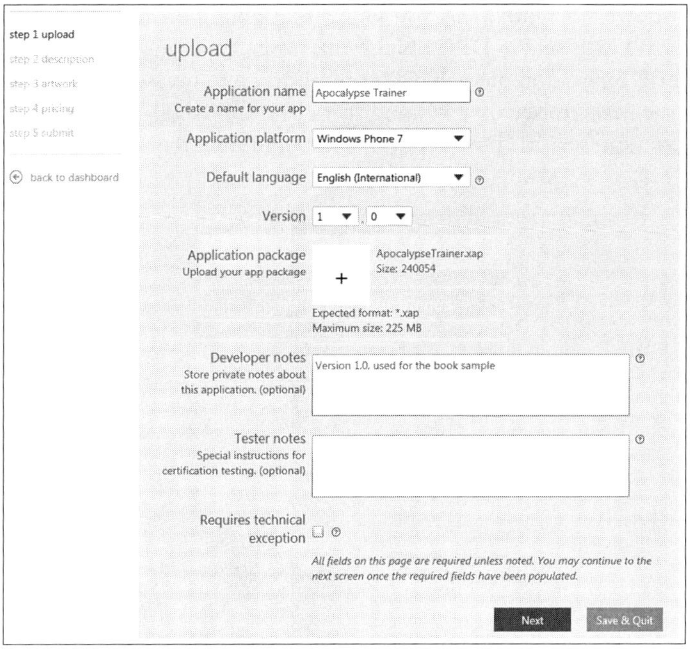

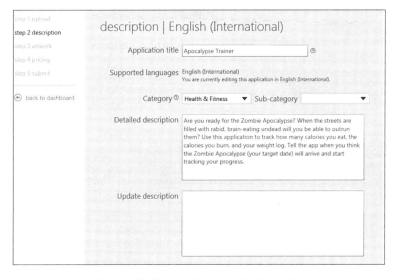

Figure 21.4   Application upload step 1.

Figure 21.5   Application upload step 2.

In step 3 (shown in Figure 21.6), you supply the application artwork. You are required to supply a 173x173-pixel (96 DPI) PNG for the large application tile, a 99x99-pixel PNG for a small application tile, a 200x200-pixel image to be used when your application is viewed in the Marketplace on a PC, and at least one 480x800-pixel screenshot. In Figure 21.6, you can see that I've supplied all the minimum requirements plus a few extra screenshots.

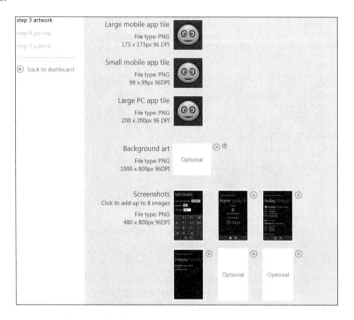

Figure 21.6   Uploading application artwork.

Remember that to get true 480x800-pixel screenshots from the emulator, you need to have the emulator set to view in Full Size. On my laptop, which is a full 1080p screen, this takes up a large portion of the screen, so you'll need to prepare for this in advance and provide enough screen real estate to see all 800 vertical pixels. This step in the submission process will reject images that are not the right size.

After you've supplied the application artwork, the description, the category, and the actual XAP package, you need to supply pricing information (shown in Figure 21.7). Here you indicate whether your application supports a trial mode, whether your application can be distributed outside your country of origin, and how much you plan to charge. Note that the application price is a drop-down box, not a free-form text box. This means that there is only a certain set of prices you can use to provide consistency throughout the Marketplace. The lowest you can charge for a paid application is 99 cents.

Finally, after you have finished providing all the details for your application, your dashboard will show all your applications and their status. As you can see from Figure 21.8, my application was ready for testing when I took this screenshot.

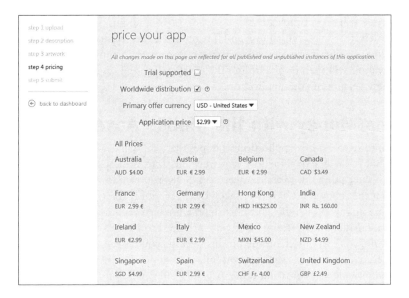

Figure 21.7   Setting application pricing.

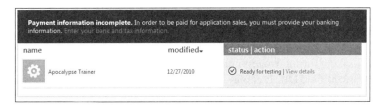

Figure 21.8   Status of application certification.

Additionally, you can see a warning message in Figure 21.8 indicating that my payment information is incomplete. In fact, I had provided the bank account information where Microsoft can deposit the millions I plan to earn as a result of hordes of Apocalypse Trainer fans downloading this app. The issue here was that it takes about 24 hours for Microsoft to validate the bank routing, account, and address information. After this information has been validated, the payment information warning will disappear from your dashboard.

That's it—at this point you're ready to go. Assuming your application passes certification, it will either autodeploy to the Marketplace or, if you choose not to autodeploy, you can manually deploy it at exactly the time you choose. (You can find the up-to-date list of certification requirements on the App Hub; I haven't listed them in this book because they changed four times while I was writing it.)

Every time you want to release a new version of your application that contains bug fixes or new features, you return to App Hub, upload a new version of your application, and go through a slightly condensed version of the process I've just described. Owners of your application will then be able to use the Marketplace app on their phones to download the new version of your application.

Earning Money with the Mobile Advertising SDK

If you plan to release a free application in hopes that you will get more downloads, but you still want to be able to somehow draw revenue from your application, you might want to consider using the Mobile Advertising SDK. You can download this SDK from Microsoft at the following URL (I've taken the liberty of making a small URL that you can just type in as you read this): http://tinyurl.com/wp7adsdk.

To use the Mobile Advertising SDK, you will need to sign up with Microsoft pub-Center (again, you can't use Chrome on this website, you'll need IE) at http://pubcenter. microsoft.com. This website is where you link your developer ID with advertising configuration and provide keywords and other targeting information for advertisements. Much like Apple's iAds SDK, all the busywork of tracking down potential advertisers and negotiating rates and payments has been taken care of on your behalf. All you need to do is use the SDK to display advertisements within your application and, assuming your application is launched often enough, you will begin receiving payments based on view impressions and "tap-through" events that occur when users tap displayed advertisements within your application.

If you're looking for information on how to utilize the SDK within your application, you need to install the SDK. It comes with its own help file that is full of tutorials and other information on configuring your pubCenter account and writing the code necessary to allow your application to participate in advertisements.

Summary

This chapter provided you with an overview of the things you need to do to prepare your application for submission to the Marketplace. After your application has been prepped, this chapter provided you with a walkthrough of submitting a real application to the Marketplace and the information you need for submission.

After having read through this entire book, whether or not you are an iOS developer, you should now have a very firm grasp of the information you need to build, test, troubleshoot, deploy, and sell Windows Phone 7 applications. I hope you find the experience of developing for Windows Phone 7 as amazing as I have, and I look forward to seeing the amazing applications you are no doubt going to build.

A

B

C

N

The Titles You Need to Build Killer Apps

informit.com/learnmac

iOS Development is evolving rapidly. So are the resources from Addison-Wesley Professional, Prentice Hall, and Sams.

From getting started with iPhone and iPad application development, to improving the user experience of your applications, to mastering Cocoa, we are updating and publishing the titles you need, when you need them, and in the formats you want!

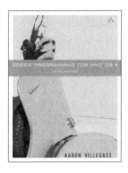   

Check informit.com/learnmac regularly to see new titles and new editions on Mac and iOS programming.

Developer's Library

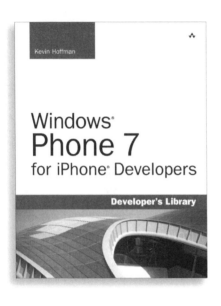